THE AMERICAN MEDICAL ASSOCIATION

MEN:
HOW TO UNDERSTAND YOUR SYMPTOMS

Editors-in-chief Charles B. Clayman, MD
Jeffrey R. M. Kunz, MD

**RANDOM HOUSE
NEW YORK**

All rights reserved under International and
Pan-American Copyright Conventions.
Published in the United States
by Random House, Inc., New York,
and simultaneously in Canada by
Random House of Canada Limited, Toronto.
Published in Great Britain in different form
by Dorling Kindersley Limited, London.

Library of Congress Cataloging-in-Publication Data
Main entry under title:

Men, how to understand your symptoms.

Includes index.
1. Symptomatology – Popular works.
2. Men – Diseases – Diagnosis – Popular works.
3. Self-examination, Medical.
I. American Medical Association.

RC69.A64   1986   616.07′2   85-25706
ISBN 0-394-74044-0

Manufactured in the United States of America

2 4 6 8 9 7 5 3

First American Edition

Preface

For most people, most of the time, that miraculous machine we call the human body functions with remarkable reliability. It does, however, require maintenance and occasional repair, and we as a people have demonstrated an increasing willingness to devote a growing share of our national resources to health. Americans spent 4 percent of the U.S. gross national product on health in 1940; today we spend over 10 percent.

At the same time, we have grown more self-reliant, recognizing that the health decisions we make on everything from watching weight to seeking medical care can affect our well-being as well as our pocketbook. The purpose of this book is to *extend* individual competence in making medical decisions about personal health.

When symptoms appear, when the body sends out signals that something is wrong, the trouble may be only a common, simple illness. It can be a minor cold or some other self-limiting ailment from which we will recover with or without medical intervention.

But minor symptoms, sometimes even a headache or a cough, may also be the first warning of something serious. The decision charts in this book enable you to interpret body signals more accurately, allowing you to distinguish between what may be a minor problem and what may not be so minor. The charts will also help you with the question that everyone has to ask from time to time: How long does a worried but sensible person wait before seeking medical help?

This book is not intended to teach you medical diagnosis; no book can do that. But it will give you a more *informed* understanding of your ailments; it will provide scientifically valid answers to everyday questions; and it will allay many of the needless anxieties that arise when signs of illness first appear. In addition, it includes illustrated sections on first aid and emergency treatment.

These self-help medical charts have been developed under medical supervision, tested on patients under real conditions and reviewed by American medical authorities. We are pleased to add this book to the American Medical Association Home Health Library, a series of books aimed at widening the health education of the American public.

James H. Sammons, M.D.
Executive Vice President
American Medical Association

American Medical Association

The American Medical Association Home Health Library

The AMA Family Medical Guide

The AMA Handbook of First Aid and Emergency Care

The AMA Guide to BackCare – Revised and Updated Edition

The AMA Guide to HeartCare – Revised and Updated Edition

The AMA Guide to WomanCare – Revised and Updated Edition

The AMA Guide to Health and Well-Being After Fifty

The AMA Guide to Better Sleep

Children: How to Understand Their Symptoms

Women: How to Understand Your Symptoms.

Contents

Introduction

The symptoms

1 General medical
page 21

2 Sex and fertility
page 115

The male body

A man is male from the moment he is conceived. This maleness is determined by the pattern of chromosomes (thread-like structures within each living cell that contain genetic information) in the fertilized egg. Every man has 23 pairs of chromosomes; 22 are the same as for women, but the 23rd pair, which is responsible for the development of internal and external genitals, is different. It consists of an X and a Y chromosome (women have two X chromosomes). Hormones secreted by the testes and other glands during fetal growth are thought to affect the development of the brain and its sense of being male. At birth, boys are, on average, slightly heavier than girls, although the male skeleton is four to five weeks less mature. The shape of the adult male body is largely due to the action of the male hormone testosterone, which during puberty is responsible for the development of features known as secondary sexual characteristics – shoulders become broader, voice deepens, the Adam's apple becomes more prominent and body hair grows on the face and chest. These changes begin later in a man than comparable changes in a pubescent woman, but they occur over a longer period of time, making men generally taller, with larger hands and feet. Men's bones are thicker than women's; this thickness provides a base for their bulkier, more powerful muscles. And the male pelvis is narrower than a woman's.

Men also differ from women in their susceptibility to certain disorders. For instance, their livers are slightly less sensitive to alcohol and so, even when weight is taken into account, a man can normally drink slightly more than a woman without damaging his liver. In general, too, men do not live as long as women; the average life expectation in the U.S. is about 71 for men and about 78 for women. This gap seems to be narrowing, however, perhaps because of the changes in the life-styles of both sexes over the past few decades.

The changing body

A man's body usually reaches maturity by the age of 18. The body's systems are fully developed and remain effective for many years, able to withstand periods of illness or injury. A hygienic life-style once maturation has occurred plays an important role in maintenance of health. Attention to how much and what you eat or drink, whether or not you smoke, and how much you exercise – these all affect the body's ability to function in a normal fashion in the years to come.

The time when natural changes associated with aging occur varies greatly from man to man. In part, this is an inherited tendency but it is also a function of how well we care for ourselves. Body systems begin to lose some of their efficiency and become more vulnerable to illness after the age of 35. This is because the specialist cells die and are not replaced, because the tissues become less elastic and more fibrous and because blood flow to various tissues may begin to lessen. Loss of elasticity with age is most obvious in the skin, and this process may be accelerated by excessive exposure to sunlight and by smoking. The healing process of minor injuries becomes noticeably slower with age and the bones of the wrist or the hip may be easily broken by minor falls. The bones tend to thin and become brittle with age (a process known as osteoporosis, whereby the body loses significant amounts of calcium). In later years, compression of the bones of the spine may lead to loss of height, and there may be loss of weight due to wasting of the muscles. Weakening of muscle fiber is unavoidable in the aging process. Since hair loss and changes in hair color are genetically determined, nothing can be done about them. Even so, if you exercise regularly throughout your life, you are likely to have the same vitality at 60 that you had at 30.

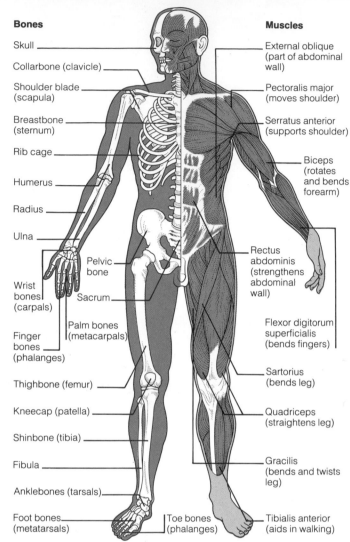

Bones
- Skull
- Collarbone (clavicle)
- Shoulder blade (scapula)
- Breastbone (sternum)
- Rib cage
- Humerus
- Radius
- Ulna
- Wrist bones (carpals)
- Finger bones (phalanges)
- Pelvic bone
- Sacrum
- Palm bones (metacarpals)
- Thighbone (femur)
- Kneecap (patella)
- Shinbone (tibia)
- Fibula
- Anklebones (tarsals)
- Foot bones (metatarsals)
- Toe bones (phalanges)

Muscles
- External oblique (part of abdominal wall)
- Pectoralis major (moves shoulder)
- Serratus anterior (supports shoulder)
- Biceps (rotates and bends forearm)
- Rectus abdominis (strengthens abdominal wall)
- Flexor digitorum superficialis (bends fingers)
- Sartorius (bends leg)
- Quadriceps (straightens leg)
- Gracilis (bends and twists leg)
- Tibialis anterior (aids in walking)

Skeleton

The bony skeleton provides the rigid structure that supports the muscles and provides a protective framework for the organs. Bone itself is made up of protein hardened with calcium salts. It is a living material with cells that are constantly replacing old bone with new material. To maintain healthy bones, you need adequate amounts of protein, calcium and vitamins – particularly vitamin D – in your diet. Male bones are generally heavier than women's.

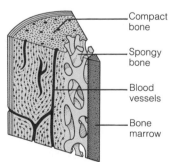

- Compact bone
- Spongy bone
- Blood vessels
- Bone marrow

Bone marrow
The marrow inside the bones is a fatty material with a plentiful blood supply. Certain bones – particularly those of the breastbone, vertebrae, ribs and pelvis – also contain blood-forming tissues that produce the red and white blood cells.

Symptoms

The most common problems affecting the skeleton in men of all ages include breakage (fractures) of the bones as a result of injury, and damage to the joints between bones as a result of inflammation, injury or wear and tear. Bone infections and tumors are rare.

Symptoms of skeletal disorders include pain, swelling, and redness and heat (inflammation) around the affected part.

See also the following diagnostic charts: **54** Back pain **55** Painful or stiff neck **56** Painful arm **57** Painful knee **58** Painful leg **59** Painful or swollen joints **60** Foot problems

Muscles

Muscles are composed of a soft tissue arranged in fibers that contract and relax to produce movement of the body and its internal organs. There are two distinct types of muscles: the voluntary muscles, which are attached to the skeleton and subject to our conscious control; and the involuntary muscles, which are responsible for movement such as the digestive tract's rhythmical contraction.

Muscles thrive on work and will remain in good condition if used regularly. Vigorous exercise increases the size of muscles and improves the circulation of blood to them, thereby increasing their capacity for still more strenuous activity. Inactivity can soon lead to weakness. Muscle disorders are rare, but can be caused by inherited chemical abnormalities or hormonal imbalances.

How muscles work

Most voluntary muscles are fixed to two or more adjacent bones, often by means of a fibrous tendon. When a muscle contracts, the bones to which it is attached move. Muscles usually work in groups where the contraction of one muscle is accompanied by the relaxation of another.

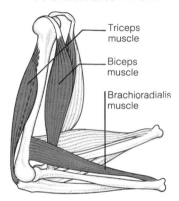

Triceps muscle

Biceps muscle

Brachioradialis muscle

Symptoms

Damage to muscles from injury normally produces pain, stiffness and sometimes swelling and inflammation. Muscles may also become weak or painful as a result of virus infection.

See also the following diagnostic charts: **54** Back pain **55** Painful or stiff neck **56** Painful arm **57** Painful knee **58** Painful leg **59** Painful or swollen joints

Respiratory system

Respiration, inhaling (breathing in) and exhaling (breathing out), allows the blood to absorb oxygen that enables the body's cells to form energy.

The respiratory system consists of the rib cage, the diaphragm, the lungs, and the tubes through which air passes on its way to and from the lungs. Air is breathed in through the nose and mouth, passes down the trachea (windpipe), and enters the lungs through a branching tree of tubes – the bronchi and bronchioles. The lungs are sponge-like organs composed of millions of air sacs (alveoli).

The respiratory system is vulnerable to repeated infection and exposure to pollutants including tobacco smoke and dust from industrial or agricultural processes.

Symptoms

The most common disorders of the respiratory tract are caused by infection, leading to inflammation of the lining of the tract or of the lung tissues themselves. This may result in coughing and the production of excessive amounts of mucus. If the breathing mechanism is severely damaged, there may be shortness of breath. Chest pain is a common symptom of respiratory infections.

See also the following diagnostic charts: **31** Runny nose **32** Sore throat **33** Hoarseness or loss of voice **34** Wheezing **35** Coughing **36** Difficulty breathing **50** Chest pain

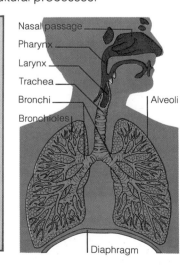

Nasal passage

Pharynx

Larynx

Trachea

Bronchi

Bronchioles

Alveoli

Diaphragm

Fat distribution

Fat is deposited in a layer under the skin and within the tissues in other parts of the body. Fat comprises up to about 15 percent of a man's weight (compared with 20 to 25 percent of a woman's) and is distributed in such a way as to give a man's body its contours. Fat is laid down when food intake is greater than is needed to fuel the body's energy requirements. It is burned when food intake fails to equal the body's energy output. Fat also acts as insulation against cold.

Both too much and too little fat can be unhealthy. Being too fat can lead to heart and circulation problems. Being too thin is less of a health risk, but may be a sign of undernourishment and can reduce your resistance to a variety of diseases. Fluctuations in the level of fat deposits are almost always the result of an imbalance between food intake and energy output.

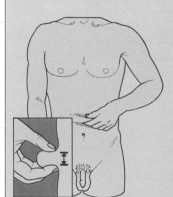

Skin-fold test

You may be too fat if a fold of skin pinched from the abdomen is thicker than 1 in. (25 mm).

Symptoms

The weight chart on p.26 shows the healthy weight for someone of your height. Weight gain or loss usually indicates a change in your level of fat deposits.

See also the following diagnostic charts: **2** Loss of weight **4** Overweight

Breathing in   Breathing out

How you breathe

As you breathe in, the diaphragm (the sheet of muscle between the chest and abdomen) contracts and flattens and the rib cage expands. This causes the lungs to expand as air is sucked in. When you breathe out, the diaphragm relaxes into a dome shape. The rib cage contracts and the lungs contract, expelling the air.

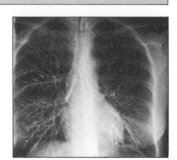

Bronchogram of the lungs

A small amount of liquid visible on X rays is trickled down the throat into the lungs; it outlines the breathing pattern of the trachea and bronchi.

Hollow center of alveoli

Flow of oxygen into red blood cells

Flow of carbon dioxide from red blood cells

Network of capillaries

The alveoli

The lungs are sponge-like organs made up of millions of air sacs known as alveoli. Each alveolar lining is surrounded by blood capillaries – tiny vessels that connect arteries with veins. Blood enters the lungs (via the pulmonary artery), going through the capillaries surrounding the alveoli, where oxygen is picked up from breathed-in air and carbon dioxide and some water vapor is given up to be breathed out.

Heart and circulation

The heart is a muscular pump with four chambers into which enter the major blood vessels carrying blood to and from the rest of the body. Blood flows in the correct direction as the heart rhythmically squeezes the chambers, making them expand and contract.

Blood circulates via the arteries and veins, carrying oxygen and nutrients (see *Blood analysis,* p.22) to all parts of the body and carrying away waste products. The arteries and their branches (arterioles) are surrounded by muscle, which allows them to dilate or contract to regulate body temperature. Good blood circulation is essential for the health of every organ in the body.

A healthy circulatory system depends on the blood vessels remaining free from obstructions such as fatty deposits or blood clots. It is also important that the pressure of the circulating blood do not exceed certain levels. High blood pressure (hypertension) may damage the blood vessels or increase their risk of blockage. For advice on reducing the risks of diseases of the heart and circulation, see *Coronary heart disease,* p.95.

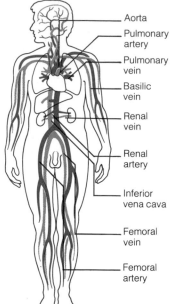

Aorta
Pulmonary artery
Pulmonary vein
Basilic vein
Renal vein
Renal artery
Inferior vena cava
Femoral vein
Femoral artery

Symptoms

The symptoms of impaired circulation depend on the organs or region affected. Heart disease may cause chest pain, palpitations or breathlessness; poor circulation to the brain may cause fainting, dizzy spells or confusion; circulation problems in the limbs may cause pain or swelling.

See also the following diagnostic charts: **10** Faintness and fainting **12** Dizziness **13** Numbness or tingling **16** Forgetfulness and confusion **36** Difficulty breathing **51** Palpitations **50** Chest pain **56** Painful arm **58** Painful leg

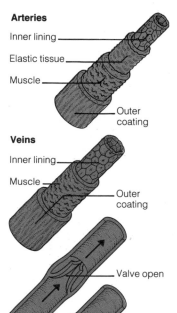

Arteries

Inner lining
Elastic tissue
Muscle
Outer coating

Veins

Inner lining
Muscle
Outer coating
Valve open
Valve closed

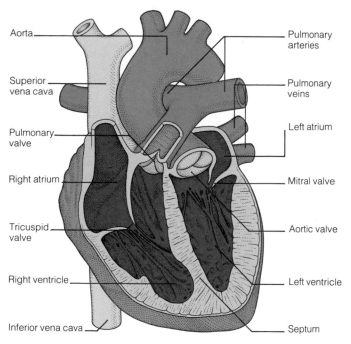

Aorta
Superior vena cava
Pulmonary valve
Right atrium
Tricuspid valve
Right ventricle
Inferior vena cava
Pulmonary arteries
Pulmonary veins
Left atrium
Mitral valve
Aortic valve
Left ventricle
Septum

The circulatory system
The circulatory system carries blood to and from every part of the body. Arteries carry oxygenated blood away from the heart; veins return "used" blood to the heart.

Arteries and veins
The walls of arteries are made up of four layers. They need to be strong because blood is forced along them under high pressure. Veins have less elastic, less muscular walls. Valves in the veins stop blood from flowing in the wrong direction.

Heart vessels
The heart is divided in two by the septum. Each side has two chambers, an atrium and a ventricle, linked by a one-way valve. The left atrium and ventricle control oxygenated blood, and those on the right control deoxygenated ("used") blood. The septum prevents the two types of blood from mixing.

Blood circulation through the heart and lungs

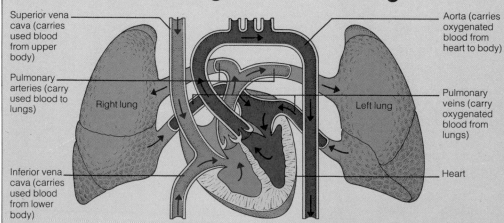

Superior vena cava (carries used blood from upper body)
Pulmonary arteries (carry used blood to lungs)
Right lung
Inferior vena cava (carries used blood from lower body)
Aorta (carries oxygenated blood from heart to body)
Pulmonary veins (carry oxygenated blood from lungs)
Left lung
Heart

Deoxygenated ("used") blood is carried back to the heart via the superior and inferior branches of the vena cava, which enters the right atrium. The blood then passes into the right ventricle, from where it is pumped along the pulmonary artery to the lungs. As blood passes through the network of small blood vessels surrounding the lungs, it absorbs oxygen from the breathed-in air and discharges carbon dioxide to be breathed out. The newly oxygenated blood then returns to the heart via the pulmonary veins, enters the left atrium and passes into the left ventricle. The oxygenated blood is then pumped from the left ventricle through the aorta to all parts of the body.

Brain and nervous system

The brain and nervous system together provide the control mechanism for conscious activities such as thought and movement, and unconscious body functions such as rhythmic heartbeating, breathing and digestion. Nerves also provide the means by which we register sensations such as sight, smell, hearing, pain, touch and temperature.

The brain and nervous system require a constant supply of oxygenated blood. Disruption of the blood flow to any part of the system is one of the most common causes of malfunctioning of the brain and nervous system, so the prevention of circulatory trouble (see *Heart and circulation,* opposite) is important. Injury, infection, degeneration, tumors and diseases of unknown cause may also affect the brain and nervous system. Certain disorders may arise out of abnormal electrical activity or chemical imbalances in the brain.

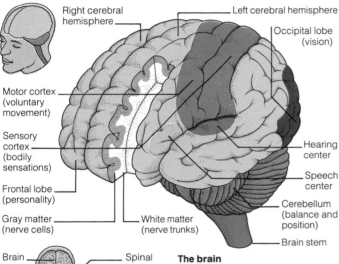

Right cerebral hemisphere — Left cerebral hemisphere

Occipital lobe (vision)

Motor cortex (voluntary movement)

Sensory cortex (bodily sensations)

Frontal lobe (personality)

Gray matter (nerve cells)

White matter (nerve trunks)

Hearing center

Speech center

Cerebellum (balance and position)

Brain stem

The brain
The brain itself is the most complex organ in the body; many aspects of its structure and function are not yet fully understood. Different parts of the brain control different activities. The two cerebral hemispheres control conscious thought and movement and interpret signals from the sensory organs. The cerebellum regulates some subconscious activities such as coordination of movement and balance. The brain stem governs vital body functons such as heartbeat and breathing.

Brain

Spinal cord

Cervical nerves

Thoracic nerves

Lumbar nerves

Sacral nerves

The nervous system
The brain and the nerve tracts of the spinal cord constitute the central nervous system. A network of peripheral nerves, named after the four regions of the spine, links the central system with other parts of the body.

Symptoms

The symptoms of brain and nervous system disorders depend on the part of the system affected. Symptoms may include pain, loss of sensation, and weakness. Brain disorders may cause a variety of psychological symptoms as well as physical symptoms such as headache, drowsiness, confusion or hallucinations.

See also the following diagnostic charts: **10** Faintness and fainting **11** Headache **12** Dizziness **13** Numbness or tingling **14** Twitching and trembling **15** Pain in the face **16** Forgetfulness and confusion **17** Difficulty speaking **19** Depression **54** Back pain

The senses

The senses are the means by which we monitor the different aspects of our environment. Five separate systems respond to different types of physical stimuli: the eyes enable us to interpret visual information; the ears monitor sound and control balance; the nose and tongue respond to different smells and tastes, respectively; and the sensory nerves in the skin allow us to feel physical contact (touch), changes in temperature, and pain.

Hearing and balance
The ear is described on p.65.

Sight
The eye is described on p.63.

Smell
Smells are detected by the olfactory nerves. These hair-like organs project into the top of the nasal cavity and absorb and analyze molecules from the breathed-in air. The sense of smell may be damaged by smoking and may be temporarily impaired by a common cold or hayfever. Permanent loss of the sense of smell may occur after nerve damage, as a result of a skull injury, or because of a disorder affecting the part of the brain responsible for interpreting smell sensations.

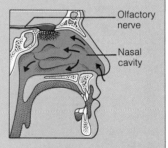

Olfactory nerve

Nasal cavity

Taste
The primary taste organs are the taste buds, located in hair-like papillae that project from the upper surface of the tongue. The taste buds for each of the four basic tastes (sweet, sour, salty and bitter) are located in a different area of the tongue. The sense of taste is closely allied to the sense of smell, which helps us to differentiate a greater range of flavors. Loss of the sense of smell is the usual cause of any impairment in the sense of taste, but certain drugs and, occasionally, a zinc deficiency may also influence our sense of taste.

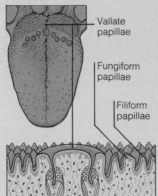

Vallate papillae

Fungiform papillae

Filiform papillae

Symptoms

The main symptom of any disorder of the senses is partial or total loss of sensitivity. There may also be pain or other symptoms affecting the sensory organ concerned.

See also the following diagnostic charts: **12** Dizziness **13** Numbness or tingling **26** Painful or irritated eye **27** Disturbed or impaired vision **28** Earache **29** Noises in the ear **30** Deafness

Touch
The sense of touch is conveyed through the nerves from the sensory receptors that lie under the surface of the skin. A different type of receptor is responsible for monitoring each of the main sensations. The number of sense receptors varies from one part of the body to another: the fingertips and the area around the mouth have a large number of receptors, whereas the skin of the middle of the back has very few. The sense of touch may be impaired by damage to the skin or the nerve endings or fibers; after any of the diseases that damage nerve fibers; or from a

more generalized condition affecting the brain and/or nervous system.

Skin surface

Free nerve endings

Nerves bundled together and leading to the spinal cord

The digestive system

The series of organs extending from the mouth to the anus responsible for carrying out the digestive process is known as the digestive tract. The digestive tract is made up of a tube in which food is broken down so that minerals, vitamins, carbohydrates, fats and proteins can be absorbed into the body and the waste products can be excreted.

The digestive organs

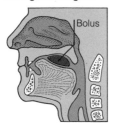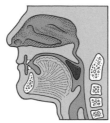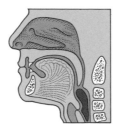

Bolus

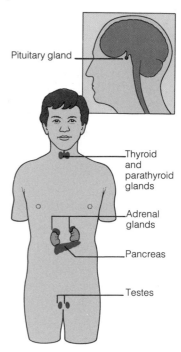

Pituitary gland

Thyroid and parathyroid glands

Adrenal glands

Pancreas

Testes

Duodenum
Liver
Pancreas
Rectum
Anus

Mouth
Digestion begins in the mouth when, as you chew food, enzymes in the saliva break down certain carbohydrates. The tongue and the muscles of the pharynx then propel the mixture of food and saliva, known as the bolus, into the esophagus and down into the stomach.

Salivary glands

Esophagus

Stomach
Food may spend several hours in the stomach being churned and partially digested by acid and more enzymes until the food becomes a semiliquid consistency called chyme. The chyme passes into the duodenum, where it is further broken down by digestive juices from the liver (via the gallbladder) and pancreas.

Small intestine
The final stage of digestion is completed in the small intestine, where the nutrients are split into chemical units small enough to pass through the wall of the intestine into the network of blood vessels and lymphatics.

Large intestine
Undigested material is passed into the large intestine (the colon), where water is absorbed, and then into the rectum, from which the undigested matter is expelled from the body.

Endoscopic view of stomach

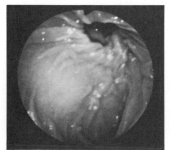

This photograph shows the lining of the stomach as the part adjacent to the duodenum. Its circular muscles are partially contracted.

Endoscopic view of duodenum

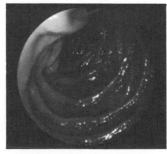

It is possible to see the characteristic circular folds of membrane which make up the surface of the duodenum. See *Endoscopy*, p.77.

Symptoms

The lining of the intestines is renewed every 24 hours so it can cope with the wide range of substances that are passed through it every day. The digestive system also reacts quickly against contaminated food, viruses or bacteria.

See also the following diagnostic charts: **2** Loss of weight **40** Vomiting **41** Recurrent vomiting **42** Abdominal pain **43** Recurrent abdominal pain **44** Swollen abdomen **45** Excess gas **46** Diarrhea **47** Constipation **48** Abnormal-looking bowel movements

The endocrine system

Endocrine glands manufacture hormones and distribute them to all parts of the body via the bloodstream. These hormones help regulate the body's internal chemistry, its responses to hunger, stress, infection and disease, and its preparation for physical activity.

Hormone-producing glands
Pituitary gland
This is a peanut-sized organ situated in the base of the brain. The pituitary gland's most important role is to stimulate and coordinate the functions of the other endocrine glands so that they produce their own hormones. In men, it also manufactures the growth hormone and hormones to control the thyroid, the volume of urine, and the activity of pigment-forming glands in the skin.

Thyroid gland
This gland is located at the front of the throat, just below the Adam's apple. It is responsible for producing the hormones that control the body's metabolism (the conversion of food into energy), and it regulates the body's internal thermostat.

Parathyroid glands
These four glands are situated behind the thyroid. The hormone they produce controls the levels of calcium and phosphorous, which are essential for healthy bones and for the nerves and muscles to work efficiently.

Adrenal glands
The adrenal glands lie immediately above the kidneys. Each adrenal gland consists of two parts: the cortex and the medulla, which have separate functions. The adrenal cortex produces steroid hormones, which help to regulate the amounts of sugar, salt and water in the body, and it influences the shape and distribution of body hair. The adrenal medulla produces adrenaline and noradrenaline, the hormones that increase the flow of blood to the muscles, heart and lungs so that they are prepared to deal with excitement or physical and mental threats.

Pancreas
The pancreas lies at the back of the abdomen behind the stomach. It produces enzymes that pass into the duodenum, where they help to digest food. It also produces the hormones insulin and glucagon, which play an important part in regulating the glucose level in the blood. Glucose is the main source of energy for all the body's cells and insulin stimulates the cells to absorb adequate amounts of glucose.

Testes
These hang in the pouch of skin known as the scrotum. The hormone they produce, testosterone, is responsible for the onset of puberty and determines the development of male characteristics such as a deep voice, body shape and hair pattern.

Symptoms

Disorders usually occur when the level of a particular hormone increases or decreases, upsetting the body's chemical balance. Any disorder and the symptoms involved depend on which hormone is affected. For instance, if production of the hormone insulin is disrupted, the most common endocrine gland disorder, diabetes mellitus, may result. Changes in hormonal levels are also responsible for the natural physical changes in your body during puberty.

See also the following diagnostic charts: **2** Loss of weight **3** Tiredness **4** Overweight **7** Excessive sweating

The lymphatic system

This system consists of the lymph glands (found mainly in the neck, armpits and groin) and the lymphatics, which connect them. The lymphatic system empties into a neck vein. Fats are absorbed into lymph vessels in the intestine. The lymph glands produce a type of white blood cell called lymphocytes, and antibodies that defend the body against infection. The glands and the spleen act as barriers to the spread of infection by trapping any infection-carrying microbes that travel along the lymphatic vessels, thus preventing them from reaching vital organs. If you have an infection, the lymph glands near the surface of the skin often become visibly swollen and sometimes painful.

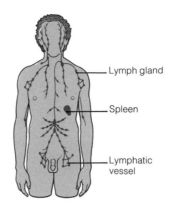

Lymph gland

Spleen

Lymphatic vessel

Symptoms

In the majority of cases, any lump or swelling beneath the surface of the skin indicates that the lymphatic system is working normally; that is, it is protecting your body against infection. In some cases, however, it may indicate a more serious underlying disorder.

See also the following diagnostic chart: **9** Lumps and swellings

The urinary system

The urinary system is responsible for filtering the blood and expelling the resulting waste fluid from the body. The organs of the urinary system consist of two kidneys, two ureters, the bladder, and the tube that leads from the bladder to the tip of the penis (the urethra).

How the urinary tract works
The kidneys are responsible for filtering waste substances from the blood. The filtered liquid passes into the central section of the kidney, the medulla, where certain chemicals are reabsorbed to maintain the levels of acids, salts and water in the body. The liquid that remains is urine. Urine trickles down the ureters into the bladder, which is kept closed by a ring of muscles (sphincter), and is periodically released from the body through the urethra.

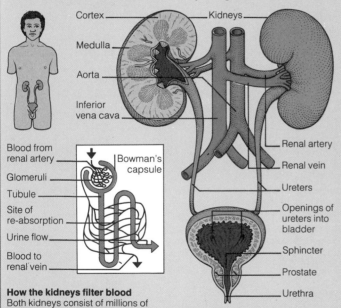

Cortex

Medulla

Aorta

Inferior vena cava

Kidneys

Blood from renal artery

Bowman's capsule

Glomeruli

Tubule

Site of re-absorption

Urine flow

Blood to renal vein

Renal artery

Renal vein

Ureters

Openings of ureters into bladder

Sphincter

Prostate

Urethra

How the kidneys filter blood
Both kidneys consist of millions of nephrons, or filtering units. Each nephron is supplied with blood from the renal artery via a cluster of minute blood vessels called glomeruli. Each cluster is almost entirely surrounded by a cup-shaped organ called a Bowman's capsule, which is joined to the tubule. This is the point where the filtration takes place: filtered material is condensed to make a small amount of urine, which then passes down to the bladder.

Symptoms

Disorders of the urinary system are fairly common, caused in most cases by infection that has led to inflammation in or near the bladder. Difficulty in passing urine or any increase in the volume of urine passed may be a symptom of a more serious underlying disorder (such as an obstruction). Any pain when you pass urine, or discharge from the urethra, may be caused by a sexually transmitted disease (p.99).

See also the following diagnostic charts: **52** General urinary problems **53** Painful urination

The reproductive system

The reproductive system is responsible for the production and delivery of sperm. The organs of the reproductive system become fully developed at puberty (between the ages of 12 and 15). They are partly external (the scrotum, which contains the testes, and the penis) and partly internal (the prostate and the various organs that collect and store sperm).

The reproductive organs

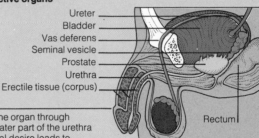

Ureter

Bladder

Vas deferens

Seminal vesicle

Prostate

Urethra

Erectile tissue (corpus)

Rectum

The penis
The penis is the organ through which the greater part of the urethra passes. Sexual desire leads to erection of the penis. The soft, spongy tissues become filled with blood, making the penis lengthen and stiffen. Partial erection can also occur during sleep when you dream.

The testes
The testes, commonly known as the testicles, have two functions: they form sperm (see *Sperm production,* p.125) and they produce the male sex hormone testosterone, which is responsible for the development of genitals, the growth of facial and body hair, and the deepening of the voice.

The prostate
The prostate gland (p.125) lies directly beneath the bladder, encircling the top part of the urethra. The fluid the prostate gland produces becomes part of the semen when you ejaculate.

Transverse section of penis

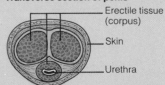

Erectile tissue (corpus)

Skin

Urethra

The three masses of erectile tissue are capable of considerable enlargement during erection, when they become engorged with blood.

Symptoms

Most disorders of the reproductive system affect the external organs. If you notice discharge from the urethra, it may be caused by a sexually transmitted disease (p.99). Blood in the semen is usually the result of rigorous sexual activity, though, in rare cases, it may be the result of a serious disorder. Any swelling with or without pain, or any change in the appearance of your testicles or penis, is a possible sign of an underlying disorder.

See also the following diagnostic charts: **61** Painful penis **62** Painful or swollen testicles

Safeguarding your health

Good health and susceptibility to disease are, to a great extent, determined by inheritance. However, whatever your family history of disease, you can improve your chances of remaining in good health by paying attention to the avoidable risk factors in your life-style – by improving your diet, reducing your alcohol intake, giving up smoking and exercising regularly. You can improve your physical well-being at any age by adopting a healthier life-style following the guidelines described here.

Diet

Diet plays a fundamental part in determining general health. To function efficiently, your body requires adequate amounts of each nutrient in the table below. The main risk of eating a typical western diet is overnutrition. Eating too many refined carbohydrates leads to obesity and eating large amounts of foods containing fats leads to heart disease. Be sure to include plenty of fruits and vegetables in your diet.

Proteins

Proteins are needed for growth, repair and replacement of body tissues. Animal products such as meat, fish, eggs and cheese (and other milk products) are high in protein, as are legumes (e.g., peas, beans, lentils).

Diet advice: Many protein-rich animal products are also high in fat, so make a point of eating nonanimal sources of protein such as peas, beans and unrefined grains as an alternative.

Carbohydrates

Carbohydrates are a major source of energy but, eaten in excess, they are stored in the body as fat. Carbohydrates are present as natural sugars and starches in cereals, grains and root vegetables.

Diet advice: Eat unrefined products (such as whole-grain bread and brown rice, which also contain fiber and other nutrients), green and yellow vegetables and potatoes. Avoid eating white bread and refined cereals.

Fats

Fats are a concentrated source of energy that provide more calories than any other food. Saturated fats are found mainly in animal products, dairy produce and eggs. Monounsaturated fats are most commonly found in poultry, margarine and olive oil. Polyunsaturated fats are found in fish, corn oil and safflower oil.

Diet advice: Intake of saturated fats should be kept to a minimum, so use vegetable fats when cooking.

Minerals

Minerals and certain salts are needed in minute quantities. These include iron, potassium, calcium and sodium (found in salt).

Diet advice: Too much salt (sodium) in the diet may be harmful.

Fiber

Fiber is the indigestible residue of plant products that passes through the digestive system.

Diet advice: While it contains no energy value or nutrients, fiber is important for healthy bowel action and may prevent colon cancer.

Vitamins

Vitamins are complex chemical compounds needed by the body in tiny quantities to regulate metabolism and to help convert carbohydrates and fats into energy.

Diet advice: Vitamins can be destroyed by lengthy cooking, so keep cooking time to a minimum and eat raw vegetables and fruit regularly.

Exercise

To be fit, you must exercise regularly. Exercise helps the body maintain mobility and body strength and conditions the heart and lungs. Physical activity makes your muscles need more oxygen – so you breathe more deeply to get oxygen into your lungs and your heart beats faster to pump blood to the muscles. There are many health benefits to be gained from exercise (see *The benefits of exercise,* p.25). The more muscles and joints you include in your exercise program and the more activities you undertake that involve a high degree of physical exertion to make you feel breathless and sweaty, the greater the benefits. Exercise is essential if you need to lose weight when it is combined with a sensible weight-reducing diet (see *How to lose weight,* p.27). Team sports and solitary exercise such as jogging are among the most popular forms of exercise, but walking and bicycling, if you do them energetically, are also good exercise. There are also psychological benefits to regular exercise. Many people sleep better, wake up more refreshed and are better able to concentrate.

Weight

Being overweight (according to the weight chart on p.26) is dangerous to your health. It increases the risk of serious disorders such as diabetes, high blood pressure, heart disease and stroke, and exaggerates the symptoms of many other disorders.

Most men can achieve and maintain an ideal weight if they follow a sensible weight-reducing diet (see *How to lose weight,* p.27) and exercise regularly (see *The benefits of exercise,* p.25). However, do not wait until you are on the verge of obesity before doing something to control your weight. It is far easier to prevent yourself from becoming overweight by eating a healthy, balanced diet than to lose weight. Try to pinch a fold of skin from your abdomen, just above your navel. If the fold is more than about 1-in. thick, look closely at your diet today.

Smoking

If you smoke, give it up. Smoking is beyond doubt the main cause of many serious illnesses (see *The dangers of smoking,* p.72), including lung cancer, emphysema and diseases of the heart and circulation. If you smoke regularly, you are probably losing about 5 minutes of life for each cigarette smoked. By giving up smoking, your chances of suffering from tobacco-related diseases lessen with each successive year. If you smoke and have children, quitting the habit will set a good example for them. Tell children the facts: smoking is a costly habit in terms of money and health.

Alcohol

Alcohol is a drug that can damage your health if consumed in large quantities. You may be putting your health at serious risk if you regularly exceed the safe limits outlined in *The effects of alcohol,* p.22, and/or if drinking ever becomes a necessity. The action of alcohol on the body and mind depends on the concentration of alcohol in the blood, so it varies from person to person according to individual weight. Men, who tend to weigh more than women, usually feel the effects of the same amount of alcohol slightly later. Factors such as the type of alcohol you drink and the speed at which you drink also affect the action of alcohol. If you want to reduce your alcohol intake but find you cannot, accept the probability that alcohol is a serious problem for you. Seek help from your physician or from an organization such as Alcoholics Anonymous, which is listed in the telephone book.

Medical checkups

Many men feel that they need only visit their physicians when they are sick. However, certain disorders such as familial disorders of the blood fats (cholesterol) and blood sugar, and high blood pressure and testicular cancer may be present in early stages without symptoms until the disease has reached a fairly advanced stage. It is then more difficult to treat. The need to visit your physician periodically varies with your age. Annual visits are more desirable after age 50.

Talk to your physician about having regular medical checkups. The record from your first medical checkup will serve as a guideline against which the significance of any further changes in your health can be measured. Your physician may use the checkup to assess your general lifestyle, to listen to your heart and breathing, to examine your eyes and ears and to perform a complete and thorough physical examination. You should also confirm with him or her that you have been immunized against infectious diseases, especially tetanus and polio.

Testing blood pressure

Systolic is the peak pressure at the moment when your heart contracts pumping out blood. Diastolic is the pressure at a moment when your heart relaxes to permit the inflow of blood. A healthy young adult has a reading of about 110/75 (systolic/diastolic), which rises by age 60 to as much as 150/90.

Your physician will place a soft cuff around your upper arm and inflate it until it is tight enough to stop the blood flow. The cuff is slowly deflated until the physician can hear (through a stethoscope) the blood forcing its way along the main artery. Your physician can then measure the amount of systolic pressure. Next the physician will deflate the cuff until he or she can hear blood flowing steadily through the now-open artery; this will be the diastolic pressure.

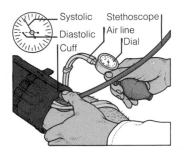

Systolic — Stethoscope
Diastolic — Air line
Cuff — Dial

NAME OF TEST AND PURPOSE	WHEN RECOMMENDED	WHEN TO BEGIN IF HEALTHY	FREQUENCY OF FOLLOW-UPS
Complete physical examination			
To check on the general health of your heart, lungs, brain and major internal organs	If you have a family history of disorders of any of these organs and as a preventive measure	Every 3 to 5 years up to age 50	Annually
Blood pressure (see above right)			
To check the condition of your heart and arteries. If there is any rise in blood pressure, this may cause serious medical problems	If you have a family history of high blood pressure, heart or kidney disease, stroke or diabetes, or if you are overweight	From the age of 20 onward	Every 3 to 5 years. Annually if you are in a high-risk group
Rectal examination			
To detect rectal and prostate cancer	If you have a family history of colon or rectal cancer	Annual digital rectal exam after age 20	After age 50 stools should be tested annually; general exam every 3 to 5 years
Serum cholesterol (blood) level			
To detect people at high risk for development of coronary artery disease	If you have a family history of coronary artery disease	At the time of your periodic physical exam in your 20s	No follow-up if first test is normal
Eye tests (see also p.62)			
Even if you can see well you should have regular vision tests	If you have difficulty seeing	From the age of 40 onward	Annually
Dental checkups			
Regular inspections are vital so that your dentist can examine your teeth, mouth and gums for signs of decay, infection or other problems	If you have not had regular check-ups, start now rather than waiting until you have a toothache or painful gums	From childhood	Every 6 months before the age of 21, then every 1 to 2 years

When you are sick

Recovery from most illnesses is more speedy if you stop work, stay at home and take things easy. There is no need to stay in bed as long as you stay in a warm environment. For the period that you feel sick, stop smoking and do not drink alcohol. Drink plenty of fluids, especially if you have a fever or diarrhea. Also, eat small, frequent meals.

When to seek medical advice

If your illness persists for more than 48 hours despite your taking self-help measures or you are worried about your symptoms, see your physician. If you have been taking your temperature, record it and the time it was taken. Keep specimens of stools, vomit or urine if they have an unusual color (especially if black or bloodstained), as this will help your physician to make a firm diagnosis. Also, try to remember when various symptoms started.

Over-the-counter medications

There are many over-the-counter medications at the pharmacy, available in almost every imaginable form. Some of them may have no direct effect on the cause of a condition but they may relieve painful or uncomfortable symptoms. For instance, some of the remedies for coughs and colds are soothing, and mild analgesics such as aspirin and aspirin substitutes relieve pain.

However, in most cases, the speed of your recovery depends more on your age and general health than on any such treatment. Nevertheless, if such "cures" make you feel better, they are unlikely to be harmful if you follow the instructions. In some cases your physician may actually recommend a particular over-the-counter preparation. If you are unsure about how to use the medication or how to receive its maximum benefit (for instance, whether you can drink alcohol or drive after taking the medication), ask your physician for advice.

Medication guide

New drugs are constantly being discovered. Many of the drugs in common use twenty years ago have been superseded by newer, safer compounds with broader applications. This medication guide is an index of major groups of drugs. It gives their uses and possible side effects and, in many cases, warnings about when they should *not* be taken.

When taking any medicine, a few precautionary measures can ensure the drug's effectiveness and safe use. Never exceed the stated dosage. Always check with your physician or pharmacist if you are unsure exactly when or how frequently the medicine should be taken (for example, some drugs work most efficiently when taken with a meal). As a general rule, avoid drinking alcohol when taking medicine, as its effects are aggravated by certain drugs. Also, even if you think it unnecessary and you *seem* to have no more symptoms, complete the prescribed course of medicine. Failure to do so may prevent complete recovery. Keep all drugs locked in a medicine cabinet (see below left).

In general, the fewer drugs you take, the better. Except for minor symptoms (such as an occasional cough or headache), you are well advised to let your physician prescribe all the medicines you need. He or she will balance the potential benefits of the medication against its side effects. Below is a guide to the more common drugs that your physician may prescribe.

Home medical supplies

Below is a list of items to keep at home to deal with common problems such as indigestion and muscle strain and a list to deal with accidents and emergencies.

Home medicine cabinet
The best place to keep prescribed medications and common, over-the-counter remedies is in a section of a medicine cabinet that can be locked. This will keep the items dry and away from children. Many over-the-counter preparations have a shelf life of 1 year and should be replaced regularly. You are likely to need:

Clinical thermometer
Antiseptic cream (cuts and scrapes)
Insect-sting reliever
Antacid liquid or tablets (indigestion)
Milk of magnesia (constipation and heartburn)
Kaolin (diarrhea)
Oil of cloves (toothache)
Motion-sickness tablets
Protective sunscreen
Calamine lotion
Petroleum jelly (chafing)
Elastic bandages
Eye wash
Aspirin or aspirin substitute

Home first-aid kit
In cases of emergency, you are likely to need additional supplies. These should be stored in a well-sealed metal or plastic box that is clearly labeled and easy for you to open. It should be kept in a dry place, out of reach of children and should include:

1 Packet of sterile cotton
2 Sterile prepared bandages (2 large, 2 medium, 2 small)
3 Sterile gauze squares in several sizes
4 Sterile triangular bandages (2)
5 Gauze bandages (2) and at least 1 crepe bandage
6 Finger-size gauze with applicator
7 Rubbing alcohol
8 Waterproof plasters in assorted sizes
9 Surgical tape in wide and narrow widths
10 Safety pins
11 Small mirror
12 Tweezers
13 Scissors

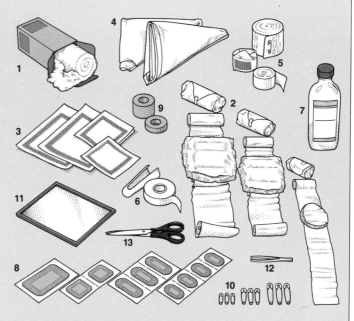

Safety note: Remember that it is important to keep all medicines safely out of the reach of children. A locked wall cabinet is usually the best place.

Medications

ANALGESICS Drugs that relieve pain. Many also reduce inflammation and fever (see ANTI-INFLAMMATORIES). There are 3 main types: simple analgesics – usually containing aspirin or acetaminophen – for mild pain; anti-inflammatories, often given for muscular aches and pains and arthritis; and narcotic analgesics – usually chemically related to morphine – for severe pain.
Possible side effects: Nausea, constipation, dizziness, dependence and development of tolerance to the drug.

ANTACIDS Drugs that neutralize stomach acid (relieving heartburn and similar conditions). They contain simple chemicals such as sodium bicarbonate, calcium carbonate, aluminum hydroxide and/or magnesium trisilicate.
Possible side effects: Belching (sodium bicarbonate preparations), constipation (aluminum or calcium preparations) and diarrhea (magnesium preparations).
Warning: Seek medical advice if you are taking other drugs. Antacids should be taken by anyone with a kidney disorder only on medical advice.

ANTIANXIETY DRUGS (sometimes called anxiolytics, sedatives or minor tranquilizers). Drugs that reduce feelings of anxiety and relax muscles. May also be used as sleeping drugs to relieve premenstrual tension.
Possible side effects: Drowsiness, dizziness, confusion, unsteadiness and lack of coordination.
Warning: Not to be taken if you intend to drive or operate potentially dangerous machinery. Antianxiety drugs may increase the effects of alcohol. They can be habit-forming and should not be used for more than a few weeks. After prolonged use, withdrawal symptoms may occur if treatment is halted abruptly.

ANTIBIOTICS Substances (that are often derived from living organisms such as molds or bacteria) that kill or inhibit the growth of bacteria in the body. Some of the newer antibiotics are synthetic versions of naturally occurring substances. Any one type of antibiotic is effective only against certain strains of bacteria; some, known as broad-spectrum antibiotics, combat a wide range of bacteria.
Possible side effects: Nausea, vomiting and diarrhea. Some people may be allergic to certain antibiotics and may experience symptoms such as rashes, fever, joint pain, swelling and wheezing. Following treatment with broad-spectrum antibiotics, secondary fungal infection (thrush) – for example, of the mouth or vagina – may sometimes occur.
Warning: Always complete a prescribed course of antibiotics. Failure to do so, even when symptoms have cleared, may lead to a recurrence of infection that is more difficult to treat (due to resistance of the bacteria to the antibiotic).

ANTICOAGULANTS (including thrombolytics). Drugs that prevent and/or disperse blood clots.
Possible side effects: Increased tendency to bleed from the nose or gums or under the skin (bruising). Blood may also appear in the urine or stool.
Warning: Anticoagulants may react more intensely with other drugs, including aspirin. Consult your physician before taking any other medicines so that the effectiveness of the anticoagulant is not altered. If you are on regular anticoagulant treatment, you will be advised to carry a warning card or ID tag.

ANTICONVULSANTS Drugs used in the prevention and treatment of epilepsy.
Possible side effects: Drowsiness, rashes, dizziness, headache, nausea and thickening of the gums.
Warning: Alcohol may increase the likelihood and severity of side effects and is best avoided, as are ANTIHISTAMINES. Consult your physician before driving and/or operating potentially dangerous machinery.

ANTIDEPRESSANTS Drugs that counter depression. These fall into two main groups: tricyclics and their derivatives, and monoamine oxidase (MAO) inhibitors. Because their side effects are likely to be more serious, MAO inhibitors are usually only prescribed for those types of severe depression that are less likely to respond to treatment with tricyclics.
Possible side effects: Drowsiness, dry mouth, blurred vision, constipation, difficulty urinating, faintness, sweating, trembling, rashes, palpitations and headaches.
Warning: MAO inhibitors react adversely with a number of foods and drugs, possibly leading to a serious rise in blood pressure. Your physician will advise you and may recommend that you carry a warning card or ID tag. During both types of antidepressant treatment, alcohol intake should be limited; ask your physician whether it is advisable to drive or operate machinery.

ANTIDIARRHEALS Drugs used to control and treat diarrhea. There are two main types: those that absorb excess water and toxins in the bowel (for example, those containing kaolin, bismuth compounds, chalk or charcoal) and those that reduce the contractions of the bowel, thus decreasing the frequency with which stools are passed (including codeine, morphine and opium mixtures).
Possible side effects: Constipation.
Warning: Antidiarrheals relieve symptoms but do not treat the underlying cause of diarrhea and may prolong the course of toxic or infectious diarrhea. They should not be taken for more than a day or so before seeking medical advice. When treating diarrhea, always drink plenty of fluids. See also REHYDRATION TREATMENTS.

ANTIEMETICS Drugs used to suppress nausea and vomiting. Most also suppress vertigo (dizziness). The main groups of drugs in this category include certain ANTIHISTAMINES (especially for nausea caused by motion sickness or by ear disorders), ANTISPASMODICS, and certain tranquilizers. Because antiemetic treatment may hinder diagnosis, such drugs are not usually prescribed when the cause of vomiting is unknown or when vomiting is unlikely to persist for longer than a day or so, as in gastroenteritis. Antiemetics are prescribed early in pregnancy only when symptoms are severe.
Possible side effects: These vary according to the drug group prescribed. Prolonged treatment with certain tranquilizers may cause involuntary movement of the facial muscles. These drugs should never be taken for more than a few days at a time.
Warning: Because most antiemetics may cause drowsiness, do not drink alcohol and seek your physician's advice before driving or operating potentially dangerous machinery.

ANTIFUNGALS Drugs used to treat fungal infections such as ringworm, athlete's foot or thrush.
Possible side effects: Oral antifungals may cause nausea, vomiting, diarrhea and/or headaches; locally applied (topical) preparations may cause irritation.
Warning: Always finish a course of antifungal treatment as prescribed; otherwise the infection may recur. Some infections, especially of the nails, may require treatment with oral antifungals for many months.

ANTIHISTAMINES Drugs mostly used to counteract the effects of histamine, one of the chemicals involved in allergic reactions. They are most often used to relieve the symptoms of seasonal hay fever, and may also clear a stuffy or runny nose, nausea or dizziness. Another class of antihistamine interferes with gastric acid secretion and is used to treat peptic ulcers.
Possible side effects: Drowsiness, dry mouth and blurred vision.
Warning: Driving or drinking alcohol should be avoided after taking an antihistamine.

ANTIHYPERTENSIVES Drugs that lower blood pressure. BETA-BLOCKERS and DIURETICS and, more recently, enzyme inhibitors or receptor blockers (which affect the action of hormones controlling blood pressure), and calcium blockers (which affect the internal chemistry of the heart and arteries) are those most commonly used.
Possible side effects: Dizziness, rashes, impotence, nightmares and lethargy.

ANTI-INFLAMMATORIES Drugs used to reduce inflammation. This is the redness, heat, swelling, pain and increased blood flow that is found in infections and in many chronic noninfective diseases such as rheumatoid arthritis and gout. Three main types of drugs are used as anti-inflammatories: ANALGESICS such as aspirin, CORTICOSTEROIDS and nonsteroidal anti-inflammatory drugs such as indomethacin which is used especially in the treatment of arthritis and muscle disorders. CORTICOSTEROIDS may be applied locally as cream or eyedrops for inflammation of the skin or eyes, but they are not generally prescribed for chronic rheumatic conditions except in unusual circumstances.
Possible side effects: Rashes and stomach irritation and occasionally bleeding, disturbances in hearing and wheezing.

ANTIPYRETICS Drugs that reduce fever. The most commonly used are aspirin and acetaminophen, which are both also ANALGESICS. This double action makes them particularly effective for relieving the symptoms of an illness such as flu.
Possible side effects: Rashes and stomach irritation and occasionally bleeding, disturbances in hearing and wheezing.

ANTISPASMODICS Drugs for reducing spasm of the bowel to relieve the pain of conditions such as irritable colon or diverticular disease.
Possible side effects: Dry mouth, palpitations, difficulty urinating, constipation and blurred vision.

ANTIVIRALS Drugs used to treat viral infections or to provide temporary protection against infections such as the flu. Few viral disorders respond to drugs, and those that do respond, such as cold sores and shingles, will do so only if treatment is started early.
Possible side effects: Antivirals used to treat cold sores, herpes genitalis and shingles may cause a stinging sensation, rashes and occasionally loss of sensation in the skin.

BETA-BLOCKERS Drugs that reduce the oxygen requirements of the heart by reducing heart rate. They are used as ANTIHYPERTENSIVES to treat angina due to exertion and to ease symptoms such as palpitations and tremors.
Possible side effects: Nausea, insomnia, tiredness and diarrhea.
Warning: Overdose can cause dizziness and fainting spells. Withdrawal from these drugs should be gradual, never abrupt. Beta-blockers are not prescribed for people who suffer from asthma or heart failure.

BRONCHODILATORS Drugs that open up the bronchial tubes within the lungs when the tubes have become narrowed by muscle spasm. Bronchodilators, taken by aerosol spray, ease breathing in diseases such as asthma. Effects usually last for 3 to 5 hours.
Possible side effects: Rapid heartbeat, palpitations, tremor, headache and dizziness.

CORTICOSTEROIDS These preparations are made from synthetic HORMONES and are used mainly as ANTI-INFLAMMATORIES (in the treatment of arthritis and other disorders), as BRONCHODILATORS (in the treatment of asthma), or as IMMUNOSUPPRESSIVES, though they may be useful for treating certain malignant neoplasms or in compensating for a deficiency of natural hormones.
Possible side effects: Weight gain, redness of the face, stomach irritation, mental disturbances and increase in body hair.

DIURETICS Drugs that increase the quantity of urine produced by the kidneys and passed out of the body, thus ridding the body of excess fluid. Diuretics reduce excess fluid that has collected in the tissues as a result of any disorder of the heart, kidneys and liver. They are useful in treating mildly raised blood pressure.
Possible side effects: Rashes, dizziness, weakness, numbness, tingling in the hands and feet and excessive loss of potassium.

HORMONES Chemicals produced naturally by the endocrine (pituitary, thyroid, adrenal, ovary/testis, pancreas or parathyroid) glands. When they are not produced naturally (because of some disorder), they can be replaced by natural or synthetic hormones (hormone replacement therapy). See SEX HORMONES.
Possible side effects: There may be an exaggeration of the secondary sexual characteristics, so estrogens given to a man may increase the size of his breasts and androgens given to a woman may cause increased body hair and deepening of the voice. Estrogens also affect blood clotting and so may cause heart attack, stroke or thrombosis in the legs.

HYPOGLYCEMICS Drugs that lower the level of glucose in the blood. Oral hypoglycemic drugs are used in the treatment of diabetes mellitus if it cannot be controlled by diet alone, and does not require treatment with injections of insulin.
Possible side effects: Loss of appetite, nausea, indigestion, numbness or tingling in the skin, fever and rashes.
Warning: If the glucose level falls too low, weakness, dizziness, pallor, sweating, increased saliva flow, palpitations, irritability and trembling may result. If such symptoms occur several hours after eating, this may indicate that the dose is too high. Report symptoms to your physician.

IMMUNOSUPPRESSIVES Drugs that prevent or reduce the body's normal reaction to invasion by disease or by foreign tissues. Immunosuppressives are used to treat autoimmune diseases (in which the body's defenses work abnormally and attack the body's own tissues) and to help prevent rejection of organ transplants.
Possible side effects: Susceptibility to infection (especially chest infections, fungal infections of the mouth and skin and virus infections) is increased. Some immunosuppressives may damage the bone marrow, causing anemia, and may cause nausea and vomiting.

LAXATIVES Drugs that increase the frequency and ease of bowel movements. They work by stimulating the bowel wall, by increasing the bulk of bowel contents or by increasing the fluid content of the stool.
Warning: Laxatives are not to be taken regularly; the bowel may become unable to work properly without them.

REHYDRATION TREATMENTS Powders or solution used to prevent and treat dehydration caused by loss of water and salts from the body as a result of diarrhea (with or without persistent vomiting). The powders and solution contain sodium chloride, glucose and other mineral salts.
Possible side effects: Fluid accumulation may occur as a result of sodium retention.

SEX HORMONES (MALE) These are responsible for development of secondary sexual characteristics. As drugs they are given to compensate for hormone deficiencies in hypopituitarism or testicular disorders. Anabolic steroids are synthetic hormones that increase muscle bulk. They are sometimes used illegally by athletes.
Possible side effects: Weight gain, weakness, loss of appetite, drowsiness and blockage of the bladder by an enlarged prostate.

VASODILATORS Drugs that dilate blood vessels. Most widely used in prevention and treatment of angina, but also for treating heart failure and circulatory disorders.
Possible side effects: Headache, palpitations, flushing, faintness, nausea, vomiting, diarrhea and stuffy nose.

How to use the charts

The 68 diagnostic charts in this book have been compiled to help you find probable reasons for your symptoms. Each chart shows in detail a single symptom – for instance, vomiting, headache or a rash – and explores the possible causes of the symptom by means of a logically organized sequence of questions, each answerable by a simple YES or NO. Your responses will lead you toward a clearly worded end point, which suggests what may be wrong and offers advice on whether your disorder requires professional attention. To see how the charts work, examine the accompanying sample chart and study the explanatory notes. In particular, make sure you understand the exact meanings of the systematized action codes that indicate the relative urgency of the need to consult a physician (see *What the instructions mean,* opposite).

Note that every chart is numbered and bears a label defining or describing the key symptom. An introductory paragraph provides further description and explanation of the purpose of the chart. Read this paragraph carefully to make sure you have chosen the most appropriate pathway toward an analysis of your problem; then proceed as indicated in the chart itself. Always begin with the first question and follow through to the end point that fits your special situation. In many cases, extensive boxed information accompanying the chart will enhance your understanding of specific diagnoses as well as likely treatment for underlying disorders. Always read through such information texts (except, of course, in emergencies, when swift action is essential).

It is important to consult the *correct* chart at the *correct* time. For instructions on how to recognize and define your symptom and how to choose the precise chart you need, turn to p. 18.

Chart group
The charts are divided into sections according to whether they cover a general medical problem or a specific area, such as *Sex and fertility*.

Chart number
Each chart has a number so that it can be easily found and cross-referenced. Occasionally, you will be advised to turn to a more appropriate chart.

Go to chart

Chart title

Chart title
A short, descriptive term for the symptom heads each chart.

Definition
Each symptom is defined in simple, nontechnical terms and an indication of when a symptom is severe enough to cause concern is given.

The questions
These are structured so that you follow either a YES or a NO pathway from each question. Follow the series of questions, answering as appropriate in your case. In almost all cases you will then arrive at a possible reason for your symptoms.

The diagnosis
Each series of questions usually leads to a possible diagnosis and the treatment you are likely to need. The diagnoses take various forms according to the potential seriousness of a complaint. For example, it takes the form of a warning in cases where you may need urgent medical attention (see *What the instructions mean,* opposite). You are usually referred to other sections of the book for further information.

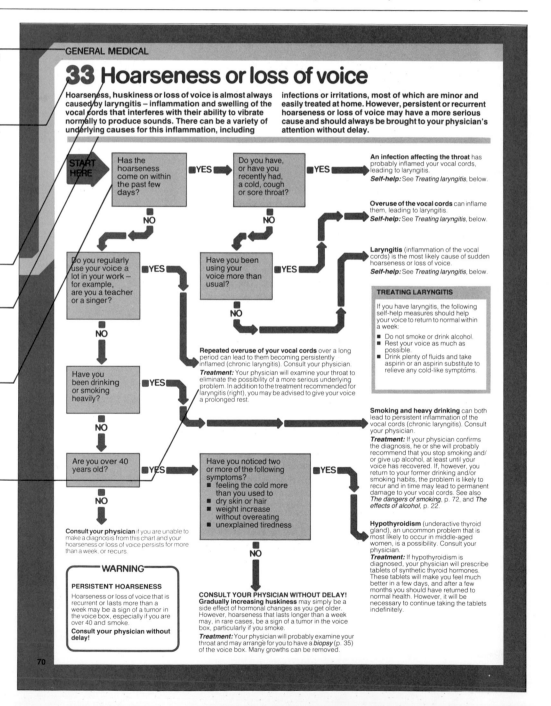

GENERAL MEDICAL

33 Hoarseness or loss of voice

Hoarseness, huskiness or loss of voice is almost always caused by laryngitis – inflammation and swelling of the vocal cords that interferes with their ability to vibrate normally to produce sounds. There can be a variety of underlying causes for this inflammation, including infections or irritations, most of which are minor and easily treated at home. However, persistent or recurrent hoarseness or loss of voice may have a more serious cause and should always be brought to your physician's attention without delay.

START HERE

Has the hoarseness come on within the past few days?
— YES → Do you have, or have you recently had, a cold, cough or sore throat? — YES → **An infection affecting the throat** has probably inflamed your vocal cords, leading to laryngitis. *Self-help:* See *Treating laryngitis*, below.

Do you regularly use your voice a lot in your work – for example, are you a teacher or a singer? — YES → Have you been using your voice more than usual? — YES → **Laryngitis** (inflammation of the vocal cords) is the most likely cause of sudden hoarseness or loss of voice. *Self-help:* See *Treating laryngitis*, below.

Overuse of the vocal cords can inflame them, leading to laryngitis. *Self-help:* See *Treating laryngitis*, below.

Repeated overuse of your vocal cords over a long period can lead to them becoming persistently inflamed (chronic laryngitis). Consult your physician. *Treatment:* Your physician will examine your throat to eliminate the possibility of a more serious underlying problem. In addition to the treatment recommended for laryngitis (right), you may be advised to give your voice a prolonged rest.

Have you been drinking or smoking heavily? — YES →

Smoking and heavy drinking can both lead to persistent inflammation of the vocal cords (chronic laryngitis). Consult your physician. *Treatment:* If your physician confirms the diagnosis, he or she will probably recommend that you stop smoking and/or give up alcohol, at least until your voice has recovered. If, however, you return to your former drinking and/or smoking habits, the problem is likely to recur and in time may lead to permanent damage to your vocal cords. See also *The dangers of smoking*, p. 72, and *The effects of alcohol*, p. 22.

Are you over 40 years old? — YES → Have you noticed two or more of the following symptoms?
■ feeling the cold more than you used to
■ dry skin or hair
■ weight increase without overeating
■ unexplained tiredness
— YES →

Hypothyroidism (underactive thyroid gland), an uncommon problem that is most likely to occur in middle-aged women, is a possibility. Consult your physician. *Treatment:* If hypothyroidism is diagnosed, your physician will prescribe tablets of synthetic thyroid hormones. These tablets will make you feel much better in a few days, and after a few months you should have returned to normal health. However, it will be necessary to continue taking the tablets indefinitely.

Consult your physician if you are unable to make a diagnosis from this chart and your hoarseness or loss of voice persists for more than a week, or recurs.

— WARNING —

PERSISTENT HOARSENESS
Hoarseness or loss of voice that is recurrent or lasts more than a week may be a sign of a tumor in the voice box, especially if you are over 40 and smoke.
Consult your physician without delay!

CONSULT YOUR PHYSICIAN WITHOUT DELAY!
Gradually increasing huskiness may simply be a side effect of hormonal changes as you get older. However, hoarseness that lasts longer than a week may, in rare cases, be a sign of a tumor in the voice box, particularly if you smoke. *Treatment:* Your physician will probably examine your throat and may arrange for you to have a *biopsy* (p. 35) of the voice box. Many growths can be removed.

TREATING LARYNGITIS
If you have laryngitis, the following self-help measures should help your voice to return to normal within a week:
■ Do not smoke or drink alcohol.
■ Rest your voice as much as possible.
■ Drink plenty of fluids and take aspirin or an aspirin substitute to relieve any cold-like symptoms.

70

WARNING: Though self-treatment is recommended for many minor disorders, remember that the charts provide only *likely* diagnoses. If you have any doubt about the diagnosis or treatment of any symptom, *always consult your physician.*

What the instructions mean

EMERGENCY
GET MEDICAL HELP NOW!

The condition may threaten life or lead to permanent disability if not given immediate medical attention. Get medical help by the fastest means possible, usually by calling an ambulance. In some cases it may be better to call your own physician or take the patient to the hospital yourself.

CALL YOUR PHYSICIAN NOW!
There is a possibility of a serious condition that may warrant immediate treatment and perhaps hospital admission. Seek medical advice immediately – day or night – usually by telephoning your physician, who will then decide on further action. If you are unable to make contact with your physician within an hour or so, emergency action (left) may be justified.

CONSULT YOUR PHYSICIAN WITHOUT DELAY!
The condition is serious and needs urgent medical assessment, but a few hours' delay in seeking treatment is unlikely to be damaging. Seek your physician's advice within 24 hours. This will usually mean telephoning for an appointment the same day.

Consult your physician.
A condition for which medical treatment is advisable, but for which reasonable delay is unlikely to lead to problems. Seek medical advice as soon as practical.

Discuss with your physician.
The condition is nonurgent and specific treatment is unlikely. However, your physician's advice may be helpful. Seek medical advice as soon as practical.

Boxed information
On most charts there are boxes containing important additional information to expand on either a diagnosis or a form of treatment. See the information and self-help boxes below.

GENERAL MEDICAL

34 Wheezing

Wheezing sometimes occurs when breathing out if you have a chest cold, and this is no cause for concern as long as breathing is otherwise normal. Such wheezing can usually be heard only through a stethoscope, but it may become more apparent to you when you exhale violently (during exercise, for example). Loud wheezing, especially if you also feel breathless or if breathing is painful, may be a sign of a number of more serious conditions, including congestive heart failure, asthma and bronchitis, which require medical attention.

START HERE → Has the wheezing started within the past few hours? → **YES** → Have you coughed up frothy pink or white phlegm? → **YES**

CALL YOUR PHYSICIAN NOW!
A dangerous buildup of fluid in the lungs, perhaps as a result of heart disease, is a possibility. Sit upright in a chair and try to keep calm; this will make breathing easier for you until help arrives.
Treatment: Keep a sample of the phlegm if possible in a glass or paper cup; this will help your physician to make a quick diagnosis of the problem. You will probably be admitted to the hospital where you will be given oxygen and drugs to assist breathing. These may include a *diuretic,* to drain fluid from the lungs, or a *bronchodilator,* to open up blocked airways in the lungs. When the lungs have cleared, treatment will depend on the underlying problem.

(wheezing NO) → Is breathing so difficult that you feel you are suffocating? → **YES**

EMERGENCY
GET MEDICAL HELP NOW!
A severe attack of asthma is a possibility.
Treatment: While waiting for help to arrive, carry out the first-aid measures described below. A severe attack usually requires hospital admission. Drugs will be given and, if necessary, the physician may use a mechanical respirator to assist breathing.

A mild attack of asthma is probably making you wheeze.
Self-help: Since asthma is most often due to an allergy, try to find which substances you are allergic to, and avoid contact with them as much as possible. Consult your physician, who will be able to prescribe drugs to prevent further attacks, and to help you when attacks occur. In addition, he or she may arrange for you to undergo special allergy tests to help identify the cause of your asthma.

(NO) → Is your temperature 100°F (38°C) or above? | 102 – 39 / 101 / 100 – 38 | → **YES**

Acute bronchitis (infection of the airways in the lungs) is a possibility.
Self-help: Take aspirin or an aspirin substitute, drink fluids and stay in a warm, humidified environment. Call your physician if you have difficulty breathing, or if you are no better in 48 hours.

(NO) → Do you wheeze a little most days? → **YES** → Do you cough up gray or greenish-yellow phlegm most days? → **YES**

Chronic bronchitis (persistent inflammation of the airways in the lungs) may be the cause of the wheezing, especially if you smoke and have had similar periods of wheezing in the past. Consult your physician.
Treatment: Your physician will advise you to give up smoking, if you are a smoker, as this is likely to make the problem worse. After tests have been done, such as a *chest X ray* (p. 73), he or she may prescribe *antibiotics.* An aerosol inhaler may help you if you suffer from breathlessness.

(NO) (NO) → **Consult your physician** if you are unable to make a diagnosis from this chart.

FIRST AID FOR ASTHMA

A severe attack of asthma, in which the person is fighting for breath and/or becomes pale and clammy with a blue tinge to the tongue or lips, is an emergency and admission to the hospital is essential. Call an ambulance or go to the emergency room of your local hospital immediately. Most people with asthma already have drugs or an inhaling apparatus, both of which should be administered. If one dose of inhalant does not quickly relieve the wheezing, it should be repeated only once.

In all cases, help the asthmatic to find the most comfortable position while you are waiting for medical help. The best position is sitting up, leaning forward on the back of a chair, and taking some of the weight on the arms (right). Plenty of fresh air will also help. A sudden severe attack of asthma can be very frightening for the family as well as the asthmatic. However, anxiety can make the attack worse, so only one other person should remain with the asthmatic and this person should be calm until help is provided.

71

WARNING
Symptoms that indicate an immediate danger to life are highlighted in these boxes. Where appropriate, steps that can be taken while waiting for medical help to arrive are explained.

FIRST AID
Where symptoms may require either simple first-aid or lifesaving measures, you will find boxed information on what action you should take.

INFORMATION
These boxes expand on the possible diagnoses and likely forms of treatment for specific symptoms. For example, several of them contain an explanation of a particular medical procedure. Where applicable, self-help treatment is included.

SELF-HELP
Where self-help measures may be effective in dealing with a symptom, advice is given on ways in which you may alleviate the problem.

How to find the correct chart

There are three ways to find the appropriate diagnostic chart for your symptom. You can use the *Pain-site map*, the *System-by-system chartfinder* or the *Chart index*, depending on the nature of the symptom, where it is located, and how easily you are able to define it. Whatever method you choose to find your chart, you will be given the title of the appropriate chart and its number.

1 Pain-site map

If you are in pain, the quickest way to find your chart is by reference to the pain-site map (below).

2 System-by-system chartfinder

If you know the body area or the body system affected, but are unsure how to define your symptom, consult the system-by-system chartfinder (opposite).

3 Chart index

When you have no difficulty naming your symptom, consult the chart index (p. 20). If you are suffering from more than one symptom, find the chart for the symptom that causes the most distress or that is most prominent.

1 Pain-site map

Consult this section to find the correct diagnostic chart for your symptom if you are suffering from pain in any part of the body. The illustrations below indicate possible areas of pain and are keyed in to the titles and numbers of the charts that deal with pain in that part of the body.

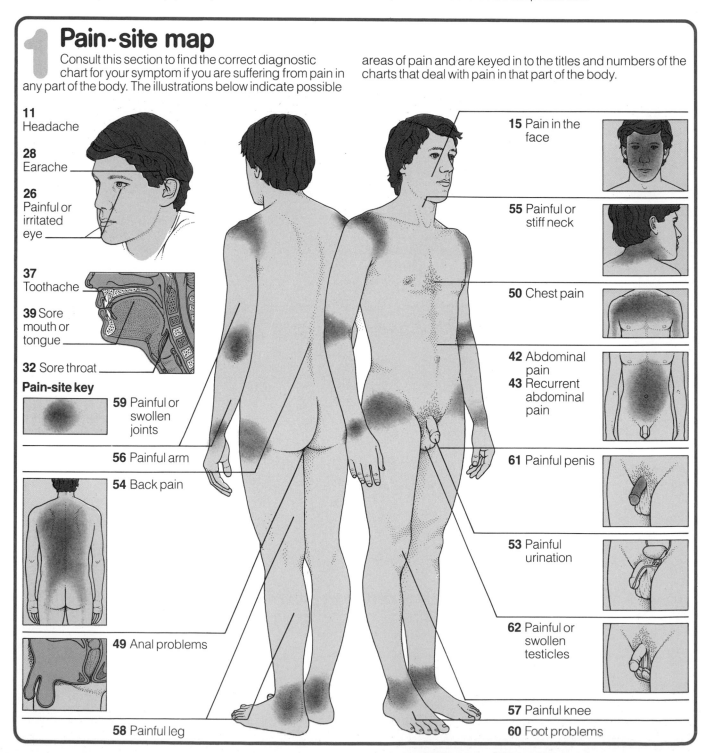

11 Headache

28 Earache

26 Painful or irritated eye

37 Toothache

39 Sore mouth or tongue

32 Sore throat

Pain-site key

59 Painful or swollen joints

56 Painful arm

54 Back pain

49 Anal problems

58 Painful leg

15 Pain in the face

55 Painful or stiff neck

50 Chest pain

42 Abdominal pain
43 Recurrent abdominal pain

61 Painful penis

53 Painful urination

62 Painful or swollen testicles

57 Painful knee

60 Foot problems

2 System-by-system chartfinder

Consult this section if you know what part of the body or which body system your symptom originates in. A list of the diagnostic charts that deal with each of the main body systems is given under each main heading. Select the chart that most closely seems to fit your symptom.

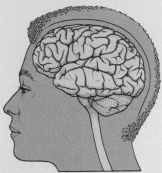

Head, brain and psychological symptoms

10 Faintness and fainting
11 Headache
12 Dizziness
13 Numbness or tingling
14 Twitching and trembling
15 Pain in the face
16 Forgetfulness and confusion
17 Difficulty speaking
18 Disturbing thoughts and feelings
19 Depression
20 Anxiety

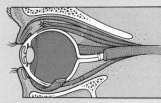

Eye and sight symptoms

26 Painful or irritated eye
27 Disturbed or impaired vision

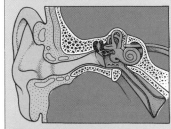

Ear and hearing symptoms

28 Earache
29 Noises in the ear
30 Deafness

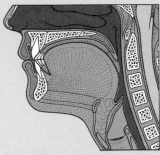

Mouth, tongue and throat symptoms

32 Sore throat
37 Toothache
38 Difficulty swallowing
39 Sore mouth or tongue

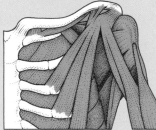

Muscle, bone and joint symptoms

54 Back pain
55 Painful or stiff neck
56 Painful arm
57 Painful knee
58 Painful leg
59 Painful or swollen joints
60 Foot problems

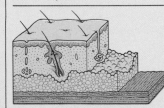

Skin, hair and nail symptoms

7 Excessive sweating
8 Itching
9 Lumps and swellings
21 Hair, scalp and nail problems
22 General skin problems
23 Spots and rashes
24 Raised spots or lumps on the skin
25 Rash with fever

General symptoms

1 Feeling under the weather
2 Loss of weight
3 Tiredness
4 Overweight
5 Difficulty sleeping
6 Fever

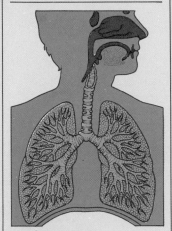

Respiratory symptoms

31 Runny nose
32 Sore throat
33 Hoarseness or loss of voice
34 Wheezing
35 Coughing
36 Difficulty breathing
50 Chest pain

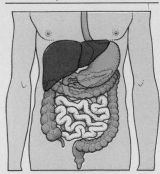

Abdominal and digestive symptoms

40 Vomiting
41 Recurrent vomiting
42 Abdominal pain
43 Recurrent abdominal pain
44 Swollen abdomen
45 Excess gas
46 Diarrhea
47 Constipation
48 Abnormal-looking bowel movements
49 Anal problems

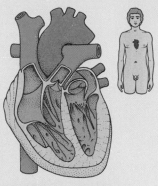

Heart symptoms

50 Chest pain
51 Palpitations

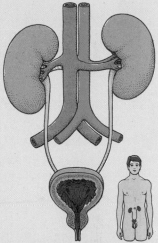

Urinary symptoms

52 General urinary problems
53 Painful urination

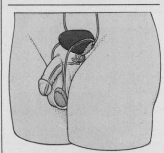

Genital symptoms

61 Painful penis
62 Painful or swollen testicles

Sexual symptoms

63 Erection difficulties
64 Premature ejaculation
65 Delayed ejaculation
66 Low sex drive
67 Contraception
68 Fertility problems

3 Chart index

Consult this index if you think that you know the correct name for your symptom. The chart titles and their numbers are listed alphabetically together with possible alternative names for symptoms (for example, *Raised temperature* for *Fever*). In this section you will also find the titles of information boxes dealing with symptoms that do not have a separate diagnostic chart.

1 General medical symptoms

1 Feeling under the weather **2** Loss of weight **3** Tiredness
4 Overweight **5** Difficulty sleeping **6** Fever **7** Excessive
sweating **8** Itching **9** Lumps and swellings **10** Faintness and
fainting **11** Headache **12** Dizziness **13** Numbness or
tingling **14** Twitching and trembling **15** Pain in the face
16 Forgetfulness and confusion **17** Difficulty speaking
18 Disturbing thoughts and feelings **19** Depression
20 Anxiety **21** Hair, scalp and nail problems **22** General skin
problems **23** Spots and rashes **24** Raised spots or lumps on
the skin **25** Rash with fever **26** Painful or irritated eye
27 Disturbed or impaired vision **28** Earache **29** Noises in the
ear **30** Deafness **31** Runny nose **32** Sore throat
33 Hoarseness or loss of voice **34** Wheezing **35** Coughing
36 Difficulty breathing **37** Toothache **38** Difficulty swallowing
39 Sore mouth or tongue **40** Vomiting **41** Recurrent vomiting
42 Abdominal pain **43** Recurrent abdominal pain **44** Swollen
abdomen **45** Excess gas **46** Diarrhea **47** Constipation
48 Abnormal-looking bowel movements **49** Anal problems
50 Chest pain **51** Palpitations **52** General urinary problems
53 Painful urination **54** Back pain **55** Painful or stiff neck
56 Painful arm **57** Painful knee **58** Painful leg **59** Painful or
swollen joints **60** Foot problems **61** Painful penis **62** Painful or
swollen testicles

1 Feeling under the weather

Sometimes you may have a vague, generalized feeling of being sick without being able to locate a specific symptom such as pain. This may be the result of a minor infection or unhealthy life-style, but occasionally it may be a sign of a more serious underlying problem that requires medical treatment.

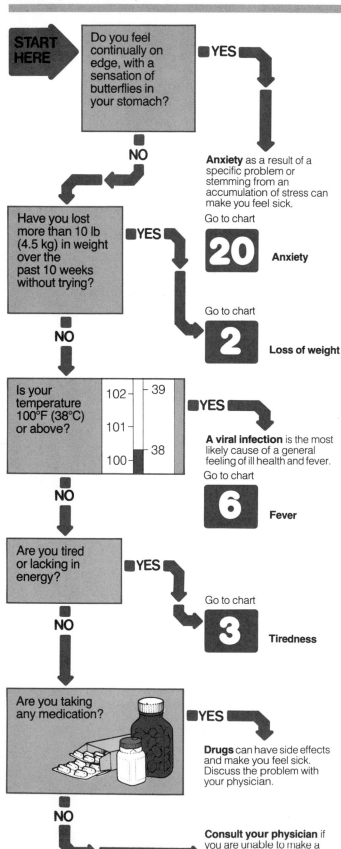

START HERE

Do you feel continually on edge, with a sensation of butterflies in your stomach?

YES →

Anxiety as a result of a specific problem or stemming from an accumulation of stress can make you feel sick.

Go to chart

20 Anxiety

NO ↓

Have you lost more than 10 lb (4.5 kg) in weight over the past 10 weeks without trying?

YES →

Go to chart

2 Loss of weight

NO ↓

Is your temperature 100°F (38°C) or above?

102 — 39
101 —
100 — 38

YES →

A viral infection is the most likely cause of a general feeling of ill health and fever.

Go to chart

6 Fever

NO ↓

Are you tired or lacking in energy?

YES →

Go to chart

3 Tiredness

NO ↓

Are you taking any medication?

YES →

Drugs can have side effects and make you feel sick. Discuss the problem with your physician.

NO ↓

Consult your physician if you are unable to make a diagnosis from this chart.

THE EFFECTS OF ALCOHOL

The main immediate effect of alcohol is to dull the reactions of the brain. In small quantities, this can produce a pleasantly relaxed feeling but in larger amounts can lead to gross impairment of memory, judgment, coordination and emotional reactions.

Alcohol also widens the blood vessels, making you feel temporarily warm. However, body heat is rapidly lost from the dilated blood vessels and this can lead to severe chilling (hypothermia).

After a heavy drinking session, you are likely to feel tired and nauseated, and may have a headache as a result of dehydration and the damaging effect of alcohol on the stomach and intestines.

Long-term effects
Regular consumption of large amounts of alcohol can lead to the following serious health problems:

- **Obesity** is likely as a result of the high-energy value of most alcoholic drinks.
- **Liver damage** (cirrhosis, when the liver can no longer process nutrients or drugs) is almost inevitable.
- **Brain shrinkage** has been observed in many heavy drinkers.
- **Addiction** with accompanying social problems is a real risk for even moderate regular drinkers.

Maximum safe alcohol intake
Anyone who regularly drinks more than 3 alcoholic drinks or goes on drinking binges is risking serious health problems. For safety, keep your drinking at a much lower level.

3 beers **OR** 3 glasses of wine **OR** 3 measures of spirits

BLOOD ANALYSIS

The blood is the principal transport medium of the body. It carries oxygen, nutrients and other vital substances to the body tissues and carries waste products away. The blood is composed of three principal parts: red cells containing the red pigment (hemoglobin), which carries oxygen; the white cells (which fight infection) and platelets (which fight infection and seal damaged blood vessels); and the plasma, a yellowish fluid in which the blood cells, nutrients, chemicals and waste products are suspended.

Modern techniques for counting the numbers of different types of blood cells contained in a blood sample – a procedure known as a blood count – can help in the diagnosis of blood disorders. And examination of the chemicals in the plasma can give clues to diseases of many other parts of the body.

Parts of the blood

Plasma

White cells and platelets

Red cells

1 **Red blood cells** carry oxygen to body cells.
2 **Platelets** seal damaged blood vessels.
3 **Lymphocytes** (a type of white blood cell) produce substances to destroy invading germs.
4 **Neutrophils** (a type of white blood cell) engulf invaders.

2 Loss of weight

Minor fluctuations in weight of only a few pounds as a result of temporary changes in the amount of exercise you take or the amount of food you eat are normal. However, more severe unintentional weight loss, especially when combined with loss of appetite or other symptoms, usually requires medical attention. Consult this chart if you have lost more than 10 lb (4.5 kg) in a period of 10 weeks or less.

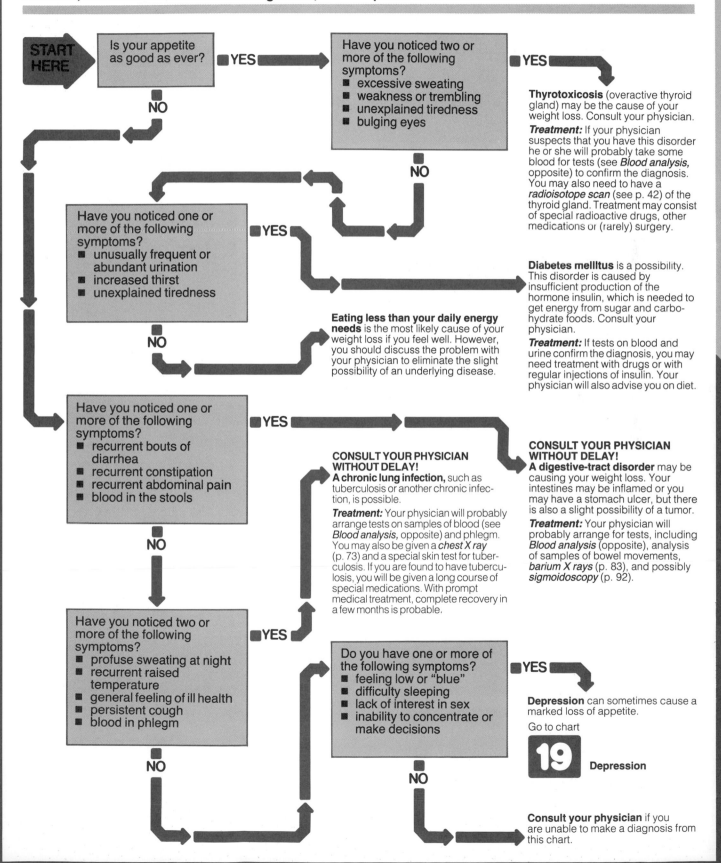

START HERE

Is your appetite as good as ever?

YES

Have you noticed two or more of the following symptoms?
- excessive sweating
- weakness or trembling
- unexplained tiredness
- bulging eyes

YES

Thyrotoxicosis (overactive thyroid gland) may be the cause of your weight loss. Consult your physician.

Treatment: If your physician suspects that you have this disorder he or she will probably take some blood for tests (see *Blood analysis,* opposite) to confirm the diagnosis. You may also need to have a *radioisotope scan* (see p. 42) of the thyroid gland. Treatment may consist of special radioactive drugs, other medications or (rarely) surgery.

NO

NO

Have you noticed one or more of the following symptoms?
- unusually frequent or abundant urination
- increased thirst
- unexplained tiredness

YES

Diabetes mellitus is a possibility. This disorder is caused by insufficient production of the hormone insulin, which is needed to get energy from sugar and carbohydrate foods. Consult your physician.

Treatment: If tests on blood and urine confirm the diagnosis, you may need treatment with drugs or with regular injections of insulin. Your physician will also advise you on diet.

Eating less than your daily energy needs is the most likely cause of your weight loss if you feel well. However, you should discuss the problem with your physician to eliminate the slight possibility of an underlying disease.

NO

Have you noticed one or more of the following symptoms?
- recurrent bouts of diarrhea
- recurrent constipation
- recurrent abdominal pain
- blood in the stools

YES

CONSULT YOUR PHYSICIAN WITHOUT DELAY!
A digestive-tract disorder may be causing your weight loss. Your intestines may be inflamed or you may have a stomach ulcer, but there is also a slight possibility of a tumor.

Treatment: Your physician will probably arrange for tests, including *Blood analysis* (opposite), analysis of samples of bowel movements, *barium X rays* (p. 83), and possibly *sigmoidoscopy* (p. 92).

CONSULT YOUR PHYSICIAN WITHOUT DELAY!
A chronic lung infection, such as tuberculosis or another chronic infection, is possible.

Treatment: Your physician will probably arrange tests on samples of blood (see *Blood analysis,* opposite) and phlegm. You may also be given a *chest X ray* (p. 73) and a special skin test for tuberculosis. If you are found to have tuberculosis, you will be given a long course of special medications. With prompt medical treatment, complete recovery in a few months is probable.

NO

Have you noticed two or more of the following symptoms?
- profuse sweating at night
- recurrent raised temperature
- general feeling of ill health
- persistent cough
- blood in phlegm

YES

Do you have one or more of the following symptoms?
- feeling low or "blue"
- difficulty sleeping
- lack of interest in sex
- inability to concentrate or make decisions

YES

Depression can sometimes cause a marked loss of appetite.

Go to chart

19 Depression

NO

NO

Consult your physician if you are unable to make a diagnosis from this chart.

3 Tiredness

Consult this chart if you feel tired or lacking in energy during the day or if you spend more time asleep than you normally do. Lethargy is a common symptom of many disorders, some trivial and some that require medical attention. Sudden severe drowsiness is always a serious symptom and requires prompt attention.

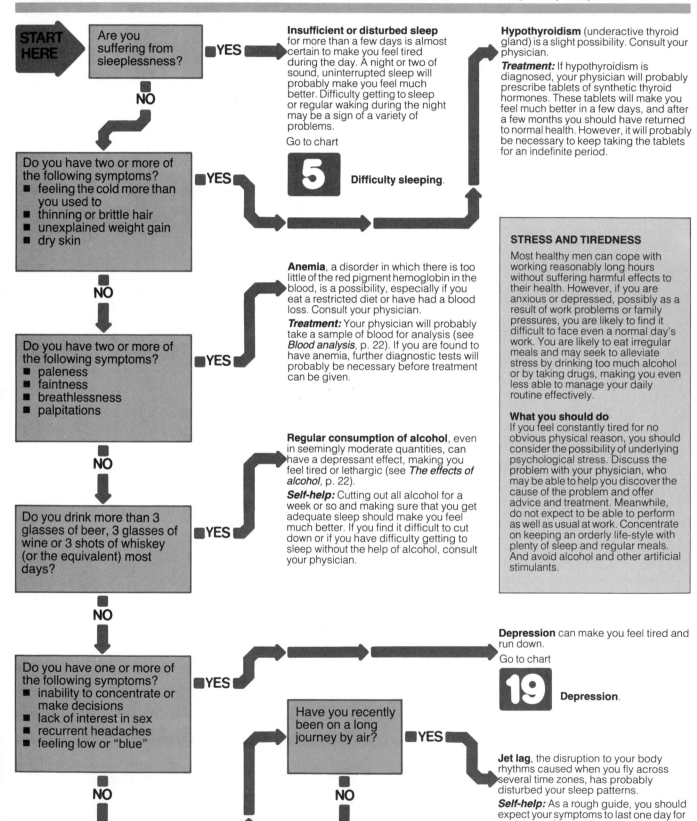

START HERE

Are you suffering from sleeplessness?

YES → **Insufficient or disturbed sleep** for more than a few days is almost certain to make you feel tired during the day. A night or two of sound, uninterrupted sleep will probably make you feel much better. Difficulty getting to sleep or regular waking during the night may be a sign of a variety of problems.

Go to chart

5 **Difficulty sleeping**.

Hypothyroidism (underactive thyroid gland) is a slight possibility. Consult your physician.

Treatment: If hypothyroidism is diagnosed, your physician will probably prescribe tablets of synthetic thyroid hormones. These tablets will make you feel much better in a few days, and after a few months you should have returned to normal health. However, it will probably be necessary to keep taking the tablets for an indefinite period.

NO

Do you have two or more of the following symptoms?
- feeling the cold more than you used to
- thinning or brittle hair
- unexplained weight gain
- dry skin

YES →

NO

Do you have two or more of the following symptoms?
- paleness
- faintness
- breathlessness
- palpitations

YES → **Anemia**, a disorder in which there is too little of the red pigment hemoglobin in the blood, is a possibility, especially if you eat a restricted diet or have had a blood loss. Consult your physician.

Treatment: Your physician will probably take a sample of blood for analysis (see *Blood analysis*, p. 22). If you are found to have anemia, further diagnostic tests will probably be necessary before treatment can be given.

NO

Do you drink more than 3 glasses of beer, 3 glasses of wine or 3 shots of whiskey (or the equivalent) most days?

YES → **Regular consumption of alcohol**, even in seemingly moderate quantities, can have a depressant effect, making you feel tired or lethargic (see *The effects of alcohol*, p. 22).

Self-help: Cutting out all alcohol for a week or so and making sure that you get adequate sleep should make you feel much better. If you find it difficult to cut down or if you have difficulty getting to sleep without the help of alcohol, consult your physician.

NO

Do you have one or more of the following symptoms?
- inability to concentrate or make decisions
- lack of interest in sex
- recurrent headaches
- feeling low or "blue"

YES → **Depression** can make you feel tired and run down.

Go to chart

19 **Depression**.

NO

Have you recently been on a long journey by air?

YES → **Jet lag**, the disruption to your body rhythms caused when you fly across several time zones, has probably disturbed your sleep patterns.

Self-help: As a rough guide, you should expect your symptoms to last one day for each hour of time difference. Meanwhile, take as much rest as you need until your sleep patterns have readjusted.

NO

Go to next page

STRESS AND TIREDNESS

Most healthy men can cope with working reasonably long hours without suffering harmful effects to their health. However, if you are anxious or depressed, possibly as a result of work problems or family pressures, you are likely to find it difficult to face even a normal day's work. You are likely to eat irregular meals and may seek to alleviate stress by drinking too much alcohol or by taking drugs, making you even less able to manage your daily routine effectively.

What you should do
If you feel constantly tired for no obvious physical reason, you should consider the possibility of underlying psychological stress. Discuss the problem with your physician, who may be able to help you discover the cause of the problem and offer advice and treatment. Meanwhile, do not expect to be able to perform as well as usual at work. Concentrate on keeping an orderly life-style with plenty of sleep and regular meals. And avoid alcohol and other artificial stimulants.

Continued from previous page

Have you been working hard without a break for several weeks?

YES

NO

Overworking for an extended period has probably caused your tiredness. However, you should also consider the possibility that stress from problems at work or at home is making you less able to cope than usual. See *Stress and tiredness*, opposite.

Self-help: Try to take some time off from your normal responsibilities, if possible, or rearrange your routine to allow yourself more time for relaxation. If a break does not make you feel any better, discuss the problem with your physician.

Have you recently recovered from an infectious illness, such as the flu or infectious mononucleosis?

YES

NO

Recovery from many such illnesses can take several weeks. During this period you are likely to feel tired and possibly depressed.

Self-help: Do not expect too much of yourself at first. Make sure you eat a nourishing diet and take things easy until you feel better again. If symptoms persist for more than a month, consult your physician.

Are you taking any medications?

YES

NO

Drugs have side effects and can make you feel tired. Discuss the problem with your physician.

Consult your physician if you are unable to make a diagnosis from this chart.

THE BENEFITS OF EXERCISE

There are sound physiological benefits to health from regular exercise. You will sleep better, wake more refreshed and feel more alert and able to concentrate. Exercising regularly will help to control your weight and help you to build up stamina, or your endurance, and "staying power," which will in turn improve your physical and mental capacity for everyday activities. Some recent research has shown that regular strenuous physical activity can help to prevent and alleviate minor depression. But, most importantly, regular exercise has been proven to help prevent *coronary heart disease* (p. 95).

How to organize your exercise routine

Three 20-minute exercise sessions a week, at regular intervals, should be sufficient to put you on the path to fitness and well-being. Choose a level of activity high enough to make you breathless, sweaty and aware of your heart beating. It is important to find an activity that interests you, otherwise you may lack the basic motivation needed to maintain the activity over a period of time. If running, swimming or cycling does not appeal to you, remember that an activity such as digging in the garden can be made just as energetic.

If you fit in any of the following categories, ask your physician before you take up any sort of strenuous activity:

- If you are over 60 years of age, or over 40 and have not exercised regularly since early adulthood;
- If you are a heavy smoker (i.e., you smoke more than 20 cigarettes most days);
- If you are seriously overweight (see *Weight chart*, p. 26);
- If you are under treatment or supervision for any health problem such as high blood pressure, heart disease, diabetes or kidney disease.

It is always advisable to do some warm-up exercises before an exercise session to prevent muscle or joint strain. Also, "cool-down" exercises help you gradually adjust to your regular routine.

Fitness values of selected common activities

This table includes a selection of sports and activities and compares their relative values for increasing physical fitness. The ratings are based on the average performance of a nonprofessional. The benefits depend on how vigorously you undertake your chosen activity.

●●●● Excellent
●●● Good
●● Fair
● Minimal

Activity	Calories consumed in 20 minutes of activity	Value in improving heart and lung fitness	Value in improving suppleness	Value in improving joint power	Value in improving muscle
Easy walking	60	●		●	●
Light gardening (weeding, etc.)	90	●		●●	●●
Golf (flat course)	90	●		●●	●
Brisk walking	100	●●		●	●●
Badminton	115	●●		●●●	●●
Horseback riding	115	●●		●●●	●●
Gymnastics	140	●●		●●●●	●●●
Heavy gardening (digging, etc.)	140	●●		●●●	●●●●
Dancing	160	●●		●●●	●
Easy jogging	160	●●●		●	●●
Tennis	160	●●●		●●●	●●
Ice skating	160	●●●		●●●	●●
Skiing (downhill)	160	●●●		●●●	●●
Skiing (cross-country)	180	●●●●		●●●	●●●
Rowing	180	●●●●		●●●	●●●●
Soccer	180	●●●		●●●	●●●
Football	180	●●●		●●	●●●
Racquetball or handball	200	●●●		●●●	●●●
Brisk jogging	210	●●●●		●●	●●
Bicycling	220	●●●●		●●●	●●●
Swimming	240	●●●●		●●●●	●●●●

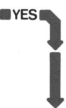

4 Overweight

Normally, fat accounts for between 10 and 20 percent of the weight of an adult man. Any more than this is both unnecessary and unhealthy, increasing the risk of diseases such as diabetes, high blood pressure and arthritis. Most people reach their ideal weight in their teens and gradually gain a little weight as they get older, reaching their heaviest at about 50. Consult this chart if you weigh more than the healthy weight for your height shown in the chart below, or if you can pinch a fold of flesh that is more than an inch thick on your abdomen. In most cases, weight gain is due simply to eating more than you need and can be remedied by a balanced reducing diet, but occasionally there may be a medical reason for putting on weight.

START HERE

Have you been overweight for most of your life?
→ **YES** →

Are both your parents overweight?
→ **YES** →

A tendency to obesity can run in families. This may be because unhealthy eating habits tend to be passed on to the younger generation. Or it may be that some physical types naturally burn energy more slowly than others and therefore need to eat less.

Self-help: Adopt a sensible weight-reducing diet such as the one suggested in the box on *How to lose weight*, opposite.

NO (from "Have you been overweight")
NO (from "Are both your parents overweight?")

Did you put on weight after giving up smoking?
→ **YES** →

Eating more than you need is likely to be the cause of your weight problem.

Self-help: You should aim to take in fewer calories (units of energy) each day than your body burns up (see *How to lose weight*, opposite).

NO

Compulsive eating as a result of psychological stress is a common problem.

Self-help: A gradual reducing diet that helps you adopt healthier long-term eating habits should help you lose your excess weight (see *How to lose weight*, opposite). However, if you are still suffering from depression or anxiety, you should discuss the problem with your physician first so that the underlying cause of your overeating can be treated.

Did you put on weight at a time when you were depressed or anxious?
→ **YES** →

Withdrawal of tobacco often causes a temporary gain in weight. This may partly be due to changes in body chemistry, but is more likely to be due to compensatory overeating.

Self-help: During the first weeks after giving up smoking do not worry about putting on weight. Wait until you have lost your intense craving for tobacco (after about 8 weeks) before adopting a weight-reducing diet (see *How to lose weight*, opposite).

NO

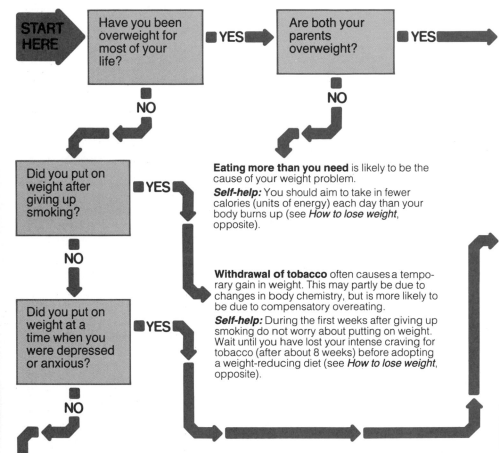

WEIGHT CHART

This chart enables you to check your actual weight against the healthy weight for your height. Rule a line across from your height on the left of the chart, and a line up from your weight on the bottom of the chart. If the point where the lines meet is in the colored central band, your weight is healthy for someone of your height.

Height: 6'4" 6'3" 6'2" 6'1" 6' 5'11" 5'10" 5'9" 5'8" 5'7" 5'6" 5'5" 5'4" 5'3" 5'2"

Underweight | Healthy weight | Overweight

Weight (lbs) 120 130 140 150 160 170 180 190 200

AGE AND INCREASING WEIGHT

As you get older you need less energy, partly because you become less active, partly for other reasons that are not yet clear. But many people do not reduce their food intake to correspond with their lower energy requirements as they get older. In addition, many men drink more alcohol than they did when they were younger, and alcohol contains calories in abundance. The result is a surplus of calories, causing increasing deposits of fatty flesh as old age approaches.

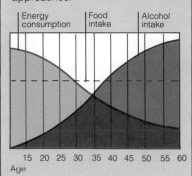

Energy consumption | Food intake | Alcohol intake

15 20 25 30 35 40 45 50 55 60
Age

Go to next page

Continued from previous page

Did the weight gain follow a change from a physically active life or strenuous job to a more sedentary lifestyle or work?

▪YES▪

Energy requirements of the body vary according to the amount of exercise your daily routine involves. For instance, if you have a desk job, your average daily calorie requirement may be approximately 2,500 calories, but if you have a more active job, you may require 3,300 calories.

Self-help: Adjusting your food intake to take account of your reduced energy requirements should help you to lose the weight you have put on. This may mean changing eating habits you have developed over many years, and it may take a little while for you to become accustomed to your new diet. See *How to lose weight*, right, for some advice on a healthy reducing diet. You should also try to incorporate some physical exercise into your new routine to help keep your muscles firm and to assist weight loss (see *The benefits of exercise*, p. 25).

NO

Have you noticed two or more of the following symptoms since you began to put on weight?
- feeling the cold more than you used to
- thinning or brittle hair
- dry skin
- unexplained tiredness

▪YES▪

Hypothyroidism (underactive thyroid gland) is a possibility. Consult your physician.

Treatment: If hypothyroidism is diagnosed, your physician will probably prescribe tablets of synthetic thyroid hormones. These tablets will help your body burn up excess fat and after a few months you should have returned to your normal weight. However, it will probably be necessary to keep on taking the tablets indefinitely.

NO

Are you taking any medications?

▪YES▪

Certain drugs, particularly steroids prescribed for problems such as asthma or rheumatoid arthritis, can cause weight gain as a side effect. Discuss the problem with your physician.

NO

Are you over 40 years old?

▪YES▪

Growing older is often accompanied by a gradual gain in weight. This is most likely because you begin to exercise less at a time in your life when your body is beginning to take longer to burn up food (see *Age and increasing weight*, opposite).

Self-help: Reduce your intake of food to correspond with your lower energy consumption (see *How to lose weight*, above).

NO

Overeating is the likely cause of your excess weight.

Self-help: Follow the recommended reducing diet (see *How to lose weight*, above). If after a month you fail to lose weight, consult your physician, who will find out if the problem is due to any underlying disorder.

HOW TO LOSE WEIGHT

If you are fat, it is because your body is not using all the energy you feed it. To lose weight you must expend more energy than you take in, first by changing your diet, second by exercising more. It is best to avoid crash diets, which have no lasting effect because they do not encourage you to adopt healthy new habits. You will find it more helpful to follow this step-by-step diet, which is designed to help you change your eating habits over time.

1 Try to cut out, or at least cut down on, all foods in group 1, the sweet or rich foods. Reduce your daily alcohol intake to no more than two 12-oz cans of beer, two 6-oz glasses of wine or 2 shots (1.5 oz) of whiskey (or the equivalent). If you drink hard liquor, use low-calorie mixers or unsweetened fruit juices. Eat normal portions of food from groups 2 and 3.

2 If you have not lost any weight after 2 weeks, stop having any group 1 foods, halve your helpings of group 2 foods and eat as much as you want from group 3. Cut down further on (or eliminate) your consumption of alcohol.

3 If you fail to lose weight after 2 more weeks, halve your helpings of group 3 foods and eat as little as possible from group 2. Consult your physician if you fail to lose weight after 4 more weeks.

Meat	Vegetables	Dairy foods	Fish	Other
Group 1 foods				
Visible fat on any meat Bacon Duck, goose Sausages, salami Pâtés		Butter Cream Ice cream		Thick gravies or sauces Fried food Sugar, candies Cakes, pies, cookies Puddings Canned fruits in syrup Dried fruits Nuts Jams, syrups Carbonated drinks Sherbets
Group 2 foods				
Lean beef Lamb Pork	Beans Lentils	Eggs Cheeses (other than cottage cheese) Whole milk	Oily fish (e.g., herring, mackerel, sardines, tuna packed in oil)	Pasta or rice Soups Breads, crackers Unsweetened cereals Margarine Polyunsaturated vegetable oils
Group 3 foods				
Poultry other than duck or goose (not including the skin)	Potatoes Vegetables (raw or lightly cooked) Clear or vegetable-only soups	Skim milk Yogurt Cottage cheese	Nonoily fish, (e.g., haddock, perch, cod) Shellfish (e.g., crab, shrimp) Tuna packed in water	Bran Fresh fruit Unsweetened fruit juice

5 Difficulty sleeping

It is quite common to have an occasional night when you find it difficult to get to sleep and this need not be a cause for concern. Consult this chart if you regularly have difficulty falling asleep at night or if you wake during the night or early in the morning (a problem sometimes known as insomnia).

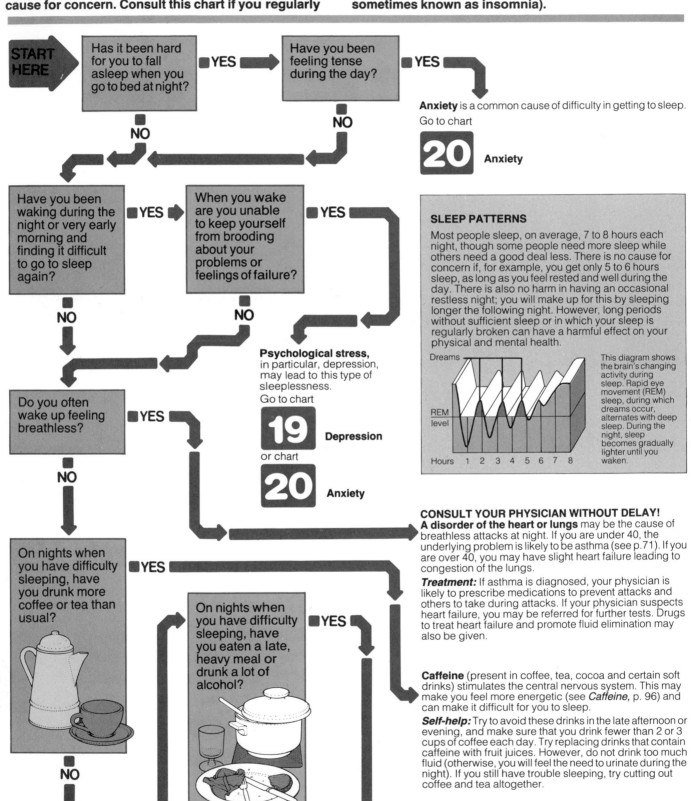

START HERE

Has it been hard for you to fall asleep when you go to bed at night?

→ **YES** → **Have you been feeling tense during the day?** → **YES** →

Anxiety is a common cause of difficulty in getting to sleep. Go to chart

20 Anxiety

NO

NO

Have you been waking during the night or very early morning and finding it difficult to go to sleep again? → **YES** → **When you wake are you unable to keep yourself from brooding about your problems or feelings of failure?** → **YES** →

NO

NO

Psychological stress, in particular, depression, may lead to this type of sleeplessness. Go to chart

19 Depression

or chart

20 Anxiety

SLEEP PATTERNS

Most people sleep, on average, 7 to 8 hours each night, though some people need more sleep while others need a good deal less. There is no cause for concern if, for example, you get only 5 to 6 hours sleep, as long as you feel rested and well during the day. There is also no harm in having an occasional restless night; you will make up for this by sleeping longer the following night. However, long periods without sufficient sleep or in which your sleep is regularly broken can have a harmful effect on your physical and mental health.

This diagram shows the brain's changing activity during sleep. Rapid eye movement (REM) sleep, during which dreams occur, alternates with deep sleep. During the night, sleep becomes gradually lighter until you waken.

Do you often wake up feeling breathless? → **YES** →

NO

CONSULT YOUR PHYSICIAN WITHOUT DELAY!
A disorder of the heart or lungs may be the cause of breathless attacks at night. If you are under 40, the underlying problem is likely to be asthma (see p.71). If you are over 40, you may have slight heart failure leading to congestion of the lungs.

Treatment: If asthma is diagnosed, your physician is likely to prescribe medications to prevent attacks and others to take during attacks. If your physician suspects heart failure, you may be referred for further tests. Drugs to treat heart failure and promote fluid elimination may also be given.

On nights when you have difficulty sleeping, have you drunk more coffee or tea than usual? → **YES** →

On nights when you have difficulty sleeping, have you eaten a late, heavy meal or drunk a lot of alcohol? → **YES** →

Caffeine (present in coffee, tea, cocoa and certain soft drinks) stimulates the central nervous system. This may make you feel more energetic (see *Caffeine,* p. 96) and can make it difficult for you to sleep.

Self-help: Try to avoid these drinks in the late afternoon or evening, and make sure that you drink fewer than 2 or 3 cups of coffee each day. Try replacing drinks that contain caffeine with fruit juices. However, do not drink too much fluid (otherwise, you will feel the need to urinate during the night). If you still have trouble sleeping, try cutting out coffee and tea altogether.

NO

NO

Eating or drinking in excess in the evening often causes sleeplessnes.

Self-help: Try eating your evening meal earlier and reducing your food and alcohol intake.

Go to next page

Continued from previous page

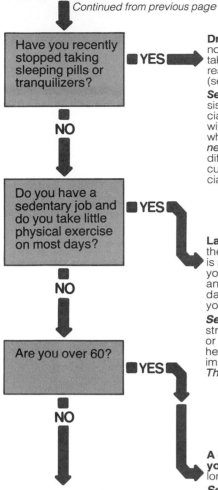

Have you recently stopped taking sleeping pills or tranquilizers?

■ **YES** ►

Drugs such as these can disrupt normal sleeping patterns, and it can take several weeks for your body to readjust after you stop taking them (see *Sleeping pills,* right).

Self-help: Try to be patient and resist the temptation to ask your physician to prescribe more pills to deal with your sleeping problem. Meanwhile, see *Preventing sleeplessness,* below. If you are still having difficulty sleeping after a month, discuss the problem with your physician.

■ **NO**

Do you have a sedentary job and do you take little physical exercise on most days?

■ **YES** ►

Lack of physical exercise during the day may mean that your body is not sufficiently tired to enable you to sleep easily. Also, stress and tension built up during the day may be making it difficult for you to relax.

Self-help: Try to get some form of strenuous exercise during the day or early evening. Not only will this help you sleep better, it will also improve your general health (see *The benefits of exercise,* p.25).

■ **NO**

Are you over 60?

■ **YES** ►

A declining need for sleep as you get older is quite normal as long as you continue to feel well.

Self-help: Try to find new activities to fill your extra waking hours. However, if your lack of sleep is making you tired or irritable, consult your physician.

■ **NO**

Consult your physician if you are unable to make a diagnosis from this chart and if the self-help measures described below do not work.

SLEEPING PILLS

If you have difficulty sleeping at night, your physician may prescribe sleeping pills. These may be useful if you cannot sleep because of pain after an injury or during an illness, or at times of emotional stress – for example, following a bereavement.

What drugs are used?

There are two main types of drug used to treat sleeplessness: antianxiety drugs and barbiturates. Both act in a similar way, but physicians usually prefer to prescribe an antianxiety drug because of the greater danger of overdose with barbiturates.

How do sleeping drugs work?

All sleeping drugs work by suppressing brain function in some way. This means that the sleep you get when taking a sleeping drug is not normal and may leave you less rested than after a natural night's sleep. This also means that if you suddenly stop taking sleeping pills after having used them regularly, you may sleep restlessly and have vivid dreams while your brain readjusts to normal *sleep patterns* (opposite).

Are sleeping pills dangerous?

Sleeping pills that are taken on your physician's advice and according to the dosage prescribed are unlikely to do you any harm, even if taken for many years. However, you may become dependent on these drugs if you take them regularly. If you wish to stop taking them, discuss this with your physician. In addition, you should consult your physician if you have difficulty waking up in the morning or if you find that your sleeping pills no longer work as effectively as before; you may need a change of drug.

People who take sleeping pills should always remember the following safety rules:

- Never take a larger dose than prescribed.
- Never drive or operate machinery before the effects of the sleeping drugs have worn off.
- Never take alcohol with these drugs; stop drinking at least 2 hours before taking a sleeping pill and do not start to drink until at least 8 hours afterward.
- Never give your sleeping pills to others, especially children.
- Never keep your tablets on your bedside table; there is a danger that you may accidentally take an additional dose when half asleep.

PREVENTING SLEEPLESSNESS

If you find that you cannot get to sleep as soon as you go to bed, try not to worry about it; this will only make matters worse. Even if you just relax or doze for a few hours you will probably be getting enough rest. The following self-help suggestions may help you get a good night's sleep:

- Try to do some form of physical exercise during the day so that your body needs rest because it is tired. A short, gentle stroll in the open air an hour or so before going to bed may also help.
- A full stomach generally is not conducive to sleep, but a warm, milky drink or even a *small* whiskey (1 ounce or less) at bedtime may help you to feel sleepy.

- Avoid heavy drinking.
- A warm bath is often relaxing. A shower may not be a good idea if it is too invigorating.
- Recreational reading, which is not associated with work or study, often makes people sleepy.
- Make sure that you are neither too hot nor too cold. Most people sleep best in a room temperature of 60 to 65°F.
- Make your environment as conducive to sleep as possible. Make sure that there are no irritating noises such as dripping faucets or knocking radiators. A comfortable bed will help (see *Preventing backache,* p.101).
- Sex may help you relax and fall asleep.

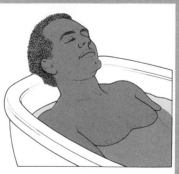

6 Fever

A fever (an abnormally high body temperature) can be a symptom of many diseases, but usually is a sign that your body is fighting infection. You may suspect that you have a fever if you feel hot or alternately shivery, hot and sweaty, and if you feel sick. To confirm that you have a

fever, take your temperature as described opposite. Consult this chart if your temperature is 100°F (38°C) or above. Call your physician at once if your temperature rises above 104°F (40°C) or remains elevated for longer than 48 hours – whatever the suspected cause.

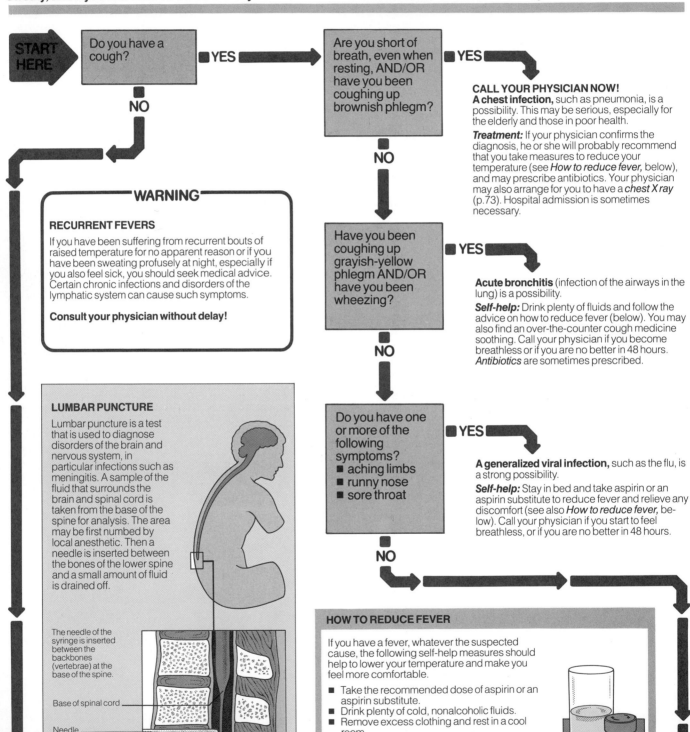

START HERE

Do you have a cough?

YES →

NO ↓

Are you short of breath, even when resting, AND/OR have you been coughing up brownish phlegm?

YES →

NO ↓

CALL YOUR PHYSICIAN NOW!
A chest infection, such as pneumonia, is a possibility. This may be serious, especially for the elderly and those in poor health.
Treatment: If your physician confirms the diagnosis, he or she will probably recommend that you take measures to reduce your temperature (see *How to reduce fever,* below), and may prescribe antibiotics. Your physician may also arrange for you to have a *chest X ray* (p.73). Hospital admission is sometimes necessary.

Have you been coughing up grayish-yellow phlegm AND/OR have you been wheezing?

YES →

NO ↓

Acute bronchitis (infection of the airways in the lung) is a possibility.
Self-help: Drink plenty of fluids and follow the advice on how to reduce fever (below). You may also find an over-the-counter cough medicine soothing. Call your physician if you become breathless or if you are no better in 48 hours. *Antibiotics* are sometimes prescribed.

Do you have one or more of the following symptoms?
■ **aching limbs**
■ **runny nose**
■ **sore throat**

YES →

NO ↓

A generalized viral infection, such as the flu, is a strong possibility.
Self-help: Stay in bed and take aspirin or an aspirin substitute to reduce fever and relieve any discomfort (see also *How to reduce fever,* below). Call your physician if you start to feel breathless, or if you are no better in 48 hours.

WARNING

RECURRENT FEVERS

If you have been suffering from recurrent bouts of raised temperature for no apparent reason or if you have been sweating profusely at night, especially if you also feel sick, you should seek medical advice. Certain chronic infections and disorders of the lymphatic system can cause such symptoms.

Consult your physician without delay!

LUMBAR PUNCTURE

Lumbar puncture is a test that is used to diagnose disorders of the brain and nervous system, in particular infections such as meningitis. A sample of the fluid that surrounds the brain and spinal cord is taken from the base of the spine for analysis. The area may be first numbed by local anesthetic. Then a needle is inserted between the bones of the lower spine and a small amount of fluid is drained off.

The needle of the syringe is inserted between the backbones (vertebrae) at the base of the spine.

Base of spinal cord

Needle

Backbone

Cerebrospinal fluid

HOW TO REDUCE FEVER

If you have a fever, whatever the suspected cause, the following self-help measures should help to lower your temperature and make you feel more comfortable.

■ Take the recommended dose of aspirin or an aspirin substitute.
■ Drink plenty of cold, nonalcoholic fluids.
■ Remove excess clothing and rest in a cool room.
■ For a high fever, sponging the body with luke-warm water and/or fanning may be helpful.

Consult your physician if your temperature continues to rise in spite of these measures.

1 *Go to next page column 1*

Go to next page column 2 2

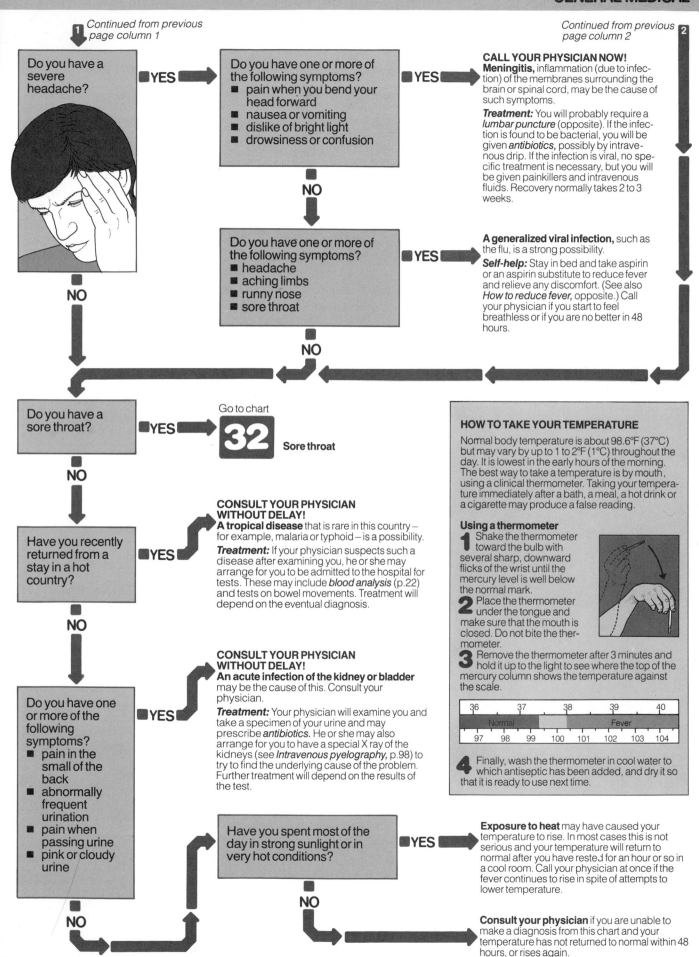

Continued from previous page column 1

1

Continued from previous page column 2

2

Do you have a severe headache?

YES → **Do you have one or more of the following symptoms?**
- pain when you bend your head forward
- nausea or vomiting
- dislike of bright light
- drowsiness or confusion

YES → **CALL YOUR PHYSICIAN NOW!**
Meningitis, inflammation (due to infection) of the membranes surrounding the brain or spinal cord, may be the cause of such symptoms.

Treatment: You will probably require a *lumbar puncture* (opposite). If the infection is found to be bacterial, you will be given *antibiotics,* possibly by intravenous drip. If the infection is viral, no specific treatment is necessary, but you will be given painkillers and intravenous fluids. Recovery normally takes 2 to 3 weeks.

NO ↓

Do you have one or more of the following symptoms?
- headache
- aching limbs
- runny nose
- sore throat

YES → **A generalized viral infection,** such as the flu, is a strong possibility.

Self-help: Stay in bed and take aspirin or an aspirin substitute to reduce fever and relieve any discomfort. (See also *How to reduce fever,* opposite.) Call your physician if you start to feel breathless or if you are no better in 48 hours.

NO ↓

NO ↓

Do you have a sore throat?

YES → Go to chart

32
Sore throat

NO ↓

Have you recently returned from a stay in a hot country?

YES → **CONSULT YOUR PHYSICIAN WITHOUT DELAY!**
A tropical disease that is rare in this country – for example, malaria or typhoid – is a possibility.

Treatment: If your physician suspects such a disease after examining you, he or she may arrange for you to be admitted to the hospital for tests. These may include *blood analysis* (p.22) and tests on bowel movements. Treatment will depend on the eventual diagnosis.

NO ↓

Do you have one or more of the following symptoms?
- pain in the small of the back
- abnormally frequent urination
- pain when passing urine
- pink or cloudy urine

YES → **CONSULT YOUR PHYSICIAN WITHOUT DELAY!**
An acute infection of the kidney or bladder may be the cause of this. Consult your physician.

Treatment: Your physician will examine you and take a specimen of your urine and may prescribe *antibiotics.* He or she may also arrange for you to have a special X ray of the kidneys (see *Intravenous pyelography,* p.98) to try to find the underlying cause of the problem. Further treatment will depend on the results of the test.

NO ↓

Have you spent most of the day in strong sunlight or in very hot conditions?

YES → **Exposure to heat** may have caused your temperature to rise. In most cases this is not serious and your temperature will return to normal after you have rested for an hour or so in a cool room. Call your physician at once if the fever continues to rise in spite of attempts to lower temperature.

NO ↓

Consult your physician if you are unable to make a diagnosis from this chart and your temperature has not returned to normal within 48 hours, or rises again.

HOW TO TAKE YOUR TEMPERATURE

Normal body temperature is about 98.6°F (37°C) but may vary by up to 1 to 2°F (1°C) throughout the day. It is lowest in the early hours of the morning. The best way to take a temperature is by mouth, using a clinical thermometer. Taking your temperature immediately after a bath, a meal, a hot drink or a cigarette may produce a false reading.

Using a thermometer

1 Shake the thermometer toward the bulb with several sharp, downward flicks of the wrist until the mercury level is well below the normal mark.

2 Place the thermometer under the tongue and make sure that the mouth is closed. Do not bite the thermometer.

3 Remove the thermometer after 3 minutes and hold it up to the light to see where the top of the mercury column shows the temperature against the scale.

36	37	38	39	40
Normal			Fever	
97	98	99	100	101	102	103	104

4 Finally, wash the thermometer in cool water to which antiseptic has been added, and dry it so that it is ready to use next time.

7 Excessive sweating

Sweating is a natural mechanism for regulating body temperature and is the normal response to hot conditions or strenuous exercise. Some people naturally sweat more than others, so, if you have always sweated profusely, there is unlikely to be anything wrong. However, sweating that is not brought on by heat or exercise or that is more profuse than you are used to may be a sign of a number of medical conditions.

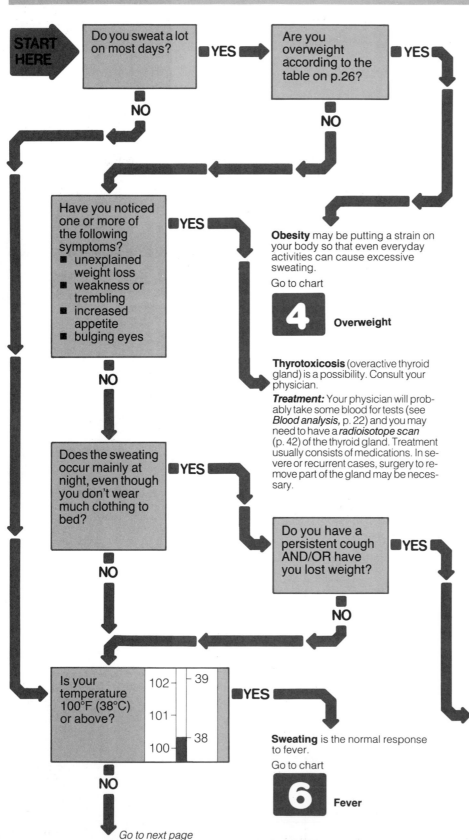

START HERE

Do you sweat a lot on most days? → **YES** → **Are you overweight according to the table on p.26?** → **YES**

NO

NO

Have you noticed one or more of the following symptoms?
- unexplained weight loss
- weakness or trembling
- increased appetite
- bulging eyes

YES

NO

Obesity may be putting a strain on your body so that even everyday activities can cause excessive sweating.

Go to chart

4 Overweight

Thyrotoxicosis (overactive thyroid gland) is a possibility. Consult your physician.

Treatment: Your physician will probably take some blood for tests (see *Blood analysis,* p. 22) and you may need to have a *radioisotope scan* (p. 42) of the thyroid gland. Treatment usually consists of medications. In severe or recurrent cases, surgery to remove part of the gland may be necessary.

Does the sweating occur mainly at night, even though you don't wear much clothing to bed? → **YES**

NO

Do you have a persistent cough AND/OR have you lost weight? → **YES**

NO

Is your temperature 100°F (38°C) or above?

102	39
101	
100	38

→ **YES**

NO

Sweating is the normal response to fever.

Go to chart

6 Fever

Go to next page

BODY ODOR

Sweat itself usually has no noticeable odor. However, if it remains on the skin for more than a few hours it may lead to body odor. This is caused by the activity of bacteria that live naturally on the surface of the skin. These flourish in the sweat, particularly that of the apocrine glands (see *Sweat glands,* opposite), which contains fats and proteins.

Preventing body odor
The most effective way to reduce body odor is to wash all over at least once a day. This will remove the stale sweat and control bacterial growth. Using an *antibacterial* soap, particularly in the areas where apocrine glands are located, will also be helpful.

Deodorants and antiperspirants
After washing, use a deodorant containing an antiperspirant, which prevents sweat from reaching the surface of the skin, under the arms. This will usually prevent body odor from building up during the day. Such deodorants may be bought in the form of a spray, a roll-on applicator or a cream. All are equally effective. However, some people may find that their skin becomes irritated by chemicals they contain, and you should change brands if this happens to you. Do not use a deodorant on broken skin.

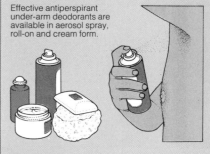

Effective antiperspirant under-arm deodorants are available in aerosol spray, roll-on and cream form.

Clothes
If sweat penetrates the fabric of your clothes, they may become a source of unpleasant odor. In addition, the bacteria that cause the odor may also in time damage the material. So, if you sweat a great deal, it is essential to wash clothes (especially those worn next to the skin) frequently.

CONSULT YOUR PHYSICIAN WITHOUT DELAY!
Tuberculosis (an infection that often starts in the lungs), or another chronic infectious disease, could be the cause of these symptoms.

Treatment: Your physician may arrange for you to have a special test for tuberculosis or a *chest X ray* (p. 73). If you are found to have tuberculosis, you will be given a long course of *antibiotics.* You may need to stay in the hospital until the infection is under control.

Continued from previous page

Did you notice the sweating after you had been drinking alcohol or taking large doses of aspirin?

YES → **Alcohol or aspirin** can cause increased sweating.

Self-help: If alcohol seems to be causing the problem, cut down on your drinking (see *The effects of alcohol,* p. 22). If aspirin taken for some other problem seems to be the cause of your sweating, ask your physician for advice.

NO ↓

Are you wearing clothes (or are your sleep clothes) made of nylon or other man-made materials?

YES → **Synthetic materials** often cause a noticeable increase in sweating. This is because they do not absorb moisture or allow your skin to breathe.

Self-help: Try wearing natural fibers, such as cotton or wool, as often as possible. In addition, make sure that your clothing is loose; this will increase the circulation of air and allow sweat to evaporate more quickly.

NO ↓

Is the excessive sweating confined to your feet or hands?

YES → **A high concentration of sweat glands** on the hands and feet (see *Sweat glands,* below) makes these parts of the body react most noticeably to increases in temperature. This is no cause for concern.

Self-help: If your hands are sweaty, wash them frequently. The problem is likely to become worse if you worry, so try to relax. Make sure that you wash and dry your feet carefully at least once a day. It is best to avoid wearing shoes and socks made of synthetic materials. If the problem is severe or causes embarrassment, consult your physician.

NO ↓

Do you notice the sweating only when you are anxious or excited?

YES → **Emotional stress** can easily cause an increase in sweating. This in itself is not a cause for concern, but, if it happens regularly or causes embarrassment, consult your physician.

Treatment: Your physician will advise you on the best method of controlling the sweating. He or she will also discuss with you the possible causes of any underlying anxiety and may recommend medication. (See also chart 20, *Anxiety.*)

NO ↓

Are you in your teens?

YES → **The development of additional (apocrine) sweat glands during puberty** (see *Sweat glands,* below) usually causes an increase in sweating that is particularly noticeable under the arms. This is quite normal.

Self-help: There is no need to be embarrassed about any increased sweating. However, you will need to wash regularly and you may want to use an antiperspirant deodorant to reduce wetness and to prevent unpleasant body odor (see *Body odor,* opposite).

NO ↓

Consult your physician if you are unable to make a diagnosis from this chart and your excessive sweating continues to worry you. There is, however, not likely to be a serious cause for this.

SWEAT GLANDS

Sweat glands are found under the skin all over the body. They produce moisture (sweat) that is carried to the surface of the skin and released through pores. Each sweat gland consists of a coiled tube deeply embedded in the dermis and subcutaneous fat (see *The structure of the skin,* p. 57). The gland is connected to the skin surface by a duct that is a continuation of the gland. The production and release of sweat is governed by nerves under the skin. There are two types of sweat glands – eccrine and apocrine glands – and these vary slightly in structure and produce different types of sweat.

Eccrine glands
Eccrine glands are found all over the body and are active from birth onward. The sweat from these glands is a clear, salty fluid.

containing various waste chemicals. It evaporates on the surface of the skin to reduce body temperature as necessary. The eccrine glands may also produce sweat in response to anxiety or fear. Eccrine glands are most concentrated on the forehead, palms and soles of the feet (see left), and profuse sweating is likely to become apparent first in these areas.

Apocrine glands
Apocrine glands become active during adolescence. They are mainly concentrated in the armpits, the groin and around the nipples (see right). These glands produce a sticky, milky fluid that contains fats and proteins. The scent from this type of gland is thought to play a role in attracting the opposite sex. But, if it is allowed to remain on the skin for long, it may interact with bacteria to produce a particularly pungent type of body odor (see *Body odor,* opposite).

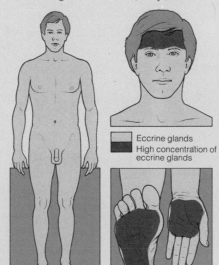

Eccrine glands
High concentration of eccrine glands

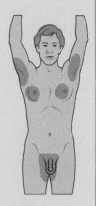

Apocrine glands

Skin cross section showing sweat gland

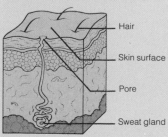

Hair
Skin surface
Pore
Sweat gland

8 Itching

Itching (skin irritation that makes you want to scratch) is usually produced by contact with certain types of fabric or with a substance to which you are sensitive. Many skin disorders that produce a rash also cause itching.

Occasionally, itching is a sign of an underlying disease or of psychological stress. Irritation is likely to be most severe if you are hot or if your skin is dry, and is likely to be made worse by rubbing or scratching.

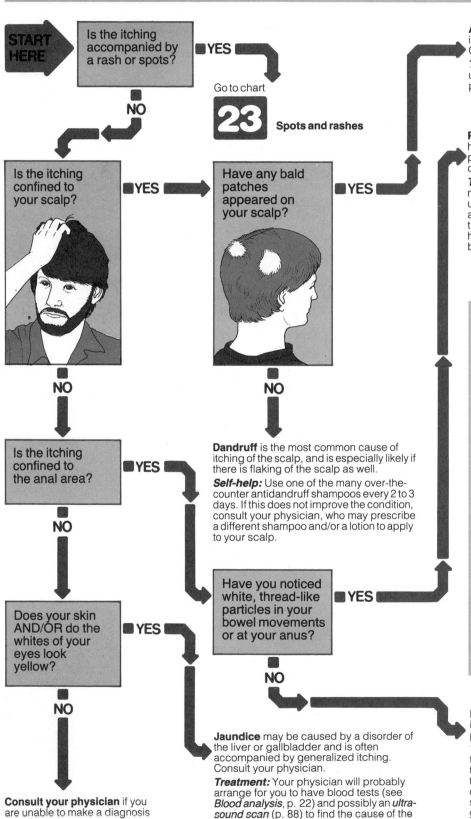

START HERE

Is the itching accompanied by a rash or spots?

YES → Go to chart **23** Spots and rashes

NO

Is the itching confined to your scalp?

YES → Have any bald patches appeared on your scalp?

NO

Is the itching confined to the anal area?

YES

NO

Does your skin AND/OR do the whites of your eyes look yellow?

YES

NO

Have you noticed white, thread-like particles in your bowel movements or at your anus?

YES

NO

A fungal infection is a possible cause of itching of the scalp and patchy hair loss. Consult your physician.

Treatment: Fungal infection of the scalp is usually treated by an *antifungal* lotion and possibly a course of antifungal tablets.

Pinworms may cause such symptoms. These harmless parasites may be passed from one person to another, or may be picked up from contaminated food. Consult your physician.

Treatment: You will probably be given medication to get rid of the worms. This is usually taken in 2 separate doses 2 weeks apart. The whole family may need to be treated. Be especially careful to wash your hands thoroughly after going to the toilet and before preparing food.

SELF-HELP FOR ITCHY SKIN

Whatever the cause of your itching, it is important to try to resist the urge to scratch, which will only further inflame and irritate the skin and may lead to infection. Try the following self-help measures:

- Keep your skin cool with frequent lukewarm baths and showers.
- Do not use bath salts or harsh detergents.
- If your skin is dry, apply some oil after your bath and use a moisturizing cream.
- Wear cotton clothing next to the skin; avoid direct contact with wool or nylon.

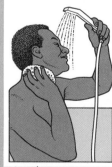

To reduce itching, take frequent lukewarm baths and showers and apply hand cream if your skin is dry.

Dandruff is the most common cause of itching of the scalp, and is especially likely if there is flaking of the scalp as well.

Self-help: Use one of the many over-the-counter antidandruff shampoos every 2 to 3 days. If this does not improve the condition, consult your physician, who may prescribe a different shampoo and/or a lotion to apply to your scalp.

Jaundice may be caused by a disorder of the liver or gallbladder and is often accompanied by generalized itching. Consult your physician.

Treatment: Your physician will probably arrange for you to have blood tests (see *Blood analysis*, p. 22) and possibly an *ultrasound scan* (p. 88) to find the cause of the trouble. Treatment will depend on the nature of the underlying disorder.

Pruritus ani is the term used to describe itching around the anus that has no obvious physical cause. Consult your physician.

Treatment: If your physician can find no cause for your itching, he or she will probably suggest the following ways to reduce the irritation. Try to resist the urge to scratch. Wash the anus carefully twice a day, using mild, unscented soap. Use only soft toilet paper and wipe gently. Avoid tight underpants made of artificial fibers; cotton is best. Your physician may also prescribe a soothing ointment.

Consult your physician if you are unable to make a diagnosis from this chart and your itching persists for longer than 3 days.

9 Lumps and swellings

Consult this chart if you notice one or more swollen areas or lumps beneath the surface of the skin. In most cases, such swellings are the result of enlargement of the lymph glands, which is a natural response to the presence of infection. You should always consult your physician about a painful or persistent swelling.

For lumps and swellings in the testicles, see chart 62, Painful or swollen testicles.

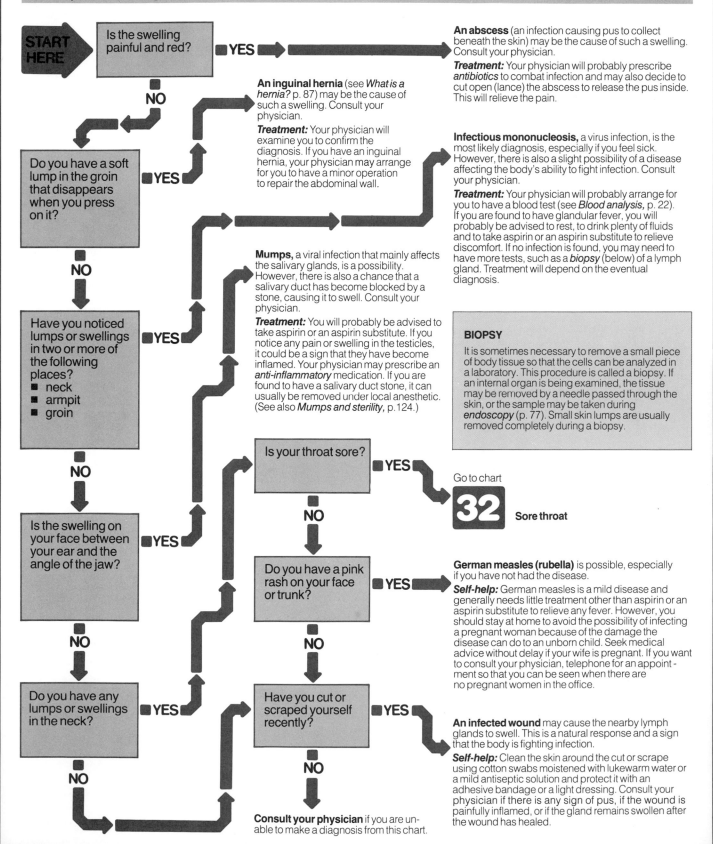

START HERE

Is the swelling painful and red?

YES ➡ **An abscess** (an infection causing pus to collect beneath the skin) may be the cause of such a swelling. Consult your physician.
Treatment: Your physician will probably prescribe *antibiotics* to combat infection and may also decide to cut open (lance) the abscess to release the pus inside. This will relieve the pain.

NO

Do you have a soft lump in the groin that disappears when you press on it?

YES ➡ **An inguinal hernia** (see *What is a hernia?* p. 87) may be the cause of such a swelling. Consult your physician.
Treatment: Your physician will examine you to confirm the diagnosis. If you have an inguinal hernia, your physician may arrange for you to have a minor operation to repair the abdominal wall.

NO

Have you noticed lumps or swellings in two or more of the following places?
■ neck
■ armpit
■ groin

YES ➡ **Mumps,** a viral infection that mainly affects the salivary glands, is a possibility. However, there is also a chance that a salivary duct has become blocked by a stone, causing it to swell. Consult your physician.
Treatment: You will probably be advised to take aspirin or an aspirin substitute. If you notice any pain or swelling in the testicles, it could be a sign that they have become inflamed. Your physician may prescribe an *anti-inflammatory* medication. If you are found to have a salivary duct stone, it can usually be removed under local anesthetic. (See also *Mumps and sterility,* p.124.)

Infectious mononucleosis, a virus infection, is the most likely diagnosis, especially if you feel sick. However, there is also a slight possibility of a disease affecting the body's ability to fight infection. Consult your physician.
Treatment: Your physician will probably arrange for you to have a blood test (see *Blood analysis,* p. 22). If you are found to have glandular fever, you will probably be advised to rest, to drink plenty of fluids and to take aspirin or an aspirin substitute to relieve discomfort. If no infection is found, you may need to have more tests, such as a *biopsy* (below) of a lymph gland. Treatment will depend on the eventual diagnosis.

BIOPSY

It is sometimes necessary to remove a small piece of body tissue so that the cells can be analyzed in a laboratory. This procedure is called a biopsy. If an internal organ is being examined, the tissue may be removed by a needle passed through the skin, or the sample may be taken during *endoscopy* (p. 77). Small skin lumps are usually removed completely during a biopsy.

NO

Is the swelling on your face between your ear and the angle of the jaw?

YES ➡

NO

Is your throat sore?

YES ➡ Go to chart **32** **Sore throat**

NO

Do you have a pink rash on your face or trunk?

YES ➡ **German measles (rubella)** is possible, especially if you have not had the disease.
Self-help: German measles is a mild disease and generally needs little treatment other than aspirin or an aspirin substitute to relieve any fever. However, you should stay at home to avoid the possibility of infecting a pregnant woman because of the damage the disease can do to an unborn child. Seek medical advice without delay if your wife is pregnant. If you want to consult your physician, telephone for an appointment so that you can be seen when there are no pregnant women in the office.

NO

Do you have any lumps or swellings in the neck?

YES ➡

NO

Have you cut or scraped yourself recently?

YES ➡ **An infected wound** may cause the nearby lymph glands to swell. This is a natural response and a sign that the body is fighting infection.
Self-help: Clean the skin around the cut or scrape using cotton swabs moistened with lukewarm water or a mild antiseptic solution and protect it with an adhesive bandage or a light dressing. Consult your physician if there is any sign of pus, if the wound is painfully inflamed, or if the gland remains swollen after the wound has healed.

NO

Consult your physician if you are unable to make a diagnosis from this chart.

10 Faintness and fainting

Fainting – a brief loss of consciousness – is usually preceded by a sensation of lightheadedness or dizziness, and you may be pale and suddenly feel cold or clammy. Such feelings of faintness may sometimes occur on their own without loss of consciousness. Faintness is usually the result of a sudden drop in blood pressure – as a result, for example, of an emotional shock – or it may be caused by an abnormally low level of sugar in the blood. Isolated episodes of fainting with no other symptoms are hardly ever a cause for concern but, if you suffer repeated fainting attacks or have additional symptoms, you should seek medical advice.

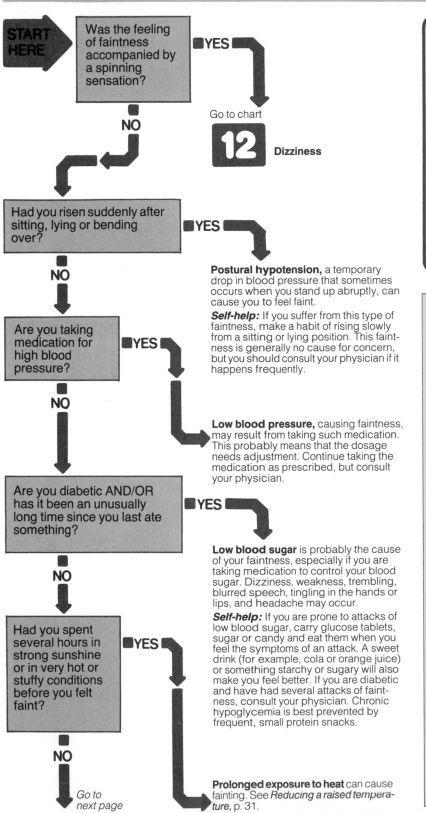

START HERE

Was the feeling of faintness accompanied by a spinning sensation?

YES → Go to chart **12** Dizziness

NO ↓

Had you risen suddenly after sitting, lying or bending over?

YES → **Postural hypotension,** a temporary drop in blood pressure that sometimes occurs when you stand up abruptly, can cause you to feel faint.
Self-help: If you suffer from this type of faintness, make a habit of rising slowly from a sitting or lying position. This faintness is generally no cause for concern, but you should consult your physician if it happens frequently.

NO ↓

Are you taking medication for high blood pressure?

YES → **Low blood pressure,** causing faintness, may result from taking such medication. This probably means that the dosage needs adjustment. Continue taking the medication as prescribed, but consult your physician.

NO ↓

Are you diabetic AND/OR has it been an unusually long time since you last ate something?

YES → **Low blood sugar** is probably the cause of your faintness, especially if you are taking medication to control your blood sugar. Dizziness, weakness, trembling, blurred speech, tingling in the hands or lips, and headache may occur.
Self-help: If you are prone to attacks of low blood sugar, carry glucose tablets, sugar or candy and eat them when you feel the symptoms of an attack. A sweet drink (for example, cola or orange juice) or something starchy or sugary will also make you feel better. If you are diabetic and have had several attacks of faintness, consult your physician. Chronic hypoglycemia is best prevented by frequent, small protein snacks.

NO ↓

Had you spent several hours in strong sunshine or in very hot or stuffy conditions before you felt faint?

YES → **Prolonged exposure to heat** can cause fainting. See *Reducing a raised temperature,* p. 31.

NO ↓ *Go to next page*

WARNING

PROLONGED LOSS OF CONSCIOUSNESS

Momentary loss of consciousness – fainting – is not usually a cause for concern if the person is breathing normally and regains consciousness within a minute or two. If someone in your presence remains unconscious for longer, or if breathing slows or becomes irregular or noisy, get medical help at once. While waiting for medical help to arrive, place the person on his stomach as shown.

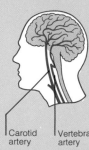

HOW BLOOD FLOWS TO THE BRAIN

The brain is more dependent on a constant supply of oxygenated blood than any other organ in the body. Temporary interruption in this supply is likely to cause the brain to malfunction, producing symptoms such as fainting and dizziness, and more serious disruption to the blood flow may cause lasting damage to brain cells.

View of the brain from beneath.

View of the brain from the side.

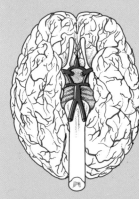

Carotid artery   Vertebral artery

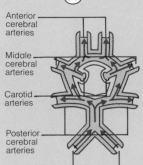

Anterior cerebral arteries
Middle cerebral arteries
Carotid arteries
Posterior cerebral arteries
Vertebral arteries

The main arteries of the brain
The brain is supplied with blood by 2 pairs of arteries in the neck: the vertebral arteries and the carotid arteries. At the bottom of the brain they join to form a circular junction from which other arteries – the anterior cerebral, the middle cerebral, and the posterior cerebral – run to all parts of the brain.

Continued from previous page

Have you noticed one or more of the following symptoms since the attack of faintness?
- numbness and/or tingling in any part of the body
- blurred vision
- confusion
- difficulty speaking
- loss of movement in your arms or legs

YES ➡ Have these symptoms now disappeared? **YES** ➡

NO ⬇

Do you have any form of heart disease AND/OR did you notice your heartbeat speed up or slow down before the onset of faintness?

YES ➡

NO ⬇

Did the faintness follow an emotional shock?

YES ➡

NO ⬇

Are you over 50 years old? **YES** ➡ Does turning your head or looking upward bring on a feeling of faintness? **YES** ➡

NO ⬇

NO ⬇

Have you been passing black, tarry stools? **YES** ➡

NO ⬇

Consult your physician if you are unable to make a diagnosis from this chart.

CALL YOUR PHYSICIAN NOW!
A stroke – a disruption in the blood supply to the brain, caused by a blocked or burst blood vessel – may be the cause of these symptoms.

Treatment: If your physician suspects that you have had a stroke, admission to the hospital for observation and tests, which may include a *CAT (computerized axial tomography) scan* (p. 39), is customary. If you are found to have had a stroke, you will probably be prescribed medication to prevent further strokes and may be given physical and occupational therapy to help restore any loss of movement. You may also be given medication to control high blood pressure and may be advised to lose weight.

CONSULT YOUR PHYSICIAN WITHOUT DELAY!
An Adams-Stokes attack (sudden alteration of the heart rhythm) could have caused the fainting. Such attacks may be a sign of an underlying disorder of heart rate or rhythm.

Treatment: If your physician suspects the possibility of such a disorder, he or she will arrange for you to undergo *electrocardiography* (p. 96). If this shows that your heart rhythms are abnormal, you will probably be prescribed medication to regulate the heart's activity.

Emotional stress can affect the nerves that control blood pressure, causing a drop in pressure that leads to faintness

CALL YOUR PHYSICIAN NOW!
Bleeding in the digestive tract, perhaps from a stomach ulcer, is a possibility.

Treatment: Your physician will probably arrange for you to have tests, such as *endoscopy* (p. 77), a *biopsy* (p. 35) of the stomach lining and a *barium X ray* (p. 83) . These tests should reveal the underlying cause of your symptoms.

CONSULT YOUR PHYSICIAN WITHOUT DELAY!
A transient ischemic attack – a temporary interruption in the blood supply to the brain, sometimes linked to a narrowing of the arteries (see *How blood flows to the brain,* opposite) – may have caused your symptoms.

Treatment: If your physician suspects that this is the problem, you will probably be referred to a specialist for tests, including *electrocardiography* (p.95). At a later stage, you may need to undergo *angiography* (p. 107) of the arteries. Treatment consists of taking steps to reduce factors that may contribute to narrowing of the arteries. These are discussed in the box on *Coronary heart disease* (p. 95). You may also be prescribed medication to control high blood pressure, if you have it, and further medication to prevent the formation of blood clots. Surgery may be necessary in some cases.

FIRST AID

Dealing with faintness
If you feel faint, lie down with your legs raised or, if this is not possible, sit with your head between your knees until you feel better.

Dealing with fainting
To help someone who has fainted, check that breathing is normal. Lay the person on his back with legs raised as high as possible above the level of the head. Hold the legs up or rest them on a chair. Loosen any tight clothing (e.g., collar or tie) and make sure that the person gets plenty of fresh air. If you are indoors, open the windows to allow air to circulate. If you are outdoors, make sure that the person is in the shade. When he regains consciousness, it is important that he remain lying down for a few minutes before attempting to get up.

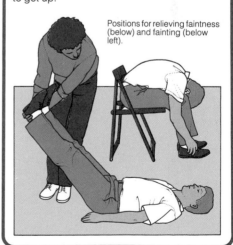
Positions for relieving faintness (below) and fainting (below left).

Cervical osteoarthritis, a disorder of the bones and joints in the neck, may affect nearby nerves and blood vessels, causing feelings of faintness. Consult your physician.

Treatment: Your physician may arrange for you to have an X ray of your neck (see *Bone X rays*, p. 103). If you are found to have a disorder, you will probably be given a collar to wear to reduce the mobility of your neck and to relieve pressure on the nerves and blood vessels. Aspirin or an aspirin substitute can be taken to relieve the discomfort.

11 Headache

From time to time nearly everyone suffers from headaches that develop gradually and clear up after a few hours, leaving no aftereffects. Headaches like this are unlikely to be a sign of any disorder and are usually caused by factors such as tension, tiredness, excessive consumption of alcohol or staying in an overheated or smoke-filled atmosphere. However, a headache that is severe, lasts for more than 24 hours, or recurs several times during one week should be brought to your physician's attention.

START HERE

Is your temperature 100°F (38°C) or above?

YES → **Many illnesses with fever** may cause a headache.

Go to chart

6 Fever

NO

Have you injured your head within the past few days?

YES → **Bruising of the brain,** or a more serious form of injury, may be the cause of your symptoms. A headache following a minor head injury will probably disappear within a few hours. You should, however, consult your physician to rule out the possibility of more serious damage to the brain or skull if the pain persists for more than a day or so. If you passed out, even for a few seconds, or if you were confused, lost your memory of the accident, or have had recurrent headaches or vomited, seek medical help at once.

Treatment: In most cases, no treatment is necessary and your physician will probably advise you to take over-the-counter painkillers to ease the headache. If your physician suspects that you have suffered some internal damage, he or she will advise you to go to the hospital where you will be fully examined and tests such as a skull X ray can be carried out. You may be admitted to the hospital and, if necessary, further investigations, including a *CAT (computerized axial tomography) scan* (opposite), may be performed to determine the extent and nature of the injury. If bleeding inside the skull or a fracture of the skull is diagnosed, surgery may be needed.

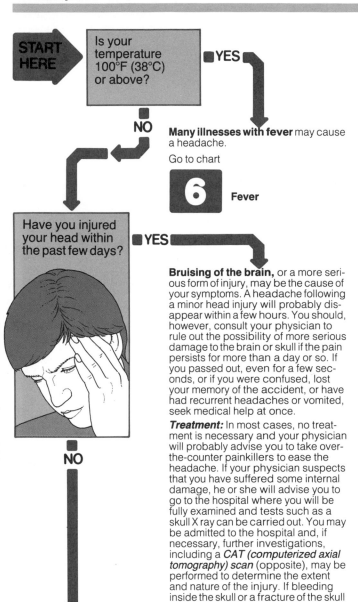

NO

Have you felt nauseated or been vomiting?

YES → **Did the headache develop before the onset of nausea or vomiting?**

NO → **YES** → **Is your vision blurred?**

YES → **CALL YOUR PHYSICIAN NOW!** **Acute glaucoma,** a serious disorder associated with increased pressure in the eye, is a possibility, especially if you are over 40.

Treatment: If your physician confirms the diagnosis, you will probably be given eye drops to allow fluid to drain from the eye. In addition, you may be given a *diuretic* to prevent fluid retention. Once the pressure has been relieved, an operation to prevent a recurrence of the problem is sometimes performed.

NO → **A headache** often follows an attack of vomiting.

Go to chart

40 Vomiting

NO

Go to next page column 1

Go to next page column 2

RELIEVING HEADACHE

Most minor headaches can be relieved by the following self-help measures:

- Take the recommended dose of aspirin or aspirin substitute.
- Take a warm bath to relieve tension.
- Rest in a quiet, darkened room.

Consult your physician if such measures fail to reduce the pain, or if pain is still present the following day.

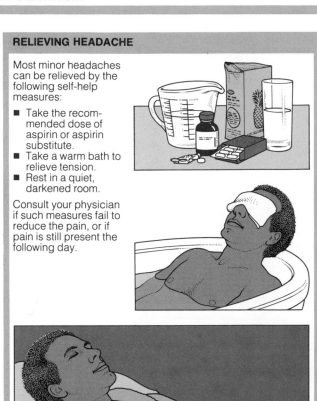

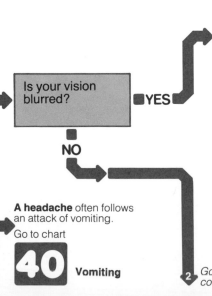

① Continued from previous page column 1

Do you have a stuffy nose?

YES

Sinusitis (inflammation of the membranes lining the air spaces in the skull) may be the cause of this problem, although it is possible that you have a common cold.

Self-help: Stay inside in a warm and humid atmosphere and take aspirin or an aspirin substitute to relieve the discomfort. If you are no better in 48 hours, consult your physician, who may prescribe *antibiotics* and *decongestants.*

NO

Did the headache occur after you had been reading or doing other close work?

YES

Muscle strain in your neck as a result of poor posture or tension from concentration is the likely cause of your headache (see *Eyestrain,* p. 60).

Self-help: In order to prevent the problem from recurring, make sure that when you read you are not sitting in an awkward position or in poor light. Periodic rest from whatever you are doing for a few minutes of relaxation will also help. If headaches recur, consult your physician, who may recommend that you have an eye test. (See *Eye testing,* p.62.)

NO

Are you sleeping poorly AND/OR are you feeling tense or under stress?

YES

Tension headaches are often caused by psychological stress.

Go to chart

20 **Anxiety**

NO

Are you currently taking any medication?

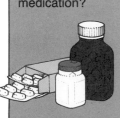

YES

Certain medications can cause headaches as a side effect. Discuss the problem with your physician.

NO

Consult your physician if you are unable to make a diagnosis from this chart and if the headache persists overnight or if you develop other symptoms.

② Continued from previous page column 2

Have you suddenly begun to have a severe, throbbing pain in one or both temples?

YES

CONSULT YOUR PHYSICIAN WITHOUT DELAY!
Temporal arteritis – inflammation of the arteries of the head – is a possibility, especially if you are over 50. Urgent treatment may be needed to prevent this condition from affecting your eyesight.

Treatment: Your physician will probably prescribe medication to reduce the inflammation and it may be necessary for you to have regular blood tests to confirm that the treatment is effective.

NO

Was your vision disturbed in any way before the onset of pain?

YES

Migraine, a recurrent, severe headache that usually occurs on one side of the head, but may occasionally be on both sides, may be the explanation for your symptoms. Migraine headaches may also be brought on by different "trigger" factors such as stress, eating cheese or chocolate, or drinking red wine. Consult your physician.

Treatment: You may find that the pain can be eased by self-help measures (see *Relieving headache,* opposite). It will also help if you can discover what causes your migraines. Your physician may be able to offer medication if self-help measures are not effective or if the attacks recur.

NO

CONSULT YOUR PHYSICIAN WITHOUT DELAY!
Unexplained headaches, especially if severe and accompanied by additional symptoms such as nausea and vomiting, should always be brought to your physician's attention.

CAT SCAN

A CAT (computerized axial tomography) scan is a safe and painless procedure that helps in the diagnosis of certain conditions. It involves hundreds of tiny X-ray pictures being taken as a camera revolves around the body. The readings are fed into a computer, which assembles them into an accurate picture of the area. CAT scans can be taken of most parts of the body, but they are especially used to diagnose brain disorders.

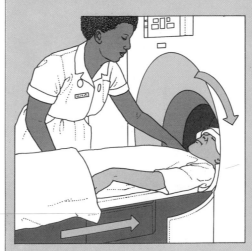

CAT scan of the head
For a CAT scan of the head (above) you will lie on a movable table with your head resting inside the machine. You will be told not to make any movement so that the pictures are not blurred.

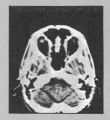

CAT scan at eyelid level
This scan shows a cross section of a normal brain at eyelid level. The front of the head is at the top, where the dark areas indicate the eye sockets and air spaces in the skull. The white areas indicate the bone.

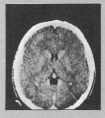

CAT scan at mid-forehead level
This scan shows a cross section of the same brain as shown above taken at mid-forehead level.

12 Dizziness

Dizziness is a feeling of unsteadiness or that everything around you is spinning. This usually occurs when you have been spinning around – for example, on a merry-go-round. If you feel dizzy for no reason, it may be a symptom of an underlying disorder and should be brought to your physician's attention.

START HERE

Have you noticed one or more of the following symptoms since you felt dizzy?
- difficulty speaking
- temporary total or partial loss of vision in one or both eyes
- weakness in your arms or legs
- numbness and/or tingling in any part of your body

YES →

Have all your symptoms now disappeared?

YES →

NO ↓

CALL YOUR PHYSICIAN NOW!

A stroke, a disruption in the blood supply to the brain caused by a blocked or burst blood vessel, may be the cause of these symptoms.

Treatment: If your physician suspects that you have had a stroke, admission to the hospital for observation and tests, which may include a *CAT (computerized axial tomography) scan* (p.39), is customary. If you are found to have had a stroke, you will probably be prescribed medication to prevent further strokes and may be given therapy to help restore any loss of movement. You may also be given medication to help control high blood pressure and may be advised to lose weight.

NO ↓

Have you been vomiting AND/OR finding it difficult to keep your balance?

YES →

Labyrinthitis, inflammation of the part of the inner ear that is responsible for maintaining balance (see *How you keep your balance,* right) due to viral infection, may cause these symptoms. Consult your physician.

Treatment: Your physician will examine your ears. If labyrinthitis is diagnosed, you will probably be prescribed *tranquilizers* to alleviate your symptoms and you will be advised to rest quietly in bed for a week or so. Most cases clear up within 3 weeks.

NO ↓

Have you noticed some loss of hearing AND/OR noises in the ear?

YES →

Ménière's disease may be the problem. This is a relatively uncommon disorder that occurs when there is an increase in the amount of fluid in the labyrinth (see *How you keep your balance,* right). Ménière's disease is most common in middle age. Consult your physician.

Treatment: Your physician will probably arrange for you to undergo tests in the hospital to confirm the diagnosis. If you are found to have Ménière's disease, you will probably be given medication to reduce the amount of fluid in the labyrinth. Your physician may also advise you to cut down on your intake of salt to reduce the frequency of further attacks. Very rarely, an operation is recommended.

NO ↓

Does turning your head or looking upward bring on dizziness?

YES →

Cervical osteoarthritis, a disorder of the bones and joints in the neck that may cause pressure on nearby nerves and blood vessels, may be the cause of this, especially if you are over 50. Consult your physician.

Treatment: Your physician may arrange for you to have an X ray of your neck. If he or she thinks that your dizziness is due to this disorder, you may be given a collar to wear for about 3 months to reduce the mobility of your neck and to relieve pressure on the nerves and blood vessels. Aspirin or an aspirin substitute can be taken to relieve any discomfort.

NO ↓

Consult your physician if you are unable to make a diagnosis from this chart.

CONSULT YOUR PHYSICIAN WITHOUT DELAY!

A transient ischemic attack – a temporary interruption in the blood supply to the brain, sometimes linked to a narrowing of the arteries (see *How blood flows to the brain,* p.36) – may have caused your symptoms.

Treatment: If your physician suspects that this is the problem, you will probably need to have tests, including *electrocardiography* (p.96). At a later stage, you may need to undergo *angiography* (p.107) or *ultrasound scanning* (p.88) of the arteries. Treatment consists of taking steps to reduce factors that may contribute to narrowing of the arteries. These are discussed in the box on *Coronary heart disease* (p.95). You may also be prescribed medication to control high blood pressure, if you have it, and further medication to prevent the formation of blood clots. Surgery may be necessary in some cases.

HOW YOU KEEP YOUR BALANCE

The brain relies on information from a structure in the inner ear called the labyrinth to help you to keep your balance. The labyrinth sends messages about your movements to the brain, where they are coordinated with other information from your eyes, limbs and muscles to assess your exact position so that your body can make adjustments to keep balanced.

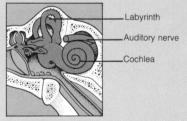

Labyrinth

Auditory nerve

Cochlea

The semicircular canals
Each of the three fluid-filled semicircular canals that make up the labyrinth lies at a right angle to the other two (above), so that whichever way you move your head – whether you shake it, nod it or tilt it – one of the canals will detect this movement and relay the information to the brain.

13 Numbness or tingling

It is normal to experience numbness or tingling if you are cold, sitting in an awkward position or sleeping on an arm. The feeling disappears as soon as you move around and is rarely a circulation problem. Numbness or tingling that occurs without apparent cause may need medical treatment.

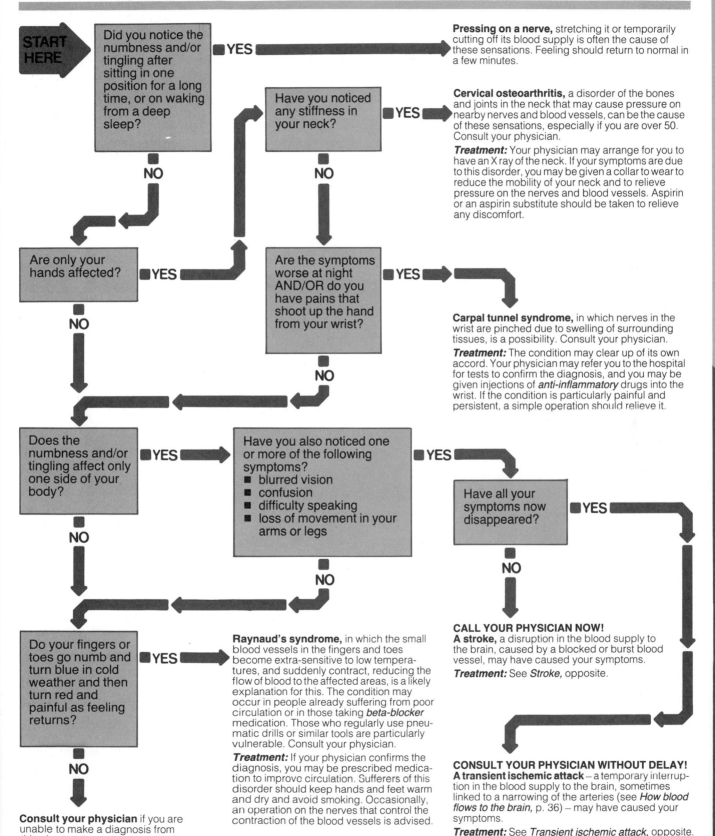

START HERE

Did you notice the numbness and/or tingling after sitting in one position for a long time, or on waking from a deep sleep?

YES → **Pressing on a nerve,** stretching it or temporarily cutting off its blood supply is often the cause of these sensations. Feeling should return to normal in a few minutes.

NO

Have you noticed any stiffness in your neck?

YES → **Cervical osteoarthritis,** a disorder of the bones and joints in the neck that may cause pressure on nearby nerves and blood vessels, can be the cause of these sensations, especially if you are over 50. Consult your physician.

Treatment: Your physician may arrange for you to have an X ray of the neck. If your symptoms are due to this disorder, you may be given a collar to wear to reduce the mobility of your neck and to relieve pressure on the nerves and blood vessels. Aspirin or an aspirin substitute should be taken to relieve any discomfort.

NO

Are only your hands affected?

YES

NO

Are the symptoms worse at night AND/OR do you have pains that shoot up the hand from your wrist?

YES → **Carpal tunnel syndrome,** in which nerves in the wrist are pinched due to swelling of surrounding tissues, is a possibility. Consult your physician.

Treatment: The condition may clear up of its own accord. Your physician may refer you to the hospital for tests to confirm the diagnosis, and you may be given injections of *anti-inflammatory* drugs into the wrist. If the condition is particularly painful and persistent, a simple operation should relieve it.

NO

Does the numbness and/or tingling affect only one side of your body?

YES → **Have you also noticed one or more of the following symptoms?**
- blurred vision
- confusion
- difficulty speaking
- loss of movement in your arms or legs

YES → **Have all your symptoms now disappeared?**

YES

NO

NO

NO

CALL YOUR PHYSICIAN NOW!
A stroke, a disruption in the blood supply to the brain, caused by a blocked or burst blood vessel, may have caused your symptoms.
Treatment: See *Stroke,* opposite.

Do your fingers or toes go numb and turn blue in cold weather and then turn red and painful as feeling returns?

YES → **Raynaud's syndrome,** in which the small blood vessels in the fingers and toes become extra-sensitive to low temperatures, and suddenly contract, reducing the flow of blood to the affected areas, is a likely explanation for this. The condition may occur in people already suffering from poor circulation or in those taking *beta-blocker* medication. Those who regularly use pneumatic drills or similar tools are particularly vulnerable. Consult your physician.

Treatment: If your physician confirms the diagnosis, you may be prescribed medication to improve circulation. Sufferers of this disorder should keep hands and feet warm and dry and avoid smoking. Occasionally, an operation on the nerves that control the contraction of the blood vessels is advised.

NO

Consult your physician if you are unable to make a diagnosis from this chart and numbness or tingling persists.

CONSULT YOUR PHYSICIAN WITHOUT DELAY!
A transient ischemic attack – a temporary interruption in the blood supply to the brain, sometimes linked to a narrowing of the arteries (see *How blood flows to the brain,* p. 36) – may have caused your symptoms.

Treatment: See *Transient ischemic attack,* opposite.

14 Twitching and trembling

Consult this chart if you experience any involuntary or uncontrolled movements of any part of your body. Such movements may range from slight occasional twitching of an eyelid or the corner of your mouth to persistent trembling or shaking – for example, of the hands, arms or head. In many cases, such movements are no cause for concern, being simply the result of tiredness, stress or an inherited tendency. Occasionally, however, twitching and trembling may be caused by problems that require medical treatment, such as excessive consumption of alcohol or a disorder of the thyroid gland. Involuntary movements that are accompanied by weakness of the affected part of the body should be brought to your physician's attention.

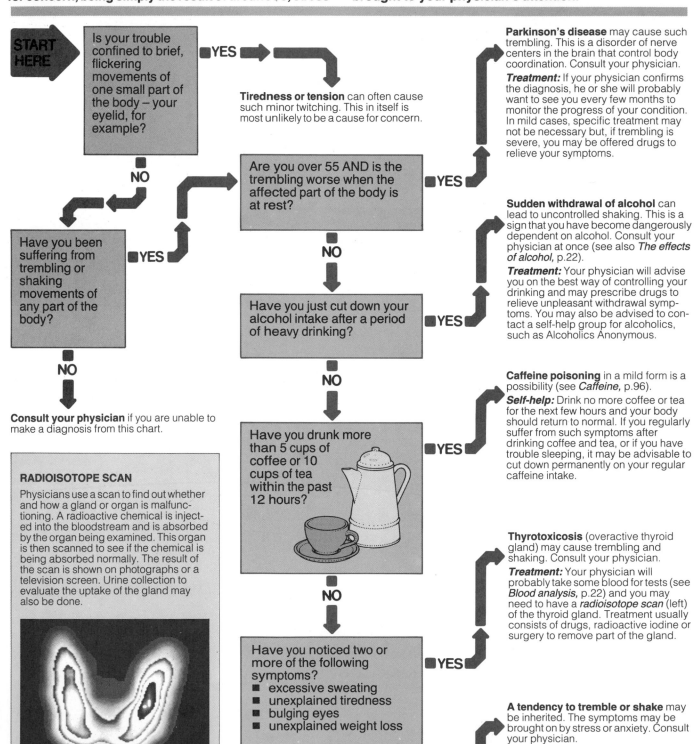

START HERE

Is your trouble confined to brief, flickering movements of one small part of the body – your eyelid, for example?

YES →

Tiredness or tension can often cause such minor twitching. This in itself is most unlikely to be a cause for concern.

NO ↓

Have you been suffering from trembling or shaking movements of any part of the body?

YES →

Are you over 55 AND is the trembling worse when the affected part of the body is at rest?

YES → **Parkinson's disease** may cause such trembling. This is a disorder of nerve centers in the brain that control body coordination. Consult your physician.

Treatment: If your physician confirms the diagnosis, he or she will probably want to see you every few months to monitor the progress of your condition. In mild cases, specific treatment may not be necessary but, if trembling is severe, you may be offered drugs to relieve your symptoms.

NO ↓

Have you just cut down your alcohol intake after a period of heavy drinking?

YES → **Sudden withdrawal of alcohol** can lead to uncontrolled shaking. This is a sign that you have become dangerously dependent on alcohol. Consult your physician at once (see also *The effects of alcohol,* p.22).

Treatment: Your physician will advise you on the best way of controlling your drinking and may prescribe drugs to relieve unpleasant withdrawal symptoms. You may also be advised to contact a self-help group for alcoholics, such as Alcoholics Anonymous.

NO ↓

NO ↓

Consult your physician if you are unable to make a diagnosis from this chart.

RADIOISOTOPE SCAN

Physicians use a scan to find out whether and how a gland or organ is malfunctioning. A radioactive chemical is injected into the bloodstream and is absorbed by the organ being examined. This organ is then scanned to see if the chemical is being absorbed normally. The result of the scan is shown on photographs or a television screen. Urine collection to evaluate the uptake of the gland may also be done.

The dark area in this scan of a thyroid gland shows a possible thyroid nodule.

Have you drunk more than 5 cups of coffee or 10 cups of tea within the past 12 hours?

YES → **Caffeine poisoning** in a mild form is a possibility (see *Caffeine,* p.96).

Self-help: Drink no more coffee or tea for the next few hours and your body should return to normal. If you regularly suffer from such symptoms after drinking coffee and tea, or if you have trouble sleeping, it may be advisable to cut down permanently on your regular caffeine intake.

NO ↓

Have you noticed two or more of the following symptoms?
- excessive sweating
- unexplained tiredness
- bulging eyes
- unexplained weight loss

YES → **Thyrotoxicosis** (overactive thyroid gland) may cause trembling and shaking. Consult your physician.

Treatment: Your physician will probably take some blood for tests (see *Blood analysis,* p.22) and you may need to have a *radioisotope scan* (left) of the thyroid gland. Treatment usually consists of drugs, radioactive iodine or surgery to remove part of the gland.

NO ↓

A tendency to tremble or shake may be inherited. The symptoms may be brought on by stress or anxiety. Consult your physician.

Treatment: Your physician will probably check your general health to reassure you that nothing is wrong. If necessary, he or she may prescribe an *anti-anxiety* drug to relieve your symptoms.

15 Pain in the face

Consult this chart if you have pain or discomfort that is limited to the area of the face and/or forehead. Facial pain may be dull and throbbing or sharp and stabbing. It is usually caused by infection or inflammation of the underlying tissues. Although it may be distressing, it is not often a sign of a serious disorder.

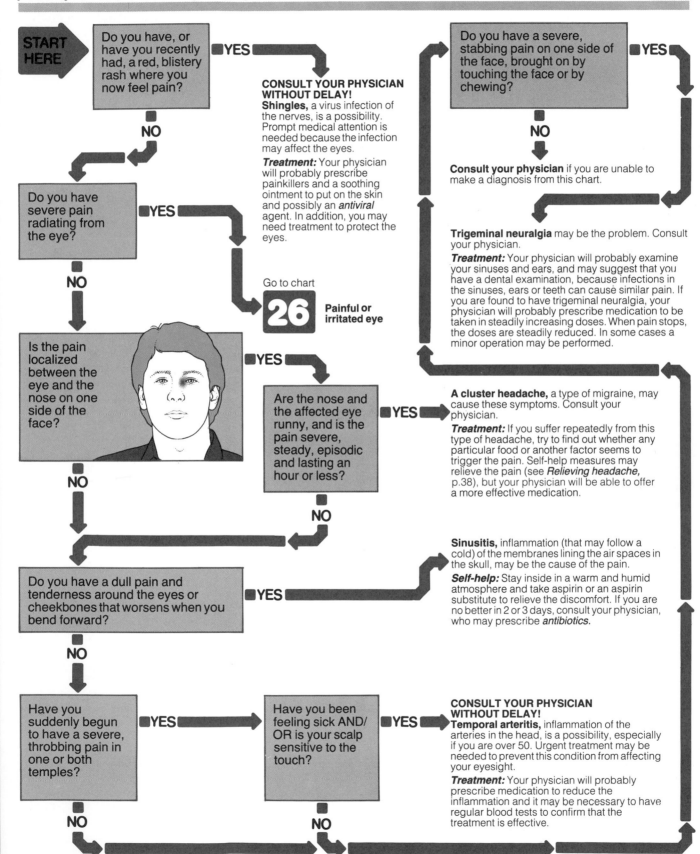

START HERE

Do you have, or have you recently had, a red, blistery rash where you now feel pain? **YES** →

NO

Do you have severe pain radiating from the eye? **YES** →

NO

Is the pain localized between the eye and the nose on one side of the face?

NO

CONSULT YOUR PHYSICIAN WITHOUT DELAY!
Shingles, a virus infection of the nerves, is a possibility. Prompt medical attention is needed because the infection may affect the eyes.
Treatment: Your physician will probably prescribe painkillers and a soothing ointment to put on the skin and possibly an *antiviral* agent. In addition, you may need treatment to protect the eyes.

Go to chart **26** **Painful or irritated eye**

YES →

Are the nose and the affected eye runny, and is the pain severe, steady, episodic and lasting an hour or less?

NO

Do you have a dull pain and tenderness around the eyes or cheekbones that worsens when you bend forward? **YES** →

NO

Have you suddenly begun to have a severe, throbbing pain in one or both temples? **YES** →

NO

Have you been feeling sick AND/OR is your scalp sensitive to the touch? **YES** →

NO

Do you have a severe, stabbing pain on one side of the face, brought on by touching the face or by chewing? **YES** →

NO

Consult your physician if you are unable to make a diagnosis from this chart.

Trigeminal neuralgia may be the problem. Consult your physician.
Treatment: Your physician will probably examine your sinuses and ears, and may suggest that you have a dental examination, because infections in the sinuses, ears or teeth can cause similar pain. If you are found to have trigeminal neuralgia, your physician will probably prescribe medication to be taken in steadily increasing doses. When pain stops, the doses are steadily reduced. In some cases a minor operation may be performed.

A cluster headache, a type of migraine, may cause these symptoms. Consult your physician.
Treatment: If you suffer repeatedly from this type of headache, try to find out whether any particular food or another factor seems to trigger the pain. Self-help measures may relieve the pain (see *Relieving headache,* p.38), but your physician will be able to offer a more effective medication.

Sinusitis, inflammation (that may follow a cold) of the membranes lining the air spaces in the skull, may be the cause of the pain.
Self-help: Stay inside in a warm and humid atmosphere and take aspirin or an aspirin substitute to relieve the discomfort. If you are no better in 2 or 3 days, consult your physician, who may prescribe *antibiotics.*

CONSULT YOUR PHYSICIAN WITHOUT DELAY!
Temporal arteritis, inflammation of the arteries in the head, is a possibility, especially if you are over 50. Urgent treatment may be needed to prevent this condition from affecting your eyesight.
Treatment: Your physician will probably prescribe medication to reduce the inflammation and it may be necessary to have regular blood tests to confirm that the treatment is effective.

16 Forgetfulness and confusion

We all suffer from mild forgetfulness and, to a lesser extent, confusion from time to time. Often such absentmindedness happens because we are tense or preoccupied. This is no cause for concern. However, if confusion comes on suddenly or if forgetfulness and confusion are so severe that they disrupt everyday life, there may be an underlying medical disorder. This chart deals with sudden or severe confusion or forgetfulness that you are aware of in yourself or in a relative or friend who may not be aware of the problem. Remember that loss of memory for recent events is a natural aging phenomenon.

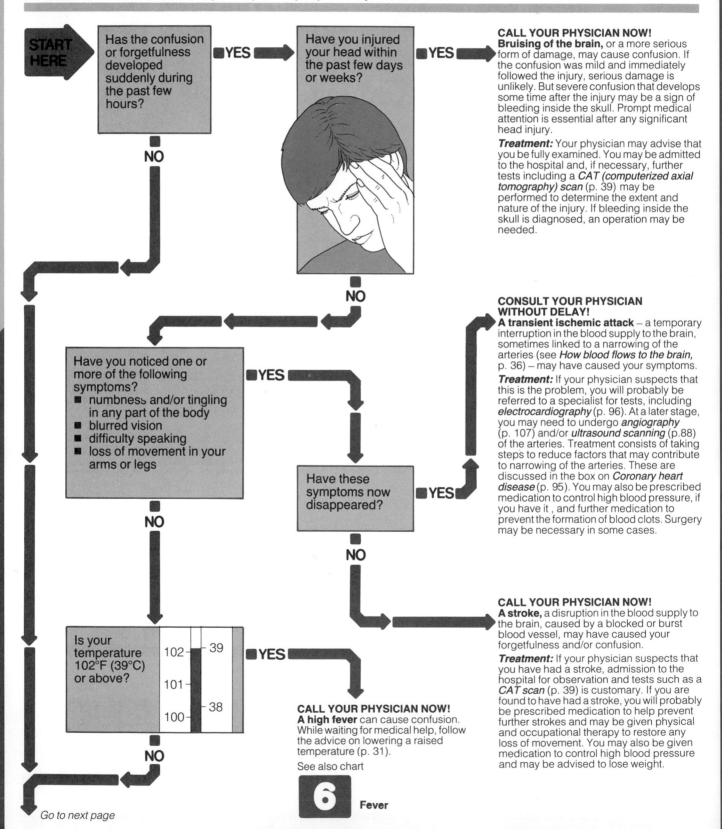

START HERE

Has the confusion or forgetfulness developed suddenly during the past few hours? — YES → **Have you injured your head within the past few days or weeks?** — YES →

CALL YOUR PHYSICIAN NOW!
Bruising of the brain, or a more serious form of damage, may cause confusion. If the confusion was mild and immediately followed the injury, serious damage is unlikely. But severe confusion that develops some time after the injury may be a sign of bleeding inside the skull. Prompt medical attention is essential after any significant head injury.

Treatment: Your physician may advise that you be fully examined. You may be admitted to the hospital and, if necessary, further tests including a *CAT (computerized axial tomography) scan* (p. 39) may be performed to determine the extent and nature of the injury. If bleeding inside the skull is diagnosed, an operation may be needed.

Have you noticed one or more of the following symptoms?
- numbness and/or tingling in any part of the body
- blurred vision
- difficulty speaking
- loss of movement in your arms or legs

— YES → **Have these symptoms now disappeared?** — YES →

CONSULT YOUR PHYSICIAN WITHOUT DELAY!
A transient ischemic attack – a temporary interruption in the blood supply to the brain, sometimes linked to a narrowing of the arteries (see *How blood flows to the brain,* p. 36) – may have caused your symptoms.

Treatment: If your physician suspects that this is the problem, you will probably be referred to a specialist for tests, including *electrocardiography* (p. 96). At a later stage, you may need to undergo *angiography* (p. 107) and/or *ultrasound scanning* (p.88) of the arteries. Treatment consists of taking steps to reduce factors that may contribute to narrowing of the arteries. These are discussed in the box on *Coronary heart disease* (p. 95). You may also be prescribed medication to control high blood pressure, if you have it , and further medication to prevent the formation of blood clots. Surgery may be necessary in some cases.

Is your temperature 102°F (39°C) or above? — YES →

CALL YOUR PHYSICIAN NOW!
A high fever can cause confusion. While waiting for medical help, follow the advice on lowering a raised temperature (p. 31).

See also chart

6 Fever

CALL YOUR PHYSICIAN NOW!
A stroke, a disruption in the blood supply to the brain, caused by a blocked or burst blood vessel, may have caused your forgetfulness and/or confusion.

Treatment: If your physician suspects that you have had a stroke, admission to the hospital for observation and tests such as a *CAT scan* (p. 39) is customary. If you are found to have had a stroke, you will probably be prescribed medication to help prevent further strokes and may be given physical and occupational therapy to restore any loss of movement. You may also be given medication to control high blood pressure and may be advised to lose weight.

Go to next page

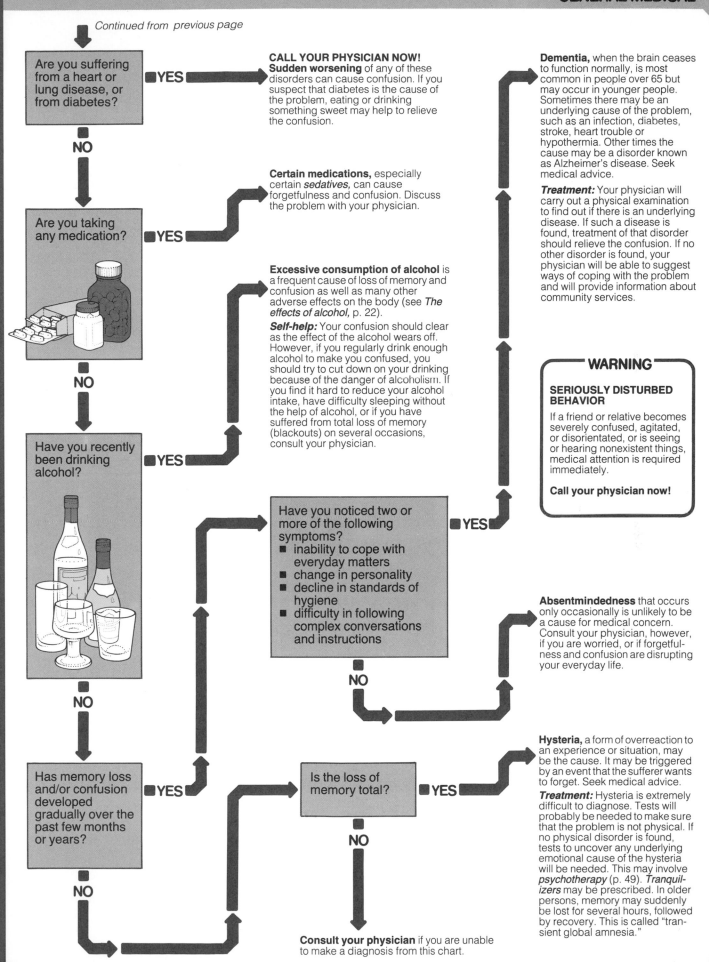

Continued from previous page

Are you suffering from a heart or lung disease, or from diabetes?

YES → **CALL YOUR PHYSICIAN NOW!**
Sudden worsening of any of these disorders can cause confusion. If you suspect that diabetes is the cause of the problem, eating or drinking something sweet may help to relieve the confusion.

NO ↓

Are you taking any medication?

YES → **Certain medications,** especially certain *sedatives,* can cause forgetfulness and confusion. Discuss the problem with your physician.

NO ↓

Have you recently been drinking alcohol?

YES → **Excessive consumption of alcohol** is a frequent cause of loss of memory and confusion as well as many other adverse effects on the body (see *The effects of alcohol,* p. 22).
Self-help: Your confusion should clear as the effect of the alcohol wears off. However, if you regularly drink enough alcohol to make you confused, you should try to cut down on your drinking because of the danger of alcoholism. If you find it hard to reduce your alcohol intake, have difficulty sleeping without the help of alcohol, or if you have suffered from total loss of memory (blackouts) on several occasions, consult your physician.

NO ↓

Have you noticed two or more of the following symptoms?
- inability to cope with everyday matters
- change in personality
- decline in standards of hygiene
- difficulty in following complex conversations and instructions

YES →

NO ↓

Has memory loss and/or confusion developed gradually over the past few months or years?

YES →

NO ↓

Is the loss of memory total?

YES →

NO ↓

Consult your physician if you are unable to make a diagnosis from this chart.

Dementia, when the brain ceases to function normally, is most common in people over 65 but may occur in younger people. Sometimes there may be an underlying cause of the problem, such as an infection, diabetes, stroke, heart trouble or hypothermia. Other times the cause may be a disorder known as Alzheimer's disease. Seek medical advice.
Treatment: Your physician will carry out a physical examination to find out if there is an underlying disease. If such a disease is found, treatment of that disorder should relieve the confusion. If no other disorder is found, your physician will be able to suggest ways of coping with the problem and will provide information about community services.

WARNING

SERIOUSLY DISTURBED BEHAVIOR

If a friend or relative becomes severely confused, agitated, or disorientated, or is seeing or hearing nonexistent things, medical attention is required immediately.

Call your physician now!

Absentmindedness that occurs only occasionally is unlikely to be a cause for medical concern. Consult your physician, however, if you are worried, or if forgetfulness and confusion are disrupting your everyday life.

Hysteria, a form of overreaction to an experience or situation, may be the cause. It may be triggered by an event that the sufferer wants to forget. Seek medical advice.
Treatment: Hysteria is extremely difficult to diagnose. Tests will probably be needed to make sure that the problem is not physical. If no physical disorder is found, tests to uncover any underlying emotional cause of the hysteria will be needed. This may involve *psychotherapy* (p. 49). *Tranquilizers* may be prescribed. In older persons, memory may suddenly be lost for several hours, followed by recovery. This is called "transient global amnesia."

17 Difficulty speaking

Consult this chart if you have or have had difficulty finding, using or defining words, or if your speech becomes slurred or unclear. Such speech difficulties may be related to disorders or medication affecting the speech centers in the brain or they may be due to a disorder of the mouth or tongue.

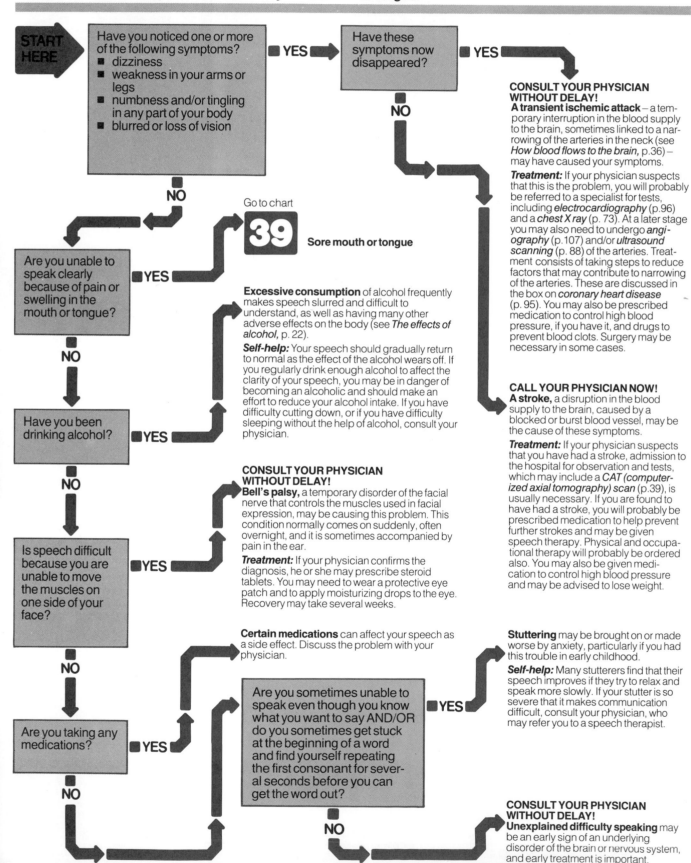

START HERE

Have you noticed one or more of the following symptoms?
- dizziness
- weakness in your arms or legs
- numbness and/or tingling in any part of your body
- blurred or loss of vision

YES → Have these symptoms now disappeared?

YES →

NO

NO

Go to chart **39** Sore mouth or tongue

Are you unable to speak clearly because of pain or swelling in the mouth or tongue?

YES →

NO

Have you been drinking alcohol?

YES →

NO

Is speech difficult because you are unable to move the muscles on one side of your face?

YES →

NO

Are you taking any medications?

YES →

NO

Are you sometimes unable to speak even though you know what you want to say AND/OR do you sometimes get stuck at the beginning of a word and find yourself repeating the first consonant for several seconds before you can get the word out?

YES →

NO

CONSULT YOUR PHYSICIAN WITHOUT DELAY!
A transient ischemic attack – a temporary interruption in the blood supply to the brain, sometimes linked to a narrowing of the arteries in the neck (see *How blood flows to the brain,* p.36) – may have caused your symptoms.

Treatment: If your physician suspects that this is the problem, you will probably be referred to a specialist for tests, including *electrocardiography* (p.96) and a *chest X ray* (p. 73). At a later stage you may also need to undergo *angiography* (p.107) and/or *ultrasound scanning* (p. 88) of the arteries. Treatment consists of taking steps to reduce factors that may contribute to narrowing of the arteries. These are discussed in the box on *coronary heart disease* (p. 95). You may also be prescribed medication to control high blood pressure, if you have it, and drugs to prevent blood clots. Surgery may be necessary in some cases.

CALL YOUR PHYSICIAN NOW!
A stroke, a disruption in the blood supply to the brain, caused by a blocked or burst blood vessel, may be the cause of these symptoms.

Treatment: If your physician suspects that you have had a stroke, admission to the hospital for observation and tests, which may include a *CAT (computerized axial tomography) scan* (p.39), is usually necessary. If you are found to have had a stroke, you will probably be prescribed medication to help prevent further strokes and may be given speech therapy. Physical and occupational therapy will probably be ordered also. You may also be given medication to control high blood pressure and may be advised to lose weight.

Excessive consumption of alcohol frequently makes speech slurred and difficult to understand, as well as having many other adverse effects on the body (see *The effects of alcohol,* p. 22).

Self-help: Your speech should gradually return to normal as the effect of the alcohol wears off. If you regularly drink enough alcohol to affect the clarity of your speech, you may be in danger of becoming an alcoholic and should make an effort to reduce your alcohol intake. If you have difficulty cutting down, or if you have difficulty sleeping without the help of alcohol, consult your physician.

CONSULT YOUR PHYSICIAN WITHOUT DELAY!
Bell's palsy, a temporary disorder of the facial nerve that controls the muscles used in facial expression, may be causing this problem. This condition normally comes on suddenly, often overnight, and it is sometimes accompanied by pain in the ear.

Treatment: If your physician confirms the diagnosis, he or she may prescribe steroid tablets. You may need to wear a protective eye patch and to apply moisturizing drops to the eye. Recovery may take several weeks.

Certain medications can affect your speech as a side effect. Discuss the problem with your physician.

Stuttering may be brought on or made worse by anxiety, particularly if you had this trouble in early childhood.

Self-help: Many stutterers find that their speech improves if they try to relax and speak more slowly. If your stutter is so severe that it makes communication difficult, consult your physician, who may refer you to a speech therapist.

CONSULT YOUR PHYSICIAN WITHOUT DELAY!
Unexplained difficulty speaking may be an early sign of an underlying disorder of the brain or nervous system, and early treatment is important.

18 Disturbing thoughts and feelings

Consult this chart if you begin to have thoughts and feelings that worry you or that seem to you or to others to be abnormal or unhealthy. Such feelings may include aggressive or sexual thoughts and unfamiliar or uncontrolled emotions. If your thoughts and feelings continue to worry you, whatever your particular problem, talk to your physician, who may be able to help you put your feelings into proper context and offer treatment where appropriate. Simply talking about your problem may make you feel better.

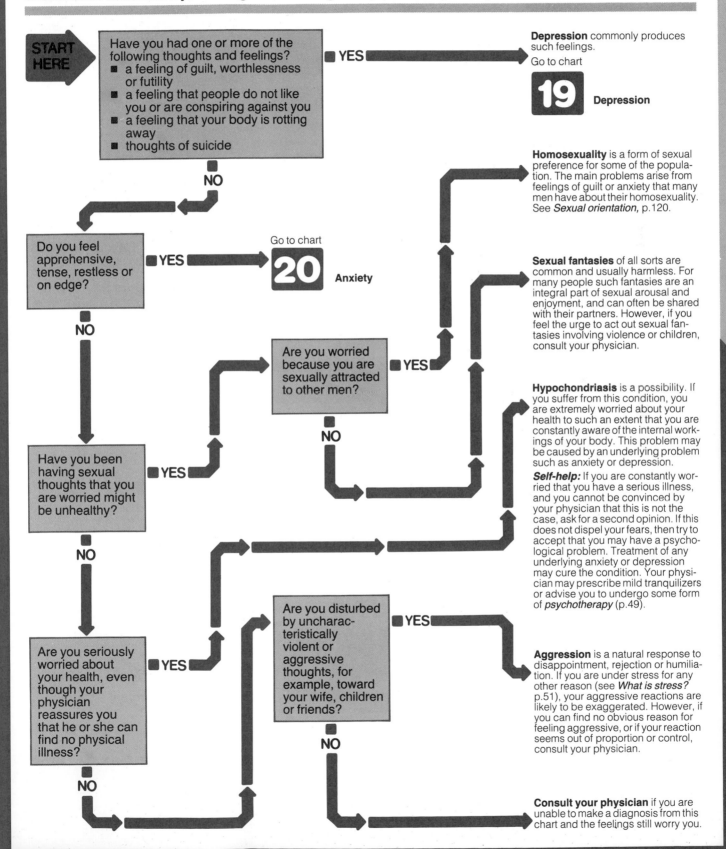

START HERE

Have you had one or more of the following thoughts and feelings?
- a feeling of guilt, worthlessness or futility
- a feeling that people do not like you or are conspiring against you
- a feeling that your body is rotting away
- thoughts of suicide

YES → **Depression** commonly produces such feelings.
Go to chart

19 Depression

NO

Do you feel apprehensive, tense, restless or on edge?

YES → Go to chart **20** Anxiety

NO

Have you been having sexual thoughts that you are worried might be unhealthy?

YES →

Are you worried because you are sexually attracted to other men?

YES → **Homosexuality** is a form of sexual preference for some of the population. The main problems arise from feelings of guilt or anxiety that many men have about their homosexuality. See *Sexual orientation,* p.120.

NO →

Sexual fantasies of all sorts are common and usually harmless. For many people such fantasies are an integral part of sexual arousal and enjoyment, and can often be shared with their partners. However, if you feel the urge to act out sexual fantasies involving violence or children, consult your physician.

NO

Are you seriously worried about your health, even though your physician reassures you that he or she can find no physical illness?

YES →

Are you disturbed by uncharacteristically violent or aggressive thoughts, for example, toward your wife, children or friends?

YES →

Hypochondriasis is a possibility. If you suffer from this condition, you are extremely worried about your health to such an extent that you are constantly aware of the internal workings of your body. This problem may be caused by an underlying problem such as anxiety or depression.

Self-help: If you are constantly worried that you have a serious illness, and you cannot be convinced by your physician that this is not the case, ask for a second opinion. If this does not dispel your fears, then try to accept that you may have a psychological problem. Treatment of any underlying anxiety or depression may cure the condition. Your physician may prescribe mild tranquilizers or advise you to undergo some form of *psychotherapy* (p.49).

Aggression is a natural response to disappointment, rejection or humiliation. If you are under stress for any other reason (see *What is stress?* p.51), your aggressive reactions are likely to be exaggerated. However, if you can find no obvious reason for feeling aggressive, or if your reaction seems out of proportion or control, consult your physician.

NO

Consult your physician if you are unable to make a diagnosis from this chart and the feelings still worry you.

19 Depression

Most people have minor ups and downs in mood, feeling particularly good one day but low the next. This is often due to an identifiable cause, and quickly passes. More severe depression, characterized by feelings of futility and guilt and often with physical symptoms such as headache, insomnia, lack of appetite, loss of weight, constipation and delusion, is sometimes brought on by some major event, such as bereavement, divorce or becoming unemployed. Some people, however, are prone to repeated attacks of depression that have no apparent cause. Also, there are certain times when we are more susceptible to depression – for instance, during adolescence, at middle age and at retirement. Depression will almost always be relieved with help.

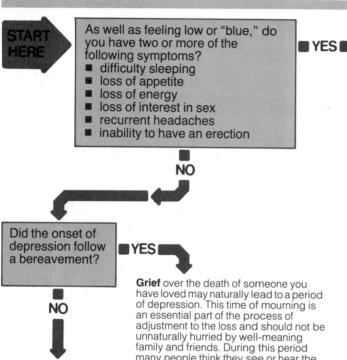

START HERE

As well as feeling low or "blue," do you have two or more of the following symptoms?
■ difficulty sleeping
■ loss of appetite
■ loss of energy
■ loss of interest in sex
■ recurrent headaches
■ inability to have an erection

YES

NO

A depressive illness is a possibility. This often develops with no apparent cause, and in the most severe cases it may be accompanied by severe psychological symptoms such as feelings of persecution, guilt and worthlessness. Some sufferers lose all energy and enthusiasm, sleep poorly and wake early. A severely depressed person may contemplate suicide. Consult your physician if you are experiencing these feelings. A threat of suicide should always be taken seriously, even if such threats have been made before (see *Suicide,* below).

Treatment: This depends on the type and severity of your symptoms. Your physician may refer you to a specialist for treatment that is likely to consist of a combination of drugs and *psychotherapy* (opposite). *Antidepressants,* if prescribed, usually begin to relieve mild depression in 2 or 3 weeks. If you are severely depressed, the specialist may recommend that you spend some time in the hospital.

Did the onset of depression follow a bereavement?

YES

NO

Grief over the death of someone you have loved may naturally lead to a period of depression. This time of mourning is an essential part of the process of adjustment to the loss and should not be unnaturally hurried by well-meaning family and friends. During this period many people think they see or hear the dead person and this is perfectly normal.

Self-help: Do not expect to return to normal within a few days or weeks. Many people take months to accept their loss. Do not, however, believe that you must not give in or that admitting to unhappiness is a sign of weakness. If depression is preventing you from coping with everyday life, or if you have difficulty sleeping, consult your physician. Sometimes *antidepressants* or *tranquilizers* are helpful.

WARNING

SUICIDE

Medical help should be sought at once if you (or someone you know) feel so depressed that you think that life is no longer worthwhile, or if you have contemplated suicide or discussed it with relatives or friends. The Samaritans, a voluntary organization specializing in helping people who are contemplating suicide, are available on the telephone 24 hours a day to offer support. Or look in the telephone book under "Suicide Prevention Service."

Seek medical help without delay!

Did your depression follow a distressing event, such as a divorce or losing your job?

YES

NO

Distressing events are often followed by a period of depression. This is known as "reactive depression." Some people react more severely than others. If your depression makes life unbearable, prevents you from coping with everyday life, begins to get worse or if your friends are clearly worried about you, consult your physician.

Treatment: This depends on the type and the severity of your symptoms. Your physician may prescribe *antidepressants,* which will usually relieve a mild depression in 2 to 3 weeks. If you are severely depressed, you may be referred to a specialist for treatment, which is likely to consist of a combination of drugs and *psychotherapy* (opposite). In some cases, it may be necessary to spend some time in the hospital, where treatment can be supervised.

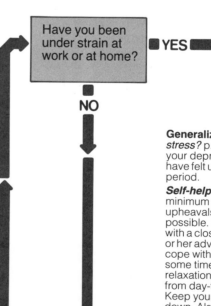

Have you been under strain at work or at home?

YES

NO

Generalized stress (see *What is stress?* p.51) may be the cause of your depression, especially if you have felt under pressure for a long period.

Self-help: Try to keep stress to a minimum by avoiding major upheavals in your life as much as possible. Discuss your feelings with a close friend and listen to his or her advice about how you might cope with your problems. Devote some time every day to physical relaxation that diverts your mind from day-to-day strain and worry. Keep your alcohol consumption down. Also, follow the advice on getting a good night's sleep (see *Preventing sleeplessness,* p.29). Consult your physician if you feel that the self-help measures are not working, or if your depression seems to be getting worse.

Go to next page

Continued from previous page

Have you recently recovered from an infectious illness, such as the flu or glandular fever?

YES

Infectious illnesses are often followed by a period of depression.

Self-help: Do not try to return to your normal routine too quickly after you have had such an illness. Make sure that you eat well and get plenty of sleep to allow your strength to build up. If your depression lasts longer than 2 weeks, consult your physician, who may prescribe an *antidepressant*.

NO

Have you been drinking alcohol every day for a prolonged period?

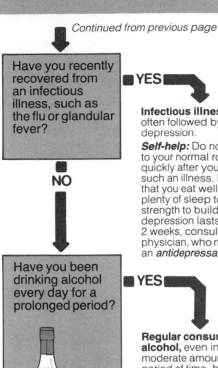

YES

Regular consumption of alcohol, even in seemingly moderate amounts over a period of time, has a depressive effect on the body and mind, and this may persist on days when you have had no alcohol (see *The effects of alcohol,* p.22).

Self-help: Your depression should clear if you stop drinking alcohol. If you find it difficult to cut down on the amount of alcohol you drink, or your depression persists or begins to get worse, consult your physician.

NO

Are you between 40 and 55 years old?

YES

Emotional instability during the middle years of life, sometimes known as mid-life crisis, commonly leads to depression. This may occur for a combination of reasons: failure to realize certain ambitions, decline in physical health or capabilities or anxiety about loss of sexual attractiveness and prowess. Such depression may be exacerbated by overeating, drinking too much alcohol and lack of exercise. Consult your physician.

Treatment: Your physician may be able to offer treatment with **antidepressant** drugs, but there is much you can do to help yourself through this difficult period. It is important to come to terms with middle age and accept that you may need help. You may find it helps to talk to family and friends about your feelings. Be careful not to neglect your physical health. If you are overweight, try losing some weight (see *How to lose weight,* p.27) and cut down on the amount of alcohol you drink. It is also a good idea to exercise regularly (see *The benefits of exercise,* p.25). If you are worried about your sexual performance, discussing it openly with your partner may help. Many specific sexual problems can be treated, so discuss these with your physician (see *Sex in later life,* p.117). See also the *Sex and fertility charts,* pp.116-125.

NO

Are you currently taking any medication?

YES

Certain drugs, especially sedatives, can cause depression. Discuss the problem with your physician.

NO

Consult your physician if you are unable to find the cause of your depression from this chart.

PSYCHOTHERAPY
Psychotherapy is the treatment of psychological problems by a therapist who encourages you to talk about your feelings and fears, and who can provide expert help and advice. This process may range from talking about your troubles with your own physician to an extended course of psychoanalysis with a psychiatrist. The more common forms of psychotherapy are described here.

Group therapy
This involves a number of sessions during which the therapist guides a discussion among a group of people with a problem in common. The advantage of group psychotherapy is that the members of the group gain strength from knowing that other people have the same problem and that they can learn from each other's experiences. There is also a certain amount of group pressure to develop a healthier attitude to personal problems and group support for this attitude to continue.

Behavior therapy
This is usually used in the treatment of specific phobias, such as fear of flying, or fear of dogs or spiders. In one form of behavior therapy known as desensitization, the sufferer is gradually helped by the therapist to overcome the fear. For example, in the case of fear of flying, the therapist encourages you to imagine the events associated with the flight – taking a bus to the airport, waiting in the terminal, dealing with the ticket agent, boarding, and finally sitting on the plane while it taxis on the runway, takes off and lands. Later, when you actually come to fly, you will feel as though you have been through it before and it will then hold no fear for you.

Another method, called flooding, involves a confrontation, under the supervision of your therapist, with the object of your fears in an extreme form – for example, a confrontation with a dog as treatment for fear of dogs. Experiencing the worst imaginable degree of exposure helps you to realize that all along there has been no real danger involved and that your fear has been exaggerated. Both methods should be attempted only under the guidance of a trained therapist.

Psychoanalysis
This form of psychotherapy, based on the belief that much human behavior is determined by early childhood conflicts, was developed in the late 19th and early 20th centuries. Psychoanalysis involves a series of meetings with a psychoanalyst during which he or she will encourage you to talk at will. He or she may ask occasional questions to guide the direction of your thoughts. By listening to your recollections, thoughts and feelings, he or she may be able to pinpoint the root of your problem and, through discussion, enable you to reach a better understanding of yourself and help you reconcile any internal conflicts.

20 Anxiety

If you are suffering from anxiety, you will feel tense and unable to concentrate, think clearly or sleep well. Some people have headaches, chest pains, palpitations, abdominal distress, backache and a general feeling of tiredness. This is often a natural reaction to a stressful situation and is only temporary. Other people, however, suffer from anxiety that comes on without apparent cause and persists for long periods.

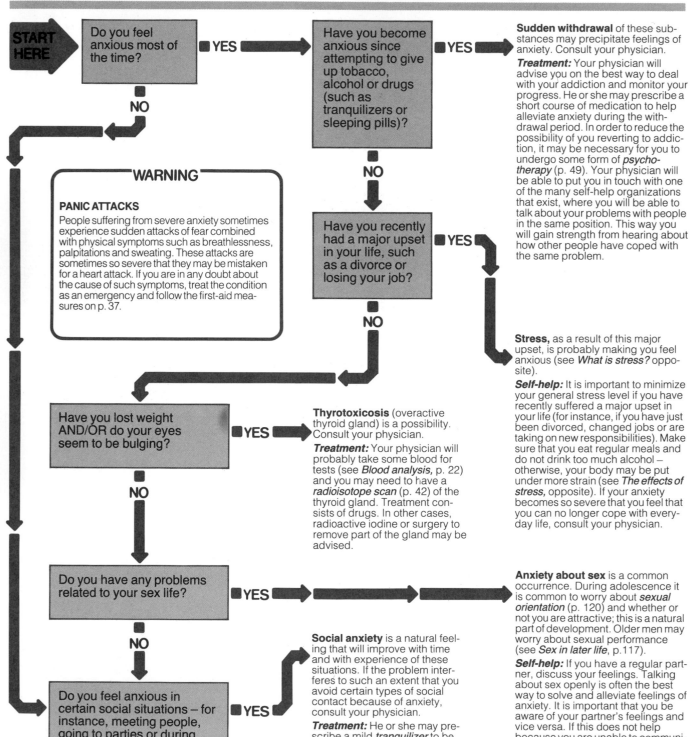

START HERE

Do you feel anxious most of the time?
— YES →

NO ↓

Have you become anxious since attempting to give up tobacco, alcohol or drugs (such as tranquilizers or sleeping pills)?
— YES →

NO ↓

Sudden withdrawal of these substances may precipitate feelings of anxiety. Consult your physician.

Treatment: Your physician will advise you on the best way to deal with your addiction and monitor your progress. He or she may prescribe a short course of medication to help alleviate anxiety during the withdrawal period. In order to reduce the possibility of you reverting to addiction, it may be necessary for you to undergo some form of *psychotherapy* (p. 49). Your physician will be able to put you in touch with one of the many self-help organizations that exist, where you will be able to talk about your problems with people in the same position. This way you will gain strength from hearing about how other people have coped with the same problem.

WARNING

PANIC ATTACKS
People suffering from severe anxiety sometimes experience sudden attacks of fear combined with physical symptoms such as breathlessness, palpitations and sweating. These attacks are sometimes so severe that they may be mistaken for a heart attack. If you are in any doubt about the cause of such symptoms, treat the condition as an emergency and follow the first-aid measures on p. 37.

Have you recently had a major upset in your life, such as a divorce or losing your job?
— YES →

NO ↓

Stress, as a result of this major upset, is probably making you feel anxious (see *What is stress?* opposite).

Self-help: It is important to minimize your general stress level if you have recently suffered a major upset in your life (for instance, if you have just been divorced, changed jobs or are taking on new responsibilities). Make sure that you eat regular meals and do not drink too much alcohol – otherwise, your body may be put under more strain (see *The effects of stress,* opposite). If your anxiety becomes so severe that you feel that you can no longer cope with everyday life, consult your physician.

Have you lost weight AND/OR do your eyes seem to be bulging?
— YES →

NO ↓

Thyrotoxicosis (overactive thyroid gland) is a possibility. Consult your physician.

Treatment: Your physician will probably take some blood for tests (see *Blood analysis,* p. 22) and you may need to have a *radioisotope scan* (p. 42) of the thyroid gland. Treatment consists of drugs. In other cases, radioactive iodine or surgery to remove part of the gland may be advised.

Do you have any problems related to your sex life?
— YES →

NO ↓

Anxiety about sex is a common occurrence. During adolescence it is common to worry about *sexual orientation* (p. 120) and whether or not you are attractive; this is a natural part of development. Older men may worry about sexual performance (see *Sex in later life,* p.117).

Self-help: If you have a regular partner, discuss your feelings. Talking about sex openly is often the best way to solve and alleviate feelings of anxiety. It is important that you be aware of your partner's feelings and vice versa. If this does not help because you are unable to communicate satisfactorily with each other, or you do not have a regular partner with whom you can talk, consult your physician, who will be able to offer helpful advice or possibly refer you for *sex counseling* (p. 116). For diagnosis of specific sex problems, see the *Sex and fertility charts,* pp.115-127.

Do you feel anxious in certain social situations – for instance, meeting people, going to parties or during interviews?
— YES →

NO ↓

Go to next page

Social anxiety is a natural feeling that will improve with time and with experience of these situations. If the problem interferes to such an extent that you avoid certain types of social contact because of anxiety, consult your physician.

Treatment: He or she may prescribe a mild *tranquilizer* to be taken just before you enter any social situation where you will feel anxious (until you gain enough confidence to do without). If your physician feels that your anxiety is severe, he or she may suggest that you undergo *psychotherapy* (p. 49) to help you overcome the problem.

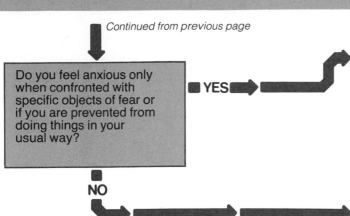

Continued from previous page

Do you feel anxious only when confronted with specific objects of fear or if you are prevented from doing things in your usual way?

YES

NO

A phobia or compulsive disorder may cause your anxiety. A phobia is an irrational fear of a specific object or situation. For instance, you may have a fear of enclosed spaces (claustrophobia). If you have a compulsive disorder, you feel an irresistible need to behave in a certain fashion, even though you may know that it is unreasonable. For example, you may feel that you have to walk to work on the same side of the street and, if prevented from doing so, you worry about it. Consult your physician.

Treatment: Your physician will try to discover the underlying cause of the problem and may be able to reassure you that your worries and fears are understandable but that it is possible to come to terms with them. He or she may decide that *antidepressants* or *tranquilizers* will help. If your symptoms are severe, he or she may refer you for *psychotherapy* (p. 49).

Consult your physician if you are unable to make a diagnosis from this chart and unexplained feelings of anxiety persist.

WHAT IS STRESS?

Stress refers to physical or mental demands that require an increased response from the body. Stress can be caused by changes in daily routine, including changes for the better – getting married or having a baby – as well as for the worse – losing a job or getting divorced. The greater the change, the more stress you will suffer. A single major event such as the death of a close relative may, on its own, equal the stress resulting from an accumulation of smaller changes such as a change in job responsibilities, a move to a new house or a vacation overseas.

The effects of stress

A certain amount of stress can be beneficial when it excites and stimulates the body and improves performance. However, as stress levels continue to rise, helpful stimulation becomes replaced by fatigue (see *Stress and tiredness,* p. 24) and, if stress is not reduced, may increase susceptibility to physical and mental illness. Everybody has a different level of tolerance to stress; some people never seem to suffer harmful effects from seemingly high levels of stress in their lives, while others can cope with only a few changes at a time without becoming anxious, depressed or physically ill.

Some of the most common disorders that may be caused by or made worse by stress are:

- Mental and emotional problems, including anxiety and depression
- Asthma
- Mouth ulcers
- Angina and some other heart conditions
- Stomach or duodenal ulcers
- Ulcerative colitis
- Irritable bowel (see p. 87)
- Stuttering
- Skin conditions, including eczema and psoriasis
- Certain forms of hair loss
- Sexual difficulties such as premature ejaculation or impotence

RELAXATION TECHNIQUES

Some people manage to remain relaxed and easy-going no matter how much strain they are under at work or at home. Others become tense and worried as a result of even minor stresses (see *What is stress?* above). If you are one of the latter type, learning to relax may help mitigate the harmful effects of stress and enable you to cope with problems more easily. Try practicing some of the simple relaxation techniques described below once or twice a day. (See also *Preventing sleeplessness,* p. 29.)

Breathing exercises

Try taking deep rather than shallow breaths. To develop the habit, sit or lie in a comfortable position and breathe deeply and slowly for one minute, counting the number of breaths you take. Try to reduce your breathing rate so that you take half as many breaths as you normally do during a minute. Try this twice daily.

Meditation

Meditation involves emptying the mind of all distractions, thoughts and worries. Try the following method:

1 Find a quiet part of the house and sit in a comfortable chair with your eyes closed.

2 Without moving your lips, repeat a word silently to yourself, paying attention only to this action. Do not choose a word that has any emotional overtones. If your mind wanders, do not fight this new train of thought but continue to focus your attention on the unspoken sound of the word. (Some people find it easier to concentrate on something visual – a door knob or a vase of flowers – rather than a word).

3 Do this for 5 minutes twice a day for a week, then gradually increase the meditation period until you can manage about 20 minutes at each session.

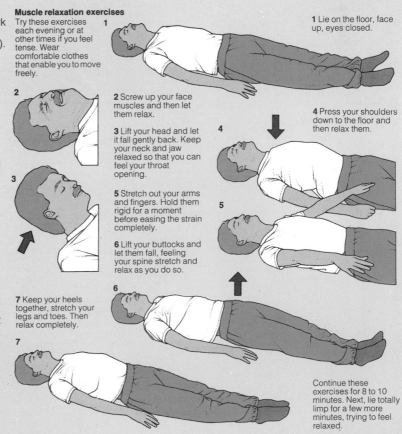

Muscle relaxation exercises
Try these exercises each evening or at other times if you feel tense. Wear comfortable clothes that enable you to move freely.

1 Lie on the floor, face up, eyes closed.

2 Screw up your face muscles and then let them relax.

3 Lift your head and let it fall gently back. Keep your neck and jaw relaxed so that you can feel your throat opening.

4 Press your shoulders down to the floor and then relax them.

5 Stretch out your arms and fingers. Hold them rigid for a moment before easing the strain completely.

6 Lift your buttocks and let them fall, feeling your spine stretch and relax as you do so.

7 Keep your heels together, stretch your legs and toes. Then relax completely.

Continue these exercises for 8 to 10 minutes. Next, lie totally limp for a few more minutes, trying to feel relaxed.

21 Hair, scalp and nail problems

Hair grows over the whole surface of the human body, except the palms and soles, and grows especially thickly on the head, in the armpits and in the genital area. Some men also have heavy hair growth on the chest, lower arms and legs. Your hair color and type are inherited, but your hair's condition may be affected by your overall health, your diet and the environment. This chart pinpoints common problems affecting hair on the head and the condition of the scalp. It also includes information on how to care for your hair and nails.

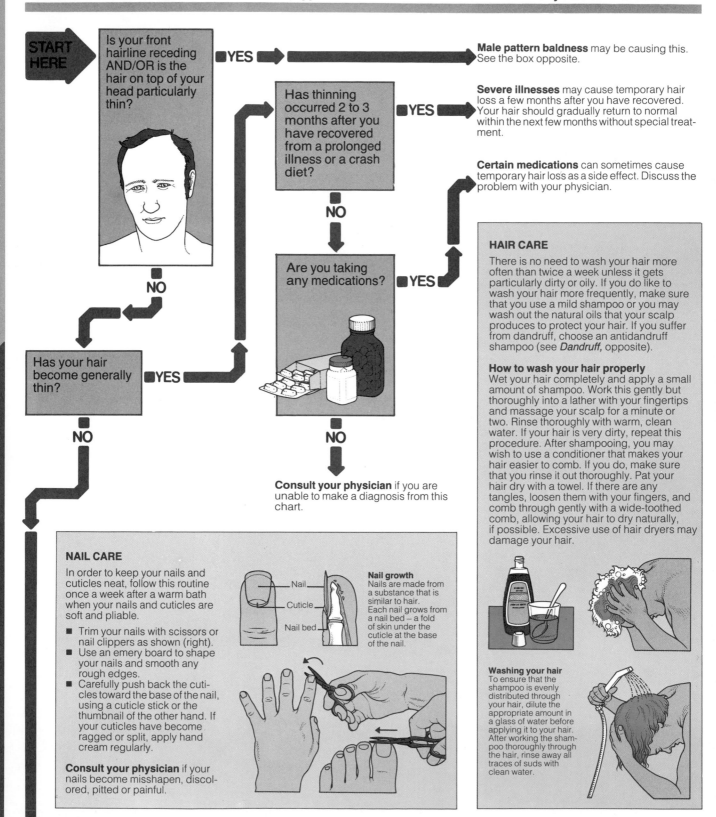

START HERE

Is your front hairline receding AND/OR is the hair on top of your head particularly thin?

YES → Male pattern baldness may be causing this. See the box opposite.

Has thinning occurred 2 to 3 months after you have recovered from a prolonged illness or a crash diet?

YES → Severe illnesses may cause temporary hair loss a few months after you have recovered. Your hair should gradually return to normal within the next few months without special treatment.

NO

Are you taking any medications?

YES → Certain medications can sometimes cause temporary hair loss as a side effect. Discuss the problem with your physician.

NO

Consult your physician if you are unable to make a diagnosis from this chart.

NO

Has your hair become generally thin?

YES

NO

HAIR CARE

There is no need to wash your hair more often than twice a week unless it gets particularly dirty or oily. If you do like to wash your hair more frequently, make sure that you use a mild shampoo or you may wash out the natural oils that your scalp produces to protect your hair. If you suffer from dandruff, choose an antidandruff shampoo (see *Dandruff,* opposite).

How to wash your hair properly
Wet your hair completely and apply a small amount of shampoo. Work this gently but thoroughly into a lather with your fingertips and massage your scalp for a minute or two. Rinse thoroughly with warm, clean water. If your hair is very dirty, repeat this procedure. After shampooing, you may wish to use a conditioner that makes your hair easier to comb. If you do, make sure that you rinse it out thoroughly. Pat your hair dry with a towel. If there are any tangles, loosen them with your fingers, and comb through gently with a wide-toothed comb, allowing your hair to dry naturally, if possible. Excessive use of hair dryers may damage your hair.

NAIL CARE

In order to keep your nails and cuticles neat, follow this routine once a week after a warm bath when your nails and cuticles are soft and pliable.

■ Trim your nails with scissors or nail clippers as shown (right).
■ Use an emery board to shape your nails and smooth any rough edges.
■ Carefully push back the cuticles toward the base of the nail, using a cuticle stick or the thumbnail of the other hand. If your cuticles have become ragged or split, apply hand cream regularly.

Consult your physician if your nails become misshapen, discolored, pitted or painful.

Nail
Cuticle
Nail bed

Nail growth
Nails are made from a substance that is similar to hair. Each nail grows from a nail bed – a fold of skin under the cuticle at the base of the nail.

Washing your hair
To ensure that the shampoo is evenly distributed through your hair, dilute the appropriate amount in a glass of water before applying it to your hair. After working the shampoo thoroughly through the hair, rinse away all traces of suds with clean water.

Go to next page

Continued from previous page

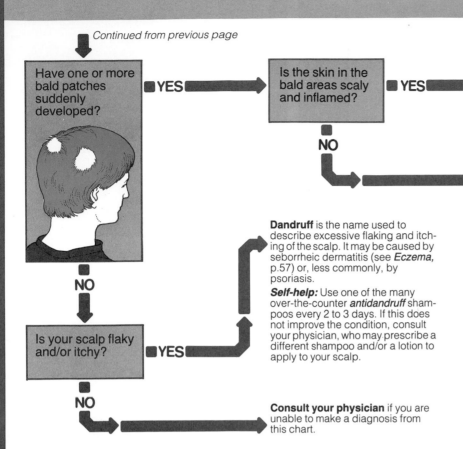

Have one or more bald patches suddenly developed? — **YES** →

Is the skin in the bald areas scaly and inflamed? — **YES** →

A fungal infection, such as ringworm, is the possible cause of this problem. Consult your physician.
Treatment: If your physician confirms the diagnosis, you will be prescribed an *antifungal* lotion and possibly a course of antifungal tablets. Your hair should return to normal in a few months. In the meantime, wash your hairbrush and comb thoroughly to prevent reinfection.

NO ↓

NO ↓

Is your scalp flaky and/or itchy? — **YES** →

Dandruff is the name used to describe excessive flaking and itching of the scalp. It may be caused by seborrheic dermatitis (see *Eczema,* p.57) or, less commonly, by psoriasis.
Self-help: Use one of the many over-the-counter *antidandruff* shampoos every 2 to 3 days. If this does not improve the condition, consult your physician, who may prescribe a different shampoo and/or a lotion to apply to your scalp.

Alopecia areata may be the reason for sudden patchy hair loss. This disease is not fully understood but it may be connected to tension or other emotional factors, such as depression and anxiety. Consult your physician to confirm the diagnosis, but often the condition disappears without treatment and new hair grows within 6 to 9 months.

NO ↓

Consult your physician if you are unable to make a diagnosis from this chart.

MALE PATTERN BALDNESS

Male pattern baldness is a natural and irreversible part of the aging process. Some men start to lose their hair as early as 20 and the majority have lost hair to some extent by the age of 60, although some men retain a full head of hair until old age. In most cases, hair loss is first noticed when the hairline at the front starts to recede. Thinning of the hair may also occur on the crown of the head. Gradually, the areas of hair loss merge to form a single bald area over the top of the head (see *The development of male pattern baldness,* right).

The causes of male pattern baldness

Male pattern baldness occurs when the rate of hair loss in certain areas exceeds the rate of hair replacement. The exact cause of male pattern baldness is not known, although it is thought to be related to an increased production of androgen, a male sex hormone that is thought to limit hair growth. The tendency to lose hair at a certain age is probably inherited. You may inherit genes for male pattern baldness from one or both sides of your family. If men on both sides of your family have become bald at an early age, you are likely to lose your hair early. If early baldness runs only on one side of the family, your chances of retaining your hair for a while longer are increased.

The cycle of hair loss and growth

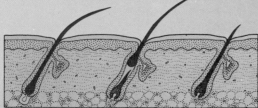

When a hair stops growing, the root forms a bulb shape and becomes detached from the base of the follicle.

The old hair then moves up the follicle and is shed. A new hair starts to form at the bottom of the follicle.

The hair may remain in the growing phase for several years.

The development of male pattern baldness

1

2

3

Concealing hair loss

Because male pattern baldness is irreversible, there is no true cure for it. There is no proof that changes in diet, or taking vitamins or minerals, can prevent or restore hair loss. Most men simply accept their changing appearance and may adopt a new hairstyle to take account of their hair loss. If you wish to conceal your baldness, there are several alternatives with varying degrees of effectiveness, largely depending on the competence of the practitioners offering the service. The least risky alternative is a simple hairpiece. Hair transplantation (below), which involves implanting hair from some other part of the body into the bald areas, is a long, expensive and painful process. If you believe that this is the best way to conceal your hair loss, get sound medical advice first, and make sure that the transplant is carried out by a reputable, qualified specialist.

Hair transplantation
In most types of hair transplant, hair from an area of thick growth (the donor site) – often the back of the head – is implanted in the bald area (recipient site). This is a lengthy and painful process. Always seek medical advice first.

 Recipient site
 Donor site

22 General skin problems

Many different types of disorders may affect the skin, including infections, inflammation, abnormal cell growth and abnormal skin coloration. Such disorders may be the result of an internal disease, exposure to an irritant or some other external factor. Symptoms of skin problems may include blemishes, lumps, rashes, a change in skin coloring or texture, itching or discomfort. Consult this chart if your symptom is not covered elsewhere in this book or if you have difficulty defining the problem.

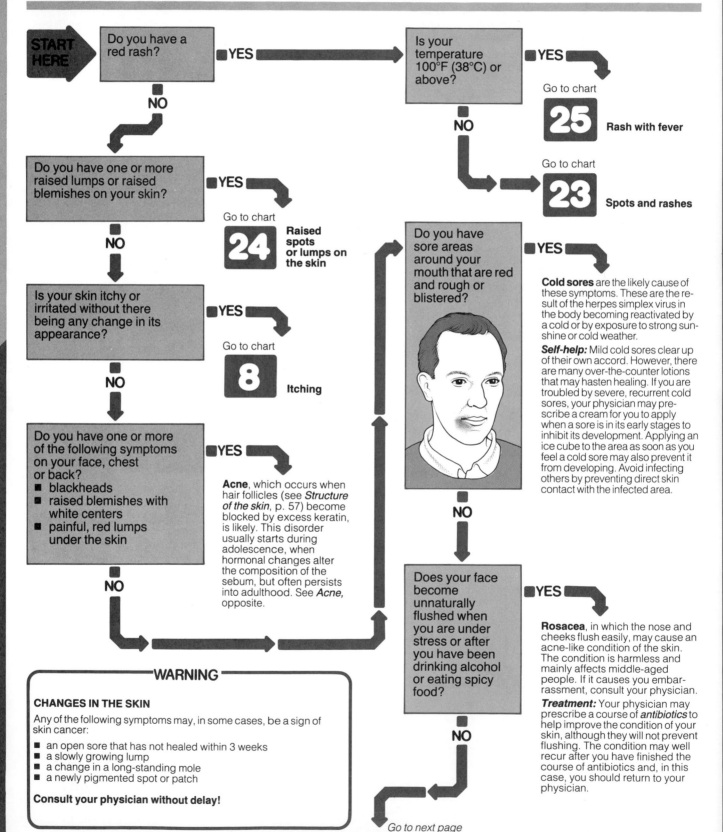

START HERE

Do you have a red rash? → **YES** → **Is your temperature 100°F (38°C) or above?** → **YES** → Go to chart **25** **Rash with fever**

↓ **NO** (from temperature) → Go to chart **23** **Spots and rashes**

Do you have a red rash? ↓ **NO**

Do you have one or more raised lumps or raised blemishes on your skin? → **YES** → Go to chart **24** **Raised spots or lumps on the skin**

↓ **NO**

Is your skin itchy or irritated without there being any change in its appearance? → **YES** → Go to chart **8** **Itching**

↓ **NO**

Do you have one or more of the following symptoms on your face, chest or back?
- blackheads
- raised blemishes with white centers
- painful, red lumps under the skin

→ **YES**

Acne, which occurs when hair follicles (see *Structure of the skin*, p. 57) become blocked by excess keratin, is likely. This disorder usually starts during adolescence, when hormonal changes alter the composition of the sebum, but often persists into adulthood. See *Acne*, opposite.

↓ **NO**

Do you have sore areas around your mouth that are red and rough or blistered? → **YES**

Cold sores are the likely cause of these symptoms. These are the result of the herpes simplex virus in the body becoming reactivated by a cold or by exposure to strong sunshine or cold weather.

Self-help: Mild cold sores clear up of their own accord. However, there are many over-the-counter lotions that may hasten healing. If you are troubled by severe, recurrent cold sores, your physician may prescribe a cream for you to apply when a sore is in its early stages to inhibit its development. Applying an ice cube to the area as soon as you feel a cold sore may also prevent it from developing. Avoid infecting others by preventing direct skin contact with the infected area.

↓ **NO**

Does your face become unnaturally flushed when you are under stress or after you have been drinking alcohol or eating spicy food? → **YES**

Rosacea, in which the nose and cheeks flush easily, may cause an acne-like condition of the skin. The condition is harmless and mainly affects middle-aged people. If it causes you embarrassment, consult your physician.

Treatment: Your physician may prescribe a course of *antibiotics* to help improve the condition of your skin, although they will not prevent flushing. The condition may well recur after you have finished the course of antibiotics and, in this case, you should return to your physician.

↓ **NO**

Go to next page

WARNING

CHANGES IN THE SKIN

Any of the following symptoms may, in some cases, be a sign of skin cancer:

- an open sore that has not healed within 3 weeks
- a slowly growing lump
- a change in a long-standing mole
- a newly pigmented spot or patch

Consult your physician without delay!

Continued from previous page

Have you recently noticed a new mole or a change in one you have had since childhood?

 YES

NO

CONSULT YOUR PHYSICIAN WITHOUT DELAY!
Moles, small, sometimes raised, pigmented spots, normally do not appear for the first time or change significantly after age 35. Most moles are harmless, but when changes occur there is a slight possibility of a malignant melanoma, a form of skin cancer.

Treatment: Even if your physician thinks that the mole is harmless, he or she may still decide to have it removed and examined under a microscope (see *Biopsy,* p. 35) for signs of cancerous cells. If cancer is confirmed, the growth will be removed, together with a wide margin of adjacent skin. A skin graft to cover the whole area will probably be carried out.

Have flat patches of very pale or very dark skin developed on your skin?

 YES

NO

Uneven skin pigmentation is usually the result of abnormal formation of the cells that produce skin pigment or of an abnormal rate of pigment production. This may sometimes be caused by a fungal infection. Consult your physician.

Treatment: Most disorders of skin pigment are harmless and require no treatment. You can disguise any disfiguring patches with make-up. If your physician suspects a fungal infection, you will be prescribed an *antifungal* cream, which will soon clear up the condition.

Do you have one or more red patches covered with silvery-white, flaky skin?

 YES

NO

Psoriasis, a disorder in which the skin cells grow unusually rapidly and form scales, is a possibility. The most common sites for this to occur are the scalp, elbows and knees, though scaly patches can also appear in the armpits, on the trunk or around the anus. Consult your physician.

Treatment: Your physician will probably prescribe a *steroid* ointment or cream to apply to the affected area. This needs to be done carefully because it may thin the unaffected skin. Alternatively, a combination of ultra-violet light treatment and medication may be recommended, or medication may be prescribed to slow down the rate of cell growth in the skin.

ACNE

Acne is the name used to describe a group of skin symptoms mainly affecting the face, chest and back, caused by blockage and infection of hair follicles (see *Structure of the skin*, p. 57). There are 3 main types of symptoms:

Blackheads These are tiny black spots caused by excess skin pigment overlying trapped sebum and skin debris in a hair follicle.

Pustules Pustules are tender, red blemishes that develop raised, white centers. They occur when excess keratin blocks a hair follicle and becomes inflamed (see right).

The development of a pustule

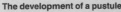

Cysts These are painful, red, fluid-filled lumps under the skin. They persist for several weeks and are more likely than other types of blemishes to lead to scarring.

Self-help
Mild acne with blackheads and the occasional pustule needs no special treatment other than ensuring that you wash your face thoroughly twice a day. Exposure to sunlight or careful use of an ultraviolet lamp often improves the condition. Avoid squeezing blemishes, as this is likely to increase the risk of infection and scarring. There are many over-the-counter preparations for acne. You may find some of these helpful. But you should avoid using anything too vigorously; this may lead to permanent skin damage.

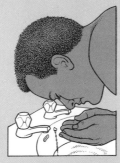

Professional treatment
If your acne is severe enough to embarrass you, if you have cystic blemishes or if there is any sign of scarring, consult your physician. Various treatments may be advised, depending on the type of acne. You may be prescribed a lotion that gently removes the top layer of skin, clearing blocked pores and preventing further blemishes from forming. Or you may be prescribed a long course of low-dose *antibiotics* that counters bacterial activity in the skin. Less commonly, a medication that alters the composition of the sebum may be prescribed. This treatment needs to be monitored carefully because of possible side effects.

Has a blistery rash appeared on one side of your body in a place in which there has been a burning sensation for a day or two?

 YES

NO

Shingles, a virus infection of the nerves, is a possibility. Consult your physician. This can be serious if the rash is on your face, because of the danger of damage to your eyes.

Treatment: Your physician will probably prescribe painkillers and a soothing ointment to put on the skin and, possibly, an *antiviral* agent. If there is any possibility of damage to the eyes, you will probably be referred to a specialist for treatment.

Do you have one or more open sores on your skin?

 YES

NO

Skin ulcers are usually caused by injury or infection, but may in some cases be encouraged by an underlying disorder such as poor circulation or diabetes.

Self-help: Keep the sore area clean, dry and, if necessary, protect it with an adhesive bandage or light dressing. Consult your physician if the sore has not healed within 3 weeks or if ulcers recur. Tests may be needed to determine the underlying cause of the trouble and determine treatment.

Consult your physician if you are unable to make a diagnosis from this chart.

23 Spots and rashes

Groups of inflamed spots or blisters, or larger areas of inflamed skin, are usually caused by infection, irritation or an allergic reaction. Such a rash may come up suddenly or develop over a period of days and may, or may not, cause discomfort or itching. Often, rashes are intensified or spread by scratching. If a rash persists for more than a day, it is wise to consult your physician for diagnosis and treatment.

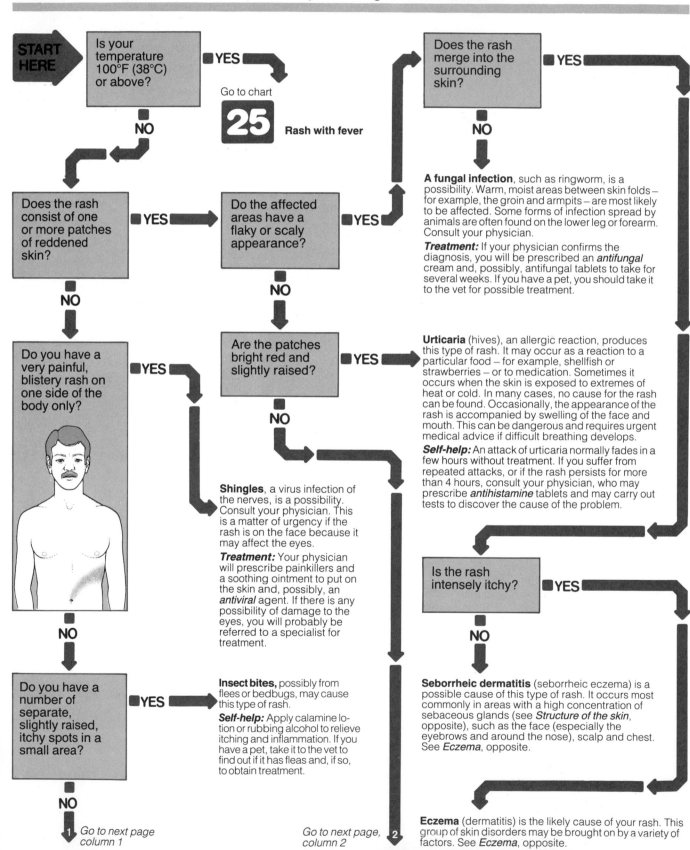

START HERE

Is your temperature 100°F (38°C) or above?

YES → Go to chart **25** Rash with fever

NO ↓

Does the rash consist of one or more patches of reddened skin?

YES → **Do the affected areas have a flaky or scaly appearance?**

YES → **Does the rash merge into the surrounding skin?**

YES →

NO ↓

A fungal infection, such as ringworm, is a possibility. Warm, moist areas between skin folds – for example, the groin and armpits – are most likely to be affected. Some forms of infection spread by animals are often found on the lower leg or forearm. Consult your physician.

Treatment: If your physician confirms the diagnosis, you will be prescribed an *antifungal* cream and, possibly, antifungal tablets to take for several weeks. If you have a pet, you should take it to the vet for possible treatment.

NO ↓ (Does the rash consist of one or more patches)

Do you have a very painful, blistery rash on one side of the body only?

NO ↓ (Do the affected areas have a flaky)

Are the patches bright red and slightly raised?

YES → **Urticaria** (hives), an allergic reaction, produces this type of rash. It may occur as a reaction to a particular food – for example, shellfish or strawberries – or to medication. Sometimes it occurs when the skin is exposed to extremes of heat or cold. In many cases, no cause for the rash can be found. Occasionally, the appearance of the rash is accompanied by swelling of the face and mouth. This can be dangerous and requires urgent medical advice if difficult breathing develops.

Self-help: An attack of urticaria normally fades in a few hours without treatment. If you suffer from repeated attacks, or if the rash persists for more than 4 hours, consult your physician, who may prescribe *antihistamine* tablets and may carry out tests to discover the cause of the problem.

YES → (Do you have a very painful, blistery)

Shingles, a virus infection of the nerves, is a possibility. Consult your physician. This is a matter of urgency if the rash is on the face because it may affect the eyes.

Treatment: Your physician will prescribe painkillers and a soothing ointment to put on the skin and, possibly, an *antiviral* agent. If there is any possibility of damage to the eyes, you will probably be referred to a specialist for treatment.

NO ↓

Is the rash intensely itchy?

YES →

NO ↓

Seborrheic dermatitis (seborrheic eczema) is a possible cause of this type of rash. It occurs most commonly in areas with a high concentration of sebaceous glands (see *Structure of the skin*, opposite), such as the face (especially the eyebrows and around the nose), scalp and chest. See *Eczema*, opposite.

Do you have a number of separate, slightly raised, itchy spots in a small area?

YES → **Insect bites,** possibly from fleas or bedbugs, may cause this type of rash.

Self-help: Apply calamine lotion or rubbing alcohol to relieve itching and inflammation. If you have a pet, take it to the vet to find out if it has fleas and, if so, to obtain treatment.

NO ↓

1 *Go to next page column 1*

Go to next page, column 2 **2**

Eczema (dermatitis) is the likely cause of your rash. This group of skin disorders may be brought on by a variety of factors. See *Eczema*, opposite.

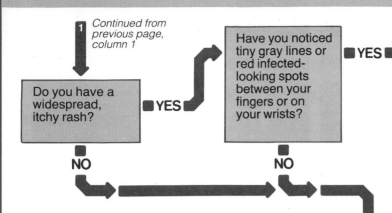

Continued from previous page, column 1

Do you have a widespread, itchy rash?

YES ▸ Have you noticed tiny gray lines or red infected-looking spots between your fingers or on your wrists?

YES ▸

Continued from previous page, column 2

Scabies, a parasitic infection, may be causing these symptoms. This is especially likely if others in the household have the same problem. Consult your physician.

Treatment: If your physician diagnoses scabies, you will need to apply a prescribed insecticide all over your body. The procedure should be repeated a few days later. Bedding and clothing should be thoroughly laundered.

NO ↓   **NO** ↓

Have you recently started to take any medication?

YES ▸ **Certain medications** may cause rashes as a side effect. Discuss the problem with your physician.

NO ↓

Consult your physician if you are unable to make a diagnosis from this chart.

STRUCTURE OF THE SKIN

Skin consists of two layers. The surface layer is known as the epidermis. Active cells at its base are continuously dividing to produce new cells, which gradually die as they fill up with a hard substance, keratin. As each cell dies, it moves up toward the surface of the skin, to be shed or worn away. This production of cells at the base of the epidermis is carefully balanced with the loss of cells at the surface of the skin. If the rate of cell replacement is altered, a skin problem develops. For instance, in psoriasis there is an abnormal buildup of surface cells being produced and pushed up from the base of the epidermis.

The underlying layer, the dermis, contains the many specialized structures that allow the skin to function properly. Here, sebaceous glands produce sebum, a waxy substance that helps to keep the surface of the skin supple. Sweat glands produce perspiration to cool you when you are hot (see *Sweat glands,* p.33). And the small blood vessels dilate in hot weather (so that the body can lose heat) and contract in cold weather (to retain heat).

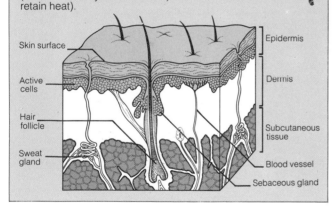

Skin surface / Epidermis / Active cells / Dermis / Hair follicle / Subcutaneous tissue / Sweat gland / Blood vessel / Sebaceous gland

BRUISING

A bruise is a discolored area of skin caused by blood leaking into the dermis (see *Structure of the skin,* above) from a blood vessel damaged by injury. A bruise is usually blue, purple or black at first, but gradually fades to yellow before disappearing.

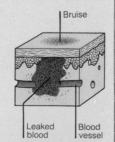

Bruise / Leaked blood / Blood vessel

Formation of a bruise A bruise forms when blood from a damaged blood vessel leaks under the skin (above).

Self-help

If you have a bruise, do not rub or massage the bruised area; this may make matters worse. Applying an ice pack (or an unopened packet of frozen vegetables) immediately after the injury may reduce the extent of bruising. If you have bruised your leg, resting with your feet up may assist healing.

When to consult your physician

Consult your physician in any of the following circumstances:

- If you feel severe pain, or if movement is restricted.
- If bruises appear without injury.
- If you bruise frequently and easily.

ECZEMA

Eczema (dermatitis) refers to a group of related conditions in which the skin becomes inflamed and itchy. The main types of eczema are described below.

Infantile (atopic) eczema

This is an allergic condition that usually appears for the first time in early infancy. It tends to get less severe and may clear up completely be early adolescence. Infantile eczema usually affects the wrists, insides of the elbows and backs of the knees but, in severe cases, the whole body may be affected. The usual treatment is to avoid harsh soaps and detergents, to use a special soap substitute and to apply oil after the bath. A rich, moisturizing cream should be applied to the affected areas. If itching is severe, your physician may prescribe medication. Mild *steroid* creams are recommended in some cases and, if the eczema becomes infected, a mixed steroid and *antibiotic* cream or antibiotics by mouth may be necessary. Skin tests may be carried out to identify factors that trigger outbreaks. Going on a special diet may help.

Contact eczema

This type of eczema is caused by a reaction to contact with a substance to which you are allergic. Certain plants, such as poison ivy or poison oak, are common causes. The skin becomes red and itchy and blisters (which break and crust over) may form. Milder forms of contact eczema may be caused by contact with certain metals – for example, nickel used in jewelry or on a watch. The rash will clear up in a week or so if the cause of the trouble is removed.

Irritant eczema

As the name suggests, this type of rash is caused by contact with irritant chemicals – for example, harsh detergents or industrial chemicals in your place of work. The skin becomes dry, red, rough and itchy. The condition usually clears up if you avoid contact with the irritants by protecting your hands with gloves. A moisturizing hand cream should soothe the affected skin, but it is advisable to consult your physician, who may prescribe a mild steroid cream to clear up the rash.

Seborrheic dermatitis

The tendency to develop this type of eczema is probably inherited. Flaky, red, but not especially itchy, patches appear in areas with a high concentration of sebaceous glands (see *Structure of the skin,* above left), such as around the nose, in the eyebrows or on the scalp and chest. Seborrheic dermatitis on the scalp is the most common cause of dandruff. Keep the affected skin clean and dry, but avoid using harsh soaps or detergents. Further treatment is often unnecessary but, if the rash is extensive, consult your physician, who may prescribe a mild cream or ointment.

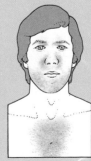

24 Raised spots or lumps on the skin

Consult this chart if you develop any raised lumps, whether they are skin-colored or pigmented (brown). In the majority of cases, such lumps are the harmless result of virus infection. Your physician will be willing to give you advice on the problem if skin lumps persist or cause you discomfort or embarrassment.

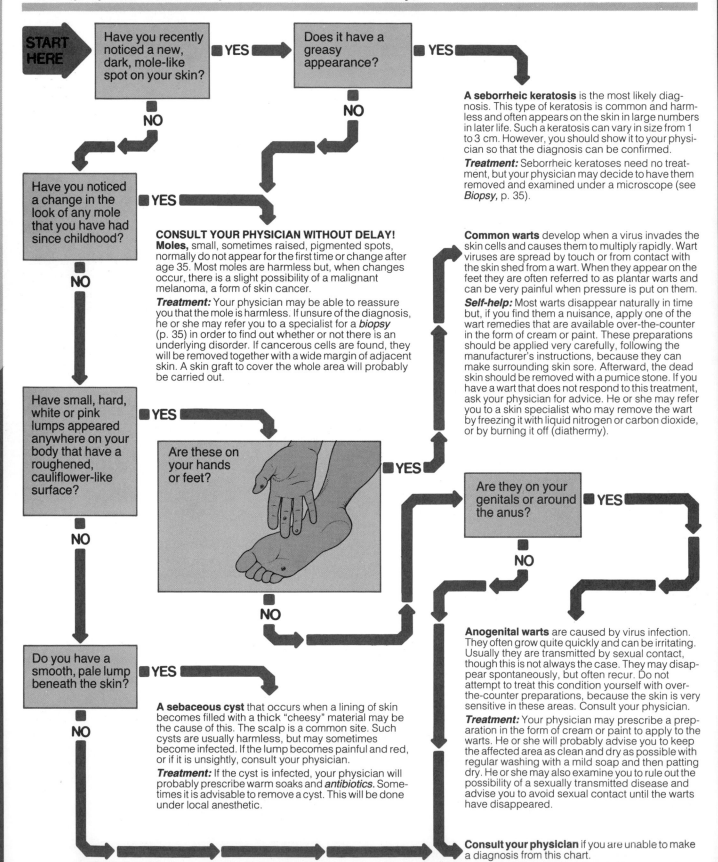

START HERE → Have you recently noticed a new, dark, mole-like spot on your skin? — **YES** → Does it have a greasy appearance? — **YES** →

A seborrheic keratosis is the most likely diagnosis. This type of keratosis is common and harmless and often appears on the skin in large numbers in later life. Such a keratosis can vary in size from 1 to 3 cm. However, you should show it to your physician so that the diagnosis can be confirmed.

Treatment: Seborrheic keratoses need no treatment, but your physician may decide to have them removed and examined under a microscope (see *Biopsy,* p. 35).

NO (from "Does it have a greasy appearance?") → **YES** →

CONSULT YOUR PHYSICIAN WITHOUT DELAY!
Moles, small, sometimes raised, pigmented spots, normally do not appear for the first time or change after age 35. Most moles are harmless but, when changes occur, there is a slight possibility of a malignant melanoma, a form of skin cancer.

Treatment: Your physician may be able to reassure you that the mole is harmless. If unsure of the diagnosis, he or she may refer you to a specialist for a *biopsy* (p. 35) in order to find out whether or not there is an underlying disorder. If cancerous cells are found, they will be removed together with a wide margin of adjacent skin. A skin graft to cover the whole area will probably be carried out.

NO (from "new dark mole-like spot") → Have you noticed a change in the look of any mole that you have had since childhood? — **YES** →

NO → Have small, hard, white or pink lumps appeared anywhere on your body that have a roughened, cauliflower-like surface? — **YES** →

Are these on your hands or feet? — **YES** →

Common warts develop when a virus invades the skin cells and causes them to multiply rapidly. Wart viruses are spread by touch or from contact with the skin shed from a wart. When they appear on the feet they are often referred to as plantar warts and can be very painful when pressure is put on them.

Self-help: Most warts disappear naturally in time but, if you find them a nuisance, apply one of the wart remedies that are available over-the-counter in the form of cream or paint. These preparations should be applied very carefully, following the manufacturer's instructions, because they can make surrounding skin sore. Afterward, the dead skin should be removed with a pumice stone. If you have a wart that does not respond to this treatment, ask your physician for advice. He or she may refer you to a skin specialist who may remove the wart by freezing it with liquid nitrogen or carbon dioxide, or by burning it off (diathermy).

Are these on your hands or feet? — **NO** →

Are they on your genitals or around the anus? — **YES** →

Are they on your genitals or around the anus? — **NO** →

Anogenital warts are caused by virus infection. They often grow quite quickly and can be irritating. Usually they are transmitted by sexual contact, though this is not always the case. They may disappear spontaneously, but often recur. Do not attempt to treat this condition yourself with over-the-counter preparations, because the skin is very sensitive in these areas. Consult your physician.

Treatment: Your physician may prescribe a preparation in the form of cream or paint to apply to the warts. He or she will probably advise you to keep the affected area as clean and dry as possible with regular washing with a mild soap and then patting dry. He or she may also examine you to rule out the possibility of a sexually transmitted disease and advise you to avoid sexual contact until the warts have disappeared.

NO (from "roughened cauliflower-like surface") → Do you have a smooth, pale lump beneath the skin? — **YES** →

A sebaceous cyst that occurs when a lining of skin becomes filled with a thick "cheesy" material may be the cause of this. The scalp is a common site. Such cysts are usually harmless, but may sometimes become infected. If the lump becomes painful and red, or if it is unsightly, consult your physician.

Treatment: If the cyst is infected, your physician will probably prescribe warm soaks and *antibiotics.* Sometimes it is advisable to remove a cyst. This will be done under local anesthetic.

NO (from "smooth, pale lump") →

Consult your physician if you are unable to make a diagnosis from this chart.

25 Rash with fever

Consult this chart if you notice any blemishes or discolored areas of skin and also have a temperature of 100°F (38°C) or above. You may have one of the infectious diseases that are more common in childhood.

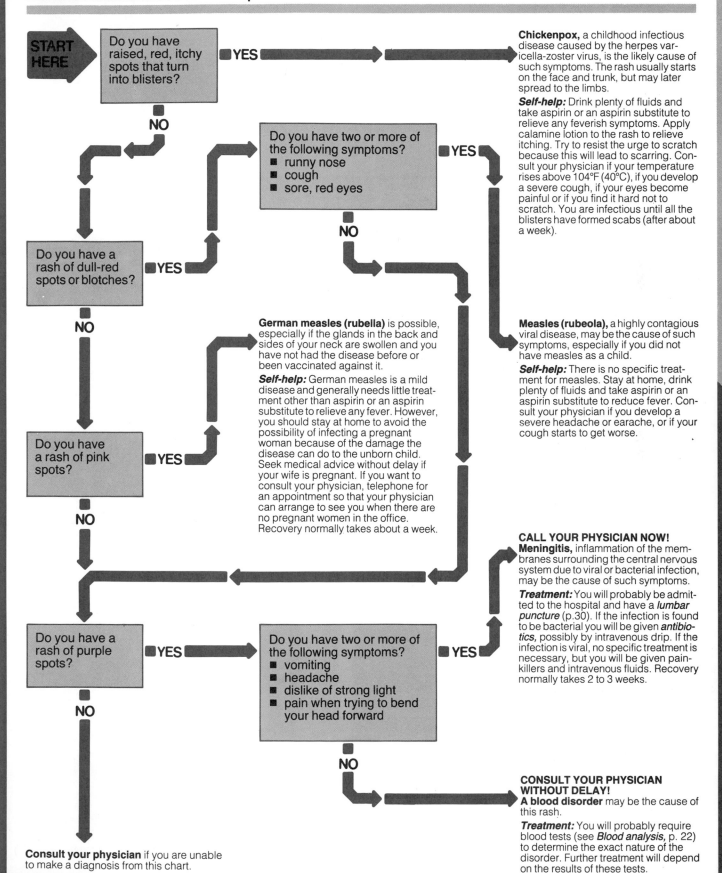

START HERE

Do you have raised, red, itchy spots that turn into blisters?
— YES →

Chickenpox, a childhood infectious disease caused by the herpes varicella-zoster virus, is the likely cause of such symptoms. The rash usually starts on the face and trunk, but may later spread to the limbs.

Self-help: Drink plenty of fluids and take aspirin or an aspirin substitute to relieve any feverish symptoms. Apply calamine lotion to the rash to relieve itching. Try to resist the urge to scratch because this will lead to scarring. Consult your physician if your temperature rises above 104°F (40°C), if you develop a severe cough, if your eyes become painful or if you find it hard not to scratch. You are infectious until all the blisters have formed scabs (after about a week).

NO

Do you have a rash of dull-red spots or blotches?
— YES

Do you have two or more of the following symptoms?
■ runny nose
■ cough
■ sore, red eyes
— YES

NO

NO

Do you have a rash of pink spots?
— YES

German measles (rubella) is possible, especially if the glands in the back and sides of your neck are swollen and you have not had the disease before or been vaccinated against it.

Self-help: German measles is a mild disease and generally needs little treatment other than aspirin or an aspirin substitute to relieve any fever. However, you should stay at home to avoid the possibility of infecting a pregnant woman because of the damage the disease can do to the unborn child. Seek medical advice without delay if your wife is pregnant. If you want to consult your physician, telephone for an appointment so that your physician can arrange to see you when there are no pregnant women in the office. Recovery normally takes about a week.

Measles (rubeola), a highly contagious viral disease, may be the cause of such symptoms, especially if you did not have measles as a child.

Self-help: There is no specific treatment for measles. Stay at home, drink plenty of fluids and take aspirin or an aspirin substitute to reduce fever. Consult your physician if you develop a severe headache or earache, or if your cough starts to get worse.

NO

Do you have a rash of purple spots?
— YES →

Do you have two or more of the following symptoms?
■ vomiting
■ headache
■ dislike of strong light
■ pain when trying to bend your head forward
— YES

CALL YOUR PHYSICIAN NOW!
Meningitis, inflammation of the membranes surrounding the central nervous system due to viral or bacterial infection, may be the cause of such symptoms.

Treatment: You will probably be admitted to the hospital and have a *lumbar puncture* (p.30). If the infection is found to be bacterial you will be given *antibiotics,* possibly by intravenous drip. If the infection is viral, no specific treatment is necessary, but you will be given painkillers and intravenous fluids. Recovery normally takes 2 to 3 weeks.

NO

NO

CONSULT YOUR PHYSICIAN WITHOUT DELAY!
A blood disorder may be the cause of this rash.

Treatment: You will probably require blood tests (see *Blood analysis,* p. 22) to determine the exact nature of the disorder. Further treatment will depend on the results of these tests.

Consult your physician if you are unable to make a diagnosis from this chart.

26 Painful or irritated eye

Pain or irritation in or around the eye may be caused by injury to the eye area or disorders of the eye or surrounding tissues. Infection and inflammation are the most com-

mon causes of eye discomfort. Disorders that threaten sight or that endanger health are uncommon, but should always be ruled out by your physician.

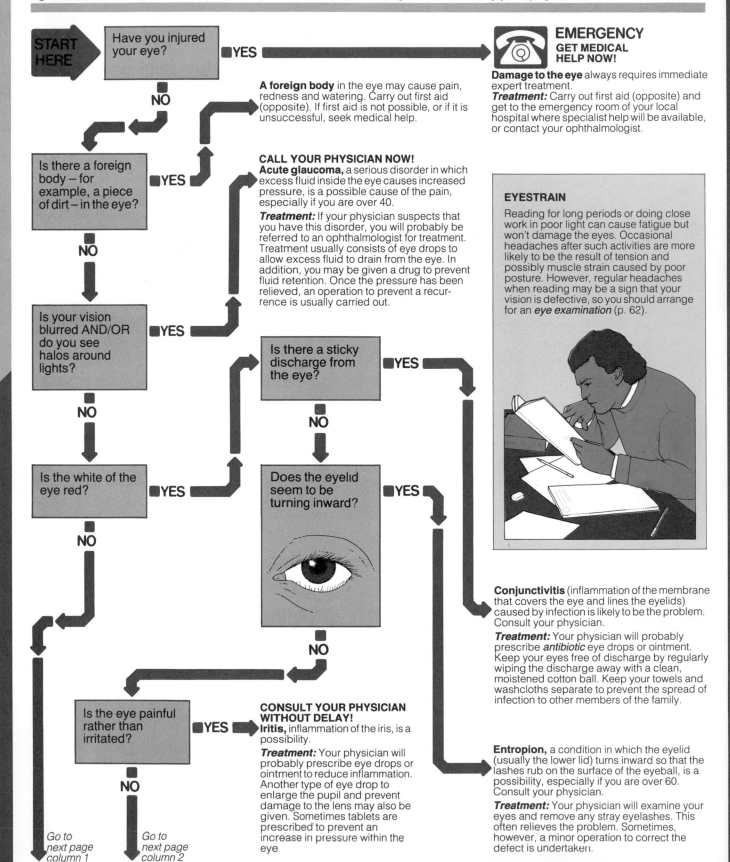

START HERE

Have you injured your eye? — **YES** →

EMERGENCY
GET MEDICAL HELP NOW!
Damage to the eye always requires immediate expert treatment.
Treatment: Carry out first aid (opposite) and get to the emergency room of your local hospital where specialist help will be available, or contact your ophthalmologist.

NO ↓

Is there a foreign body – for example, a piece of dirt – in the eye? — **YES** →

A foreign body in the eye may cause pain, redness and watering. Carry out first aid (opposite). If first aid is not possible, or if it is unsuccessful, seek medical help.

NO ↓

Is your vision blurred AND/OR do you see halos around lights? — **YES** →

CALL YOUR PHYSICIAN NOW!
Acute glaucoma, a serious disorder in which excess fluid inside the eye causes increased pressure, is a possible cause of the pain, especially if you are over 40.
Treatment: If your physician suspects that you have this disorder, you will probably be referred to an ophthalmologist for treatment. Treatment usually consists of eye drops to allow excess fluid to drain from the eye. In addition, you may be given a drug to prevent fluid retention. Once the pressure has been relieved, an operation to prevent a recurrence is usually carried out.

NO ↓

Is the white of the eye red? — **YES** →

Is there a sticky discharge from the eye? — **YES** →

NO ↓

NO ↓

Does the eyelid seem to be turning inward? — **YES** →

NO ↓

Is the eye painful rather than irritated? — **YES** →

CONSULT YOUR PHYSICIAN WITHOUT DELAY!
Iritis, inflammation of the iris, is a possibility.
Treatment: Your physician will probably prescribe eye drops or ointment to reduce inflammation. Another type of eye drop to enlarge the pupil and prevent damage to the lens may also be given. Sometimes tablets are prescribed to prevent an increase in pressure within the eye

NO ↓

Go to next page column 1

Go to next page column 2

EYESTRAIN

Reading for long periods or doing close work in poor light can cause fatigue but won't damage the eyes. Occasional headaches after such activities are more likely to be the result of tension and possibly muscle strain caused by poor posture. However, regular headaches when reading may be a sign that your vision is defective, so you should arrange for an *eye examination* (p. 62).

Conjunctivitis (inflammation of the membrane that covers the eye and lines the eyelids) caused by infection is likely to be the problem. Consult your physician.
Treatment: Your physician will probably prescribe *antibiotic* eye drops or ointment. Keep your eyes free of discharge by regularly wiping the discharge away with a clean, moistened cotton ball. Keep your towels and washcloths separate to prevent the spread of infection to other members of the family.

Entropion, a condition in which the eyelid (usually the lower lid) turns inward so that the lashes rub on the surface of the eyeball, is a possibility, especially if you are over 60. Consult your physician.
Treatment: Your physician will examine your eyes and remove any stray eyelashes. This often relieves the problem. Sometimes, however, a minor operation to correct the defect is undertaken.

Continued from previous page, column 1

Continued from previous page, column 2

Are your eyelids red and itchy? — **YES**

NO

Do you have a red lump on the eyelid? — **YES**

NO

Blepharitis (inflammation and scaling of the lid margins) may cause itchy eyelids and occurs with *dandruff* (p. 53). See a physician.
Treatment: Your physician will probably prescribe ointment to apply to the lids, and may recommend bathing the lids in warm salt water. Treat dandruff in your hair using an antidandruff shampoo.

A sty or chalazion (a boil-like infection at the base of an eyelash) is likely.
Self-help: A sty will usually either burst, and release pus, or dry up within a week without special treatment other than warm soaks. If the sty bursts, carefully wipe away the pus using a clean cotton ball each time you wipe. Consult your physician if a sty fails to heal within a week, if the eye itself becomes red and painful, or if stys recur.

Has your eye been watering? — **YES**

NO

Dry eye, a condition in which the eye fails to produce enough tears, is possible. Consult your physician.
Treatment: If dry eye is confirmed, your physician will prescribe eye drops of artificial tears, which you can use as frequently as you like in order to reduce discomfort.

Eye irritation may be caused by exposure to chemical fumes, or by an allergic reaction (for example, to pollen), or it may be caused by viral conjunctivitis.
Self-help: There is no specific treatment for any of these conditions. Avoiding the irritant in the first two cases will bring relief. However, it may be difficult to trace an allergen. Your physician may be able to help. Viral conjunctivitis will get better without treatment, but while it persists you will need to be careful to avoid spreading the infection to others. So keep a separate towel and washcloth.

Consult your physician if you are unable to make a diagnosis from this chart.

FIRST AID FOR EYE INJURIES

If you suffer an injury to your eye or eyelid, rapid action is essential. Except in the case of a foreign body that has been successfully removed from the eye, go to the emergency room of your local hospital or to an ophthalmologist by the fastest means possible, as soon as you have carried out first aid.

Cuts to the eye or eyelid
Cover the injured eye with a clean pad (such as a folded handkerchief) and hold it lightly in place with a bandage. Apply no pressure. Cover the other eye to prevent movement of the eyeball. Seek medical help.

Blows to the eye area
Carry out first aid as for a cut eye (above) but use a cold compress instead of a dry pad over the eye.

Corrosive chemicals in the eye
If you spill any harsh chemical (for example, bleach or household cleaner) in the eye, immediately flood the eye with large quantities of cold running water. Tilt your head with the injured eye downward so that the water runs from the inside outward. Keep the eyelids apart with your fingers. When all traces of the chemical have been removed, lightly cover the eye with a clean pad and seek medical help.

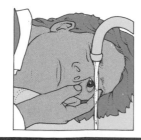

Foreign body in the eye
Never attempt to remove any of the following:

- an object that is embedded in the eyeball
- a chip of metal
- a particle over the colored part of the eye

In any of these cases, cover both eyes as described for cuts to the eye or eyelid (left) and seek medical help. Other foreign bodies – for example, specks of dirt or eyelashes floating on the white of the eye or inside the lids – may be removed as follows:

1 If you can see the particle on the white of the eye or inside the lower lid, pick it off using the moistened corner of a handkerchief (below), or cotton-tipped swab.

2 If you cannot see the particle, pull the upper lid down over the lower lid and hold it for a moment (far right). This may dislodge the particle. If the particle remains, it may be on the inside of the upper lid. If you are alone, seek medical help. Another person may be able to remove the foreign body as in step 3.

3 Ask the person to look down. Hold the lashes of the upper lid and pull it down. Place a match or cotton-tipped swab over the upper lid and fold the lid back over it (right). If the particle is now visible, carefully pick it off as in step 1 (far right).

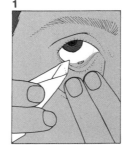

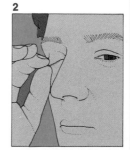

If you do not succeed in removing the foreign body, lightly cover the injured eye and seek medical help.

27 Disturbed or impaired vision

This chart deals with any change in your vision, including blurring, seeing double, seeing flashing lights or floating spots, and loss of part or all of your field of vision. Any such change in vision should be brought to your physician's attention promptly to rule out the possibility of a sight-threatening eye disorder. Successful treatment of many such disorders may depend on catching the disease in its early stages.

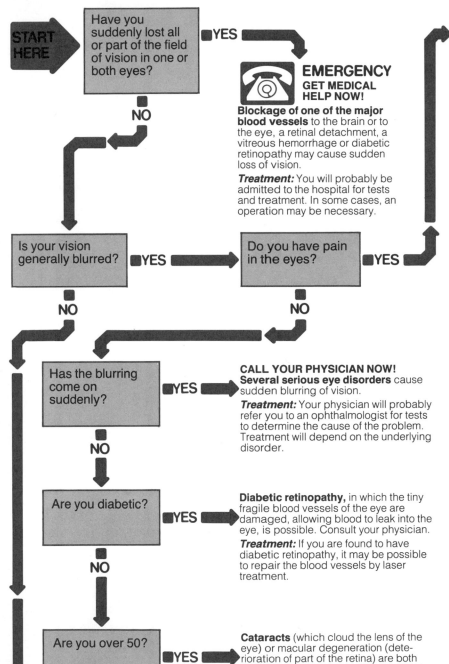

START HERE

Have you suddenly lost all or part of the field of vision in one or both eyes?

YES →

NO ↓

EMERGENCY
GET MEDICAL HELP NOW!

Blockage of one of the major blood vessels to the brain or to the eye, a retinal detachment, a vitreous hemorrhage or diabetic retinopathy may cause sudden loss of vision.

Treatment: You will probably be admitted to the hospital for tests and treatment. In some cases, an operation may be necessary.

Is your vision generally blurred?

YES →

NO ↓

Do you have pain in the eyes?

YES →

NO ↓

Has the blurring come on suddenly?

YES →

CALL YOUR PHYSICIAN NOW!
Several serious eye disorders cause sudden blurring of vision.

Treatment: Your physician will probably refer you to an ophthalmologist for tests to determine the cause of the problem. Treatment will depend on the underlying disorder.

NO ↓

Are you diabetic?

YES →

Diabetic retinopathy, in which the tiny fragile blood vessels of the eye are damaged, allowing blood to leak into the eye, is possible. Consult your physician.

Treatment: If you are found to have diabetic retinopathy, it may be possible to repair the blood vessels by laser treatment.

NO ↓

Are you over 50?

YES →

Cataracts (which cloud the lens of the eye) or macular degeneration (deterioration of part of the retina) are both possible causes of blurred vision in this age group. Consult your physician.

Treatment: If you have a mild cataract, you may need only to have special glasses. In more severe cases, an operation to remove the affected lens and replace it with a plastic lens is often recommended. Macular degeneration, another cause of impaired vision, can, in some cases, be halted by laser treatment. In other cases, special glasses may improve vision.

NO ↓

A variety of eye disorders may cause blurring of vision. Consult your physician, who may refer you to an ophthalmologist for tests and treatment.

Go to next page

CALL YOUR PHYSICIAN NOW!

Acute glaucoma (narrow angle glaucoma) is a possibility, especially if you are over 40. This is a serious disorder in which obstruction of the normal draining mechanism causes a buildup of fluid, and a consequent increase in pressure in the eye.

Treatment: If your physician suspects this disorder, you will probably be referred to an ophthalmologist for treatment. Treatment usually consists of drugs to help lower the pressure within the eye and to relieve pain. You will also probably be given eye drops to help fluid drain from the eye. Later on you may need to have an operation to prevent a recurrence of the problem.

EYE TESTING

You should have your eyes tested routinely every 2 years. The ophthalmologist will test your sight in various ways. He or she will test the sharpness of your vision by asking you to read letters on a Snellen chart. The result of the test is given as two figures. The first refers to the distance in feet – usually 20 feet – at which you are asked to read the letters. The second figure refers to the lowermost row of letters that you were able to read correctly, and indicates the optimum distance in feet at which a person with normal vision could read that row. So the result 20/40 means that the lowest row of letters that you were able to read at a distance of 20 feet is one that a person with normal vision would read at 40 feet.

The ophthalmologist also looks at each eye through an instrument called an ophthalmoscope to check that the back of the eye looks normal and make sure there are no signs of a general disorder. Also, he or she will test the balance of the muscles that control the movements of the eyes.

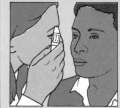

Eye examination
The ophthalmologist looks at each eye through an instrument called an ophthalmoscope (left). With this, he or she can check that the back of the eye looks normal and that there are no signs of an underlying condition.

COLOR BLINDNESS

Color blindness is a term used to describe the hereditary inability to distinguish between certain colors. All the colors we see are thought to be made up of combinations of red, green and blue – the basic colors in the light rays that enter our eyes. Literal color blindness in which everything is seen in shades of gray is rare. The most common defect, which primarily affects men, is an inability to distinguish between red and green. Most people learn to live with this minor disability without problems. However, perfect color vision is required for certain jobs – for example, that of an airline pilot – and anyone applying for such a job will be required to have a full eye examination, including tests for color vision.

Continued from previous page

Have you developed double vision? ■ **YES** ➡ **Do your eyes seem to be bulging or staring?** ■ **YES** ➡

NO ⬇ **NO** ⬇

Exophthalmos, a condition in which the eyes protrude, is a possibility. Consult your physician.

Treatment: Your physician will probably arrange for tests to find out if an underlying disorder, such as an overactive thyroid gland (see *thyrotoxicosis,* p. 42), is causing this condition. Treatment of thyrotoxicosis may consist of special radioactive drugs, other medications or surgery.

An eye muscle problem may have developed. This is the result of lack of coordination between the muscles responsible for the movement of both eyes. Consult your physician.

Have you been seeing flashing lights, floating spots AND/OR suffering other visual disturbances? ■ **YES** ➡ **Has this happened before AND did a severe headache follow?** ■ **YES** ➡

NO ⬇ **NO** ⬇

Treatment: Your physician will probably arrange for you to have tests to find the underlying cause of the problem. These may include measuring your blood pressure, blood and urine analysis, a skull X ray, and possibly a *CAT (computerized axial tomography) scan* (p.39) of the brain. While you are awaiting the results of such tests, your physician may suggest that you wear a patch over one eye to prevent double vision. Long-term treatment will depend on the underlying cause of the strabismus.

CONSULT YOUR PHYSICIAN WITHOUT DELAY!
Retinal detachment, a disorder in which the lining of the back of the eye is torn, may cause such symptoms in its early stages.

Treatment: The earlier treatment of this problem is started, the greater the chance of success. If the disorder is in its early stages, cryosurgery or sometimes laser treatment may be possible. Otherwise conventional surgery may be necessary. Following retinal detachment in one eye, there is a considerable risk of it developing in the other. Your other eye will therefore also be examined and treatment carried out if necessary.

Migraine (recurrent severe headaches) may be preceded by a warning period in which you may experience visual disturbances. Consult your physician.

Treatment: If you suffer from migraines regularly, try to find out if any particular food or other factor seems to trigger the headaches, so that you can avoid it. The self-help measures suggested on p. 38 may help to relieve the pain. Your physician will be able to offer more effective drug treatment if the attacks recur.

Consult your physician if you are unable to make a diagnosis from this chart.

THE STRUCTURE OF THE EYE

The eye is a complex and delicate structure. The eyeball itself consists of 3 layers:

The sclera, the tough outer layer, is visible as the white of the eye. It is protected at the front by the conjunctiva, a transparent membrane that also lines the inner surface of the eyelids. The colored portion, the iris, is covered by the cornea.

The choroid layer beneath the sclera is rich in blood vessels that supply the retina (the light-sensitive inner lining of the eyeball) with oxygen. At the front of the eye, the choroid layer thickens to form the ciliary body, a circle of muscle that supports and controls the lens. In front of the ciliary body lies the iris, which contains muscular fibers that control the amount of light that passes through the lens. The area between the iris and the cornea is filled with watery fluid known as the aqueous humor.

The retina is the innermost layer of the eyeball. It contains the light-sensitive nerve cells that pick up images and transmit the information through the optic nerve to the brain. The inner part of the eyeball is filled with a thick jelly-like substance called the vitreous humor.

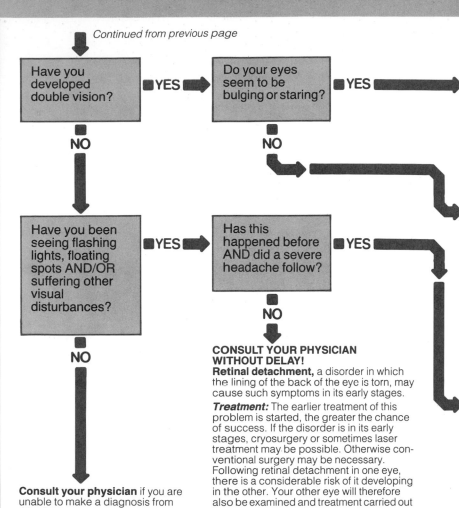

Sclera, Conjunctiva, Eyelids, Aqueous humor, Cornea, Pupil, Eyelashes, Iris, Ciliary body, Vitreous humor

Eye muscles, Retina, Optic nerve, Lens, Choroid layer

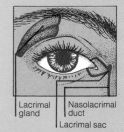

Lacrimal gland, Nasolacrimal duct, Lacrimal sac

Tear glands and ducts
Tears are produced in the lacrimal glands above each eyeball and drain away along tear ducts into the lacrimal sac, and via the nasolacrimal duct into the nose.

CONTACT LENSES

In recent years, contact lenses have become a popular alternative to eyeglasses as a means of correcting defects in vision such as near-sightedness or farsightedness. There are 2 main types of lens: the hard lens, which is made of hard-wearing plastic, but may be uncomfortable for some people; and the soft lens, which is often more comfortable, but is more easily damaged and not so long lasting. Your ophthalmologist will help you decide which type of lens is most suitable.

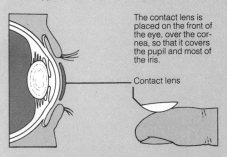

The contact lens is placed on the front of the eye, over the cornea, so that it covers the pupil and most of the iris.

Contact lens

Care of contact lenses
All types of contact lenses need regular and careful cleaning to remove dirt and prevent the buildup of protein deposits on the lens. If this is not done there is a danger of infection and permanent damage to the eye. Always use the special cleaning and soaking solutions recommended for your type of lens, and follow your ophthalmologist's advice on care of your lenses precisely.

28 Earache

Earache may vary from a dull, throbbing sensation to a sharp, stabbing pain that can be most distressing. It is a common symptom in childhood, but occurs much less frequently in adults. Pain in the ear is usually caused by infection and normally requires medical attention and antibiotic treatment.

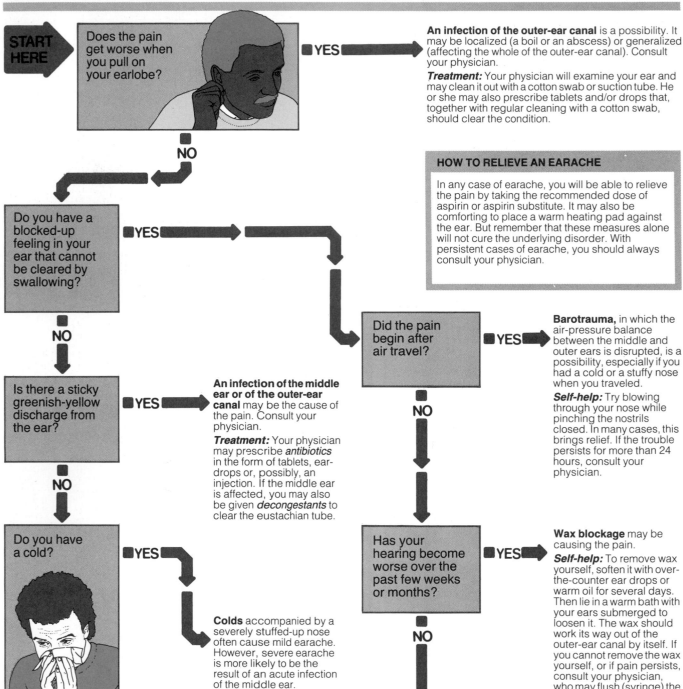

START HERE

Does the pain get worse when you pull on your earlobe?

YES →

An infection of the outer-ear canal is a possibility. It may be localized (a boil or an abscess) or generalized (affecting the whole of the outer-ear canal). Consult your physician.

Treatment: Your physician will examine your ear and may clean it out with a cotton swab or suction tube. He or she may also prescribe tablets and/or drops that, together with regular cleaning with a cotton swab, should clear the condition.

NO

Do you have a blocked-up feeling in your ear that cannot be cleared by swallowing?

YES →

HOW TO RELIEVE AN EARACHE

In any case of earache, you will be able to relieve the pain by taking the recommended dose of aspirin or aspirin substitute. It may also be comforting to place a warm heating pad against the ear. But remember that these measures alone will not cure the underlying disorder. With persistent cases of earache, you should always consult your physician.

NO

Is there a sticky greenish-yellow discharge from the ear?

YES →

An infection of the middle ear or of the outer-ear canal may be the cause of the pain. Consult your physician.

Treatment: Your physician may prescribe *antibiotics* in the form of tablets, eardrops or, possibly, an injection. If the middle ear is affected, you may also be given *decongestants* to clear the eustachian tube.

Did the pain begin after air travel?

YES →

Barotrauma, in which the air-pressure balance between the middle and outer ears is disrupted, is a possibility, especially if you had a cold or a stuffy nose when you traveled.

Self-help: Try blowing through your nose while pinching the nostrils closed. In many cases, this brings relief. If the trouble persists for more than 24 hours, consult your physician.

NO

NO

Do you have a cold?

YES →

Colds accompanied by a severely stuffed-up nose often cause mild earache. However, severe earache is more likely to be the result of an acute infection of the middle ear.

Self-help: If the pain is mild, follow the advice on *treating a cold* (p. 68). If pain persists or becomes severe, consult your physician, who may prescribe *decongestant* nose drops or spray and, possibly, *antibiotics*.

Has your hearing become worse over the past few weeks or months?

YES →

Wax blockage may be causing the pain.

Self-help: To remove wax yourself, soften it with over-the-counter ear drops or warm oil for several days. Then lie in a warm bath with your ears submerged to loosen it. The wax should work its way out of the outer-ear canal by itself. If you cannot remove the wax yourself, or if pain persists, consult your physician, who may flush (syringe) the ear with warm water to wash away the blockage. Never attempt to lever the wax out yourself by poking a pointed instrument into your ear, as this may tear a hole in the eardrum or the skin of the canal.

NO

An acute infection of the middle ear is a possibility. This may have occurred as a result of blockage of the eustachian tube. Consult your physician.

Treatment: Your physician may prescribe decongestant nose drops or spray, to help unblock the eustachian tube and to allow restoration of normal ear pressure. In addition, you may be given *antibiotics* to clear up a bacterial infection.

NO

Consult your physician if you are unable to make a diagnosis from this chart.

29 Noises in the ear

If you sometimes hear noises inside your ears, such as buzzing, ringing or hissing, you are probably suffering from a symptom known as tinnitus. This symptom can indicate a variety of ear disorders.

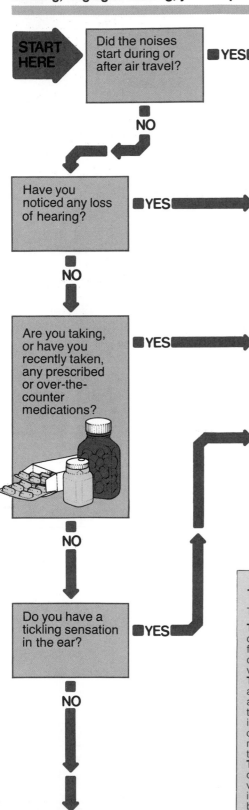

START HERE

Did the noises start during or after air travel?

YES ▶

Barotrauma, in which the air-pressure balance between the middle and outer ears is disrupted, is a possibility, especially if you had a cold or a blocked nose when you traveled.
Self-help: Try blowing through your nose while pinching the nostrils closed. In many cases, this restores hearing to normal. If the trouble persists for more than 24 hours, consult your physician.

NO

Have you noticed any loss of hearing?

YES ▶

Deafness often occurs together with noises in the ear.

Go to chart

30 Deafness

NO

Are you taking, or have you recently taken, any prescribed or over-the-counter medications?

YES ▶

Certain drugs can cause noises in the ear as a side effect. Discuss the problem with your physician.

An insect, or other foreign body, may be trapped in your outer-ear canal.
Self-help: Carry out the first-aid suggestions described above right. If these are not effective, consult your physician. Never attempt to remove anything by inserting an object into the ear.

NO

Do you have a tickling sensation in the ear?

YES ▶

NO

Consult your physician if you are unable to make a diagnosis from this chart, especially if associated with hearing loss, dizziness, headache or ear pressure.

FIRST AID FOR AN INSECT IN THE EAR

If an insect has become trapped in your ear, you can safely try to remove it by tilting your head so that the affected side is uppermost and then pouring warm olive oil, mineral oil or baby oil into the ear (it is easiest if someone helps you do this). After 15 to 20 minutes, the insect should then float out. Alternatively, you can simply lie back in a bath with your ears submerged. If these measures do not succeed in removing the insect, consult your physician.

As you pour water into the ear, gently pull the ear up and back.

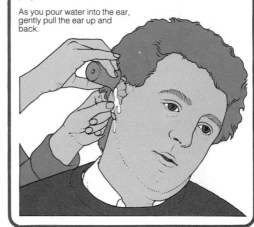

THE STRUCTURE OF THE EAR

The ear is made up of three main parts:

The outer ear, includes the external part of the ear, the pinna, which collects and funnels sound waves along the outer-ear canal to the eardrum, which then vibrates.
The middle ear contains the eardrum and three small bones (hammer, anvil and stirrup) that transmit the vibrations of the eardrum to the inner ear. Air pressure in the middle ear is kept normal by means of the eustachian tube that links the middle-ear cavity to the back of the throat.
The inner ear is filled with fluid and contains the cochlea, which converts the vibrations from the middle ear into nerve impulses. These are passed to the brain by the auditory nerve. The inner ear also contains the labyrinth (semicircular canals), which controls the body's balance.

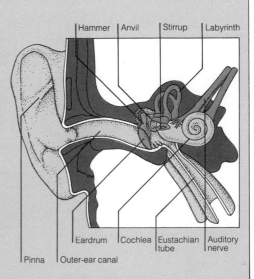

Hammer | Anvil | Stirrup | Labyrinth

Pinna | Outer-ear canal | Eardrum | Cochlea | Eustachian tube | Auditory nerve

30 Deafness

Deafness – decreased ability to hear some or all sounds – may come on gradually over a period of months or years, or may occur suddenly over a matter of days or hours. One or both ears may be affected. In most cases, deafness is the result of infection or wax blockage and can be treated.

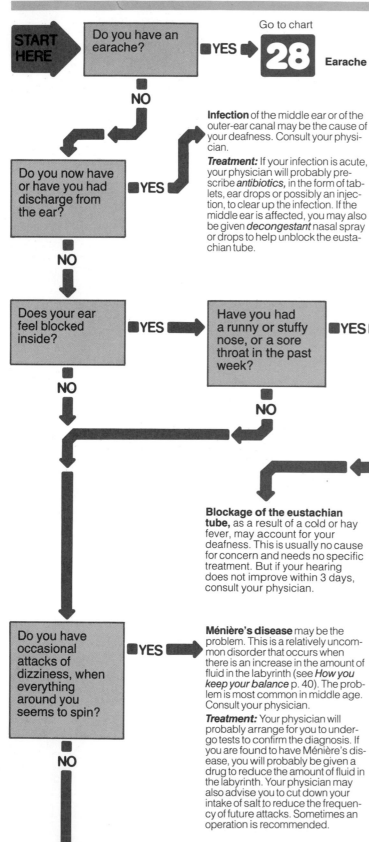

START HERE → **Do you have an earache?**

YES → Go to chart **28** Earache

NO ↓

Do you now have or have you had discharge from the ear?

YES → **Infection** of the middle ear or of the outer-ear canal may be the cause of your deafness. Consult your physician.

Treatment: If your infection is acute, your physician will probably prescribe *antibiotics,* in the form of tablets, ear drops or possibly an injection, to clear up the infection. If the middle ear is affected, you may also be given *decongestant* nasal spray or drops to help unblock the eustachian tube.

NO ↓

Does your ear feel blocked inside?

YES → **Have you had a runny or stuffy nose, or a sore throat in the past week?**

YES →

NO ↓

Blockage of the eustachian tube, as a result of a cold or hay fever, may account for your deafness. This is usually no cause for concern and needs no specific treatment. But if your hearing does not improve within 3 days, consult your physician.

NO ↓

Do you have occasional attacks of dizziness, when everything around you seems to spin?

YES → **Ménière's disease** may be the problem. This is a relatively uncommon disorder that occurs when there is an increase in the amount of fluid in the labyrinth (see *How you keep your balance* p. 40). The problem is most common in middle age. Consult your physician.

Treatment: Your physician will probably arrange for you to undergo tests to confirm the diagnosis. If you are found to have Ménière's disease, you will probably be given a drug to reduce the amount of fluid in the labyrinth. Your physician may also advise you to cut down your intake of salt to reduce the frequency of future attacks. Sometimes an operation is recommended.

NO ↓

Go to next page

HEARING TESTS

If, after examining you, your physician suspects that your hearing is impaired, he or she may refer you for specialized hearing tests such as audiometry and acoustic impedance testing.

Audiometry
The first part of this test measures your ability to hear sounds conducted through the air. You are asked to listen through headphones, one ear at a time, to different pitches of sound. Each sound is played first at an inaudible level, then the volume is gradually increased until you signal that you can hear it.

The second part of the test measures your ability to hear the same sounds conducted through the bones in your head. For this test you wear a special headset that vibrates against your skull, usually behind the ear.

The third part of the test measures your ability to understand and repeat certain words.

The results of the tests are recorded on an audiogram and show what sounds you have difficulty hearing.

In the first part of the test, your ability to hear sound through headphones is measured (above). In the second part of the test, you wear a special headset behind your ears that transmits vibrations through the bones in your skull (right).

Acoustic impedance testing
Acoustic impedance testing is used to assess the movement of the eardrum, which may be impaired as a result of a disorder of the middle ear. A special probe containing a sound transmitter and receiver is inserted into the outer-ear canal. Air is pumped through the probe and the ability of the eardrum to reflect sound emitted by the sound transmitter at different air pressure levels is measured. From the results it is possible to determine the ease with which sound is transmitted through the eardrum and into the inner ear.

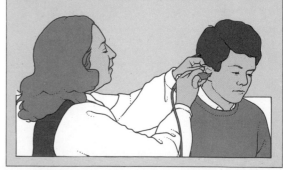

Continued from previous page

Do you regularly spend time listening to loud music, for example, at rock concerts or discos, or through headphones; are you often exposed to loud noise at work; or are you exposed to loud noise through hobbies involving power tools or firearms?

YES →

Repeated exposure to loud noise has probably caused your hearing loss. Even noise levels that do not cause discomfort can result in permanent damage to your hearing. Headphones can be particularly dangerous, since it is easy to have the volume too high (to overcome external noises such as traffic) without realizing it.

Self-help: Take appropriate steps to avoid noise exposure. Keep well away from the speakers at rock concerts and discos, and reduce the volume on your headphones so that others in the same room cannot hear the music. If you work in noisy surroundings (in a factory, for example), your employer should supply you with ear protectors, or you can buy your own earplugs. You should consult your physician, who may arrange for you to have special hearing tests and, if necessary, recommend a hearing aid.

NO ↓

Have you recently taken any prescribed or over-the-counter medications?

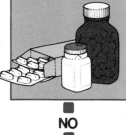

YES →

Certain drugs can cause deafness as a side effect. Discuss the problem with your physician.

NO ↓

Has your hearing been getting worse over a period of several weeks or more?

NO ↓

YES →

Have other members of your family suffered from gradual hearing loss?

NO ↓

Wax blockage may be the cause of your deafness.

Self-help: To remove wax yourself, soften it with over-the-counter ear drops or warm oil for several days. Then lie in a warm bath with your ears submerged to loosen the wax, which should work its way out of the outer ear by itself. If you cannot remove the wax this way, do not attempt to lever it out by poking a pointed instrument into your ear. Consult your physician, who will flush (syringe) the ear with warm water to wash away the blockage.

YES →

Are you over 50 years old?

NO ↓

Otosclerosis, a disorder that affects the working of the bones in the middle ear, may be the problem. This type of deafness usually affects young adults. Consult your physician.

Treatment: If your physician suspects otosclerosis, he or she will probably arrange for you to undergo *hearing tests* (opposite). If you have serious loss of hearing in one or both ears, a *stapedectomy* (above) may be recommended.

YES →

Presbycusis, gradual loss of hearing as you get older, is common, especially if other members of your family have become deaf in later years. Consult your physician.

Treatment: Your physician may refer you for *hearing tests* (opposite). If these confirm the diagnosis, you will probably be offered a hearing aid.

STAPEDECTOMY

Stapedectomy is an operation on the stirrup bone in the middle ear that is often carried out in severe cases of otosclerosis. Usually the operation produces a marked improvement in hearing but, unfortunately, in a small proportion of cases it results in complete deafness in that ear.

The operation
During the operation, the eardrum is moved aside and the stirrup, one of the three tiny bones in the middle ear that is immobilized by the disease, is replaced by a metal or plastic substitute. This improves the conduction of sound through the middle ear.

Stapedectomy usually involves a hospital stay of 2 to 3 days and convalescence at home for another week or so. You may feel dizzy for a few days following the operation.

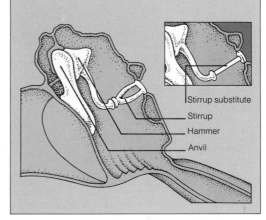

Stirrup substitute
Stirrup
Hammer
Anvil

NO ↓

Consult your physician if you are unable to make a diagnosis from this chart.

31 Runny nose

Blockage of the nose by a thick or watery discharge is probably one of the most familiar symptoms. It is nearly always caused by irritation of the delicate mucous mem-brane lining of the nose. This is usually the result of infection, but may sometimes occur as an allergic reaction. A runny nose rarely indicates a serious disorder.

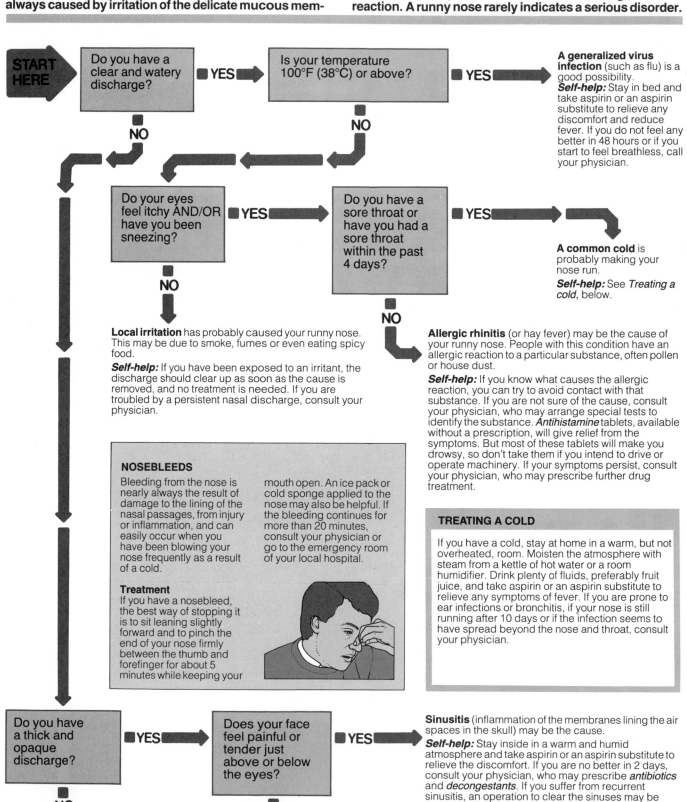

START HERE

Do you have a clear and watery discharge? — **YES** → **Is your temperature 100°F (38°C) or above?** — **YES** → **A generalized virus infection** (such as flu) is a good possibility.
Self-help: Stay in bed and take aspirin or an aspirin substitute to relieve any discomfort and reduce fever. If you do not feel any better in 48 hours or if you start to feel breathless, call your physician.

NO / **NO**

Do your eyes feel itchy AND/OR have you been sneezing? — **YES** → **Do you have a sore throat or have you had a sore throat within the past 4 days?** — **YES** → **A common cold** is probably making your nose run.
Self-help: See *Treating a cold*, below.

NO

Local irritation has probably caused your runny nose. This may be due to smoke, fumes or even eating spicy food.
Self-help: If you have been exposed to an irritant, the discharge should clear up as soon as the cause is removed, and no treatment is needed. If you are troubled by a persistent nasal discharge, consult your physician.

NO

Allergic rhinitis (or hay fever) may be the cause of your runny nose. People with this condition have an allergic reaction to a particular substance, often pollen or house dust.
Self-help: If you know what causes the allergic reaction, you can try to avoid contact with that substance. If you are not sure of the cause, consult your physician, who may arrange special tests to identify the substance. *Antihistamine* tablets, available without a prescription, will give relief from the symptoms. But most of these tablets will make you drowsy, so don't take them if you intend to drive or operate machinery. If your symptoms persist, consult your physician, who may prescribe further drug treatment.

NOSEBLEEDS

Bleeding from the nose is nearly always the result of damage to the lining of the nasal passages, from injury or inflammation, and can easily occur when you have been blowing your nose frequently as a result of a cold.

mouth open. An ice pack or cold sponge applied to the nose may also be helpful. If the bleeding continues for more than 20 minutes, consult your physician or go to the emergency room of your local hospital.

Treatment

If you have a nosebleed, the best way of stopping it is to sit leaning slightly forward and to pinch the end of your nose firmly between the thumb and forefinger for about 5 minutes while keeping your

TREATING A COLD

If you have a cold, stay at home in a warm, but not overheated, room. Moisten the atmosphere with steam from a kettle of hot water or a room humidifier. Drink plenty of fluids, preferably fruit juice, and take aspirin or an aspirin substitute to relieve any symptoms of fever. If you are prone to ear infections or bronchitis, if your nose is still running after 10 days or if the infection seems to have spread beyond the nose and throat, consult your physician.

Do you have a thick and opaque discharge? — **YES** → **Does your face feel painful or tender just above or below the eyes?** — **YES** → **Sinusitis** (inflammation of the membranes lining the air spaces in the skull) may be the cause.
Self-help: Stay inside in a warm and humid atmosphere and take aspirin or an aspirin substitute to relieve the discomfort. If you are no better in 2 days, consult your physician, who may prescribe *antibiotics* and *decongestants*. If you suffer from recurrent sinusitis, an operation to clear the sinuses may be recommended.

NO / **NO**

Consult your physician if you are unable to make a diagnosis from this chart.

A common cold, virus infection of the nasal passages, is probably making your nose run.
Self-help: See *Treating a cold*, above.

32 Sore throat

Most people suffer from a painful, rough or raw feeling in the throat at times. This is usually the result of a minor infection or local irritation, and almost always disappears within a day or so without medical treatment.

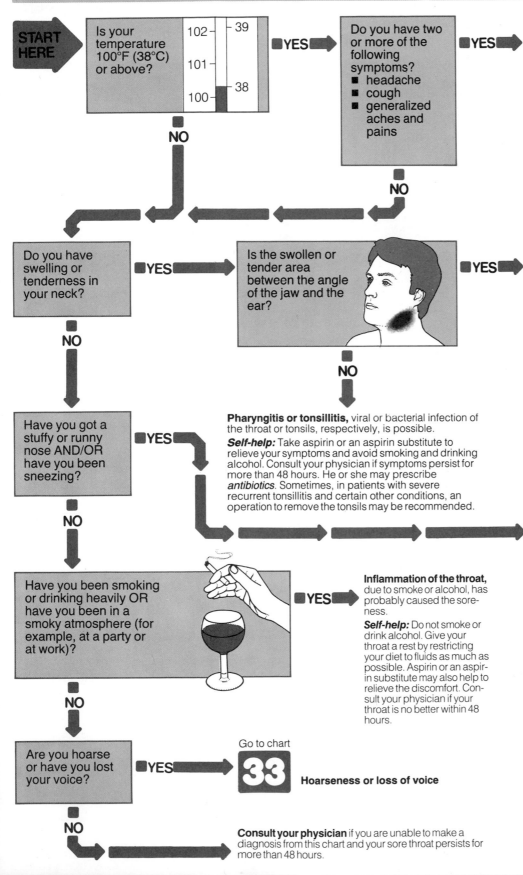

START HERE

Is your temperature 100°F (38°C) or above?

102 — 39
101 —
100 — 38

YES → Do you have two or more of the following symptoms?
■ headache
■ cough
■ generalized aches and pains

YES → **A generalized virus infection,** such as flu, is a strong possibility.
Self-help: Stay in bed and take aspirin or an aspirin substitute to relieve any discomfort and reduce fever. If you do not feel any better in 48 hours, or if you develop further symptoms (such as a rash), call your physician.

NO

NO

Do you have swelling or tenderness in your neck?

YES → Is the swollen or tender area between the angle of the jaw and the ear?

YES → **Mumps,** a virus infection that mainly affects the salivary glands, but that can also cause inflammation of other glands, especially the testicles, is a possibility. This diagnosis is particularly likely if you have not had the disease before. Consult your physician.
Self-help: You will probably be advised to stay in bed and take aspirin or an aspirin substitute to relieve the discomfort and reduce any fever. If you have pain or swelling in the testicles, it could be a sign that they have become inflamed. In this case your physician may prescribe *anti-inflammatory* drugs. See also *Mumps and sterility,* p. 124.

NO

NO

Pharyngitis or tonsillitis, viral or bacterial infection of the throat or tonsils, respectively, is possible.
Self-help: Take aspirin or an aspirin substitute to relieve your symptoms and avoid smoking and drinking alcohol. Consult your physician if symptoms persist for more than 48 hours. He or she may prescribe *antibiotics.* Sometimes, in patients with severe recurrent tonsillitis and certain other conditions, an operation to remove the tonsils may be recommended.

Have you got a stuffy or runny nose AND/OR have you been sneezing?

YES

NO

A common cold, virus infection of the nasal passages, is probably responsible for your sore throat.
Self-help: See *Treating a cold,* opposite.

Have you been smoking or drinking heavily OR have you been in a smoky atmosphere (for example, at a party or at work)?

YES → **Inflammation of the throat,** due to smoke or alcohol, has probably caused the soreness.
Self-help: Do not smoke or drink alcohol. Give your throat a rest by restricting your diet to fluids as much as possible. Aspirin or an aspirin substitute may also help to relieve the discomfort. Consult your physician if your throat is no better within 48 hours.

NO

Are you hoarse or have you lost your voice?

YES → Go to chart **33** **Hoarseness or loss of voice**

NO

Consult your physician if you are unable to make a diagnosis from this chart and your sore throat persists for more than 48 hours.

HOW TO RELIEVE A SORE THROAT

If you have a sore throat, you can reduce the inflammation by taking frequent cold drinks. Aspirin or an aspirin substitute, taken by mouth or as a gargle, may also be helpful. Do not smoke or drink alcohol, and, if your throat is very sore, avoid solid food. There are many over-the-counter throat lozenges and gargles available, but a salt water gargle is probably the best. While there is no medical evidence that these reduce inflammation, you may find them soothing and they are unlikely to do you any harm.

33 Hoarseness or loss of voice

Hoarseness, huskiness or loss of voice is almost always caused by laryngitis – inflammation and swelling of the vocal cords that interferes with their ability to vibrate normally to produce sounds. There can be a variety of underlying causes for this inflammation, including infections or irritations, most of which are minor and easily treated at home. However, persistent or recurrent hoarseness or loss of voice may have a more serious cause and should always be brought to your physician's attention without delay.

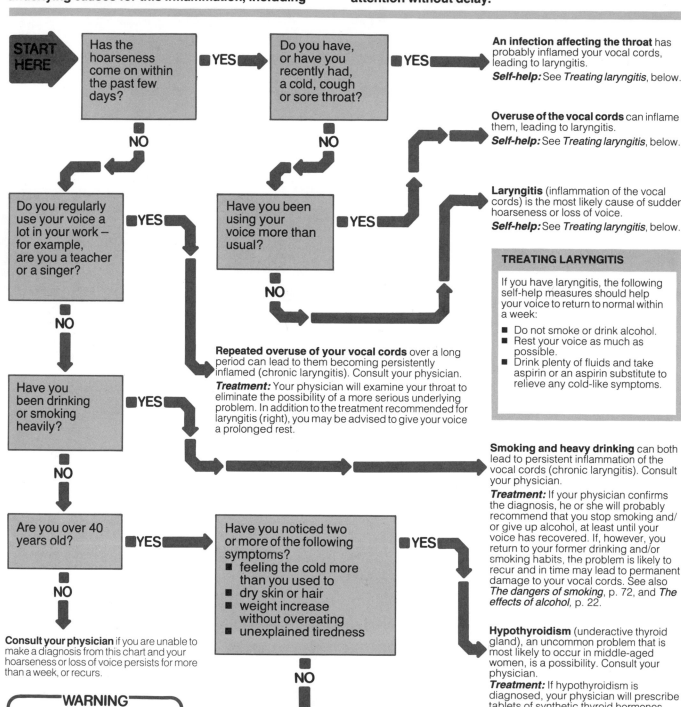

START HERE

Has the hoarseness come on within the past few days?

YES →

Do you have, or have you recently had, a cold, cough or sore throat?

YES →

An infection affecting the throat has probably inflamed your vocal cords, leading to laryngitis.
Self-help: See *Treating laryngitis*, below.

NO ↓

NO ↓

Do you regularly use your voice a lot in your work – for example, are you a teacher or a singer?

YES →

Have you been using your voice more than usual?

YES →

Overuse of the vocal cords can inflame them, leading to laryngitis.
Self-help: See *Treating laryngitis*, below.

Laryngitis (inflammation of the vocal cords) is the most likely cause of sudden hoarseness or loss of voice.
Self-help: See *Treating laryngitis*, below.

NO ↓

NO ↓

TREATING LARYNGITIS

If you have laryngitis, the following self-help measures should help your voice to return to normal within a week:

- Do not smoke or drink alcohol.
- Rest your voice as much as possible.
- Drink plenty of fluids and take aspirin or an aspirin substitute to relieve any cold-like symptoms.

Repeated overuse of your vocal cords over a long period can lead to them becoming persistently inflamed (chronic laryngitis). Consult your physician.
Treatment: Your physician will examine your throat to eliminate the possibility of a more serious underlying problem. In addition to the treatment recommended for laryngitis (right), you may be advised to give your voice a prolonged rest.

Have you been drinking or smoking heavily?

YES →

Smoking and heavy drinking can both lead to persistent inflammation of the vocal cords (chronic laryngitis). Consult your physician.
Treatment: If your physician confirms the diagnosis, he or she will probably recommend that you stop smoking and/or give up alcohol, at least until your voice has recovered. If, however, you return to your former drinking and/or smoking habits, the problem is likely to recur and in time may lead to permanent damage to your vocal cords. See also *The dangers of smoking*, p. 72, and *The effects of alcohol*, p. 22.

NO ↓

Are you over 40 years old?

YES →

Have you noticed two or more of the following symptoms?
- feeling the cold more than you used to
- dry skin or hair
- weight increase without overeating
- unexplained tiredness

YES →

Hypothyroidism (underactive thyroid gland), an uncommon problem that is most likely to occur in middle-aged women, is a possibility. Consult your physician.
Treatment: If hypothyroidism is diagnosed, your physician will prescribe tablets of synthetic thyroid hormones. These tablets will make you feel much better in a few days, and after a few months you should have returned to normal health. However, it will be necessary to continue taking the tablets indefinitely.

NO ↓

NO ↓

Consult your physician if you are unable to make a diagnosis from this chart and your hoarseness or loss of voice persists for more than a week, or recurs.

CONSULT YOUR PHYSICIAN WITHOUT DELAY!
Gradually increasing huskiness may simply be a side effect of hormonal changes as you get older. However, hoarseness that lasts longer than a week may, in rare cases, be a sign of a tumor in the voice box, particularly if you smoke.
Treatment: Your physician will probably examine your throat and may arrange for you to have a *biopsy* (p. 35) of the voice box. Many growths can be removed.

┌─── **WARNING** ───┐

PERSISTENT HOARSENESS

Hoarseness or loss of voice that is recurrent or lasts more than a week may be a sign of a tumor in the voice box, especially if you are over 40 and smoke.
Consult your physician without delay!

34 Wheezing

Wheezing sometimes occurs when breathing out if you have a chest cold, and this is no cause for concern as long as breathing is otherwise normal. Such wheezing can usually be heard only through a stethoscope, but it may become more apparent to you when you exhale violently (during exercise, for example). Loud wheezing, especially if you also feel breathless or if breathing is painful, may be a sign of a number of more serious conditions, including congestive heart failure, asthma and bronchitis, which require medical attention.

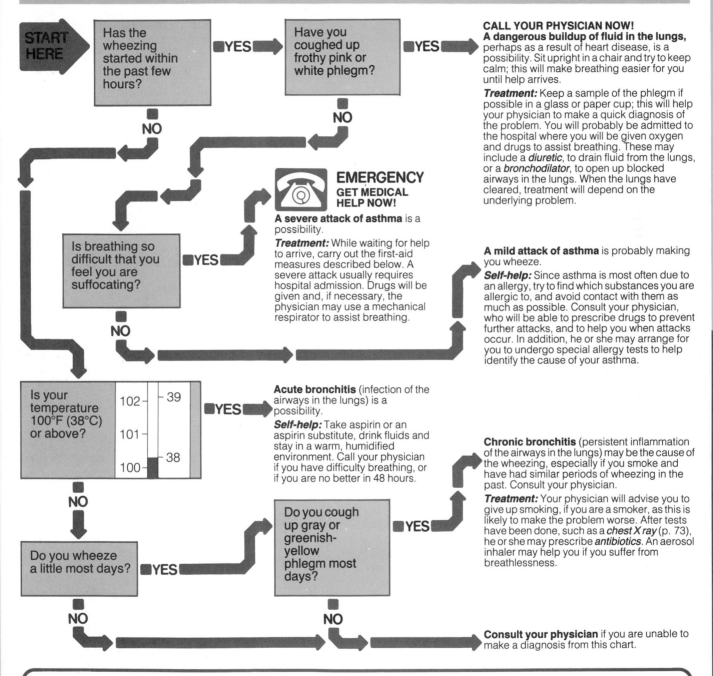

START HERE

Has the wheezing started within the past few hours?

YES →

Have you coughed up frothy pink or white phlegm?

YES →

CALL YOUR PHYSICIAN NOW!
A dangerous buildup of fluid in the lungs, perhaps as a result of heart disease, is a possibility. Sit upright in a chair and try to keep calm; this will make breathing easier for you until help arrives.

Treatment: Keep a sample of the phlegm if possible in a glass or paper cup; this will help your physician to make a quick diagnosis of the problem. You will probably be admitted to the hospital where you will be given oxygen and drugs to assist breathing. These may include a *diuretic*, to drain fluid from the lungs, or a *bronchodilator*, to open up blocked airways in the lungs. When the lungs have cleared, treatment will depend on the underlying problem.

NO (wheezing) / NO (phlegm)

EMERGENCY
GET MEDICAL HELP NOW!

A severe attack of asthma is a possibility.

Treatment: While waiting for help to arrive, carry out the first-aid measures described below. A severe attack usually requires hospital admission. Drugs will be given and, if necessary, the physician may use a mechanical respirator to assist breathing.

Is breathing so difficult that you feel you are suffocating?

YES →

NO ↓

A mild attack of asthma is probably making you wheeze.

Self-help: Since asthma is most often due to an allergy, try to find which substances you are allergic to, and avoid contact with them as much as possible. Consult your physician, who will be able to prescribe drugs to prevent further attacks, and to help you when attacks occur. In addition, he or she may arrange for you to undergo special allergy tests to help identify the cause of your asthma.

Is your temperature 100°F (38°C) or above?

102 —	— 39
101 —	
100 —	— 38

YES →

Acute bronchitis (infection of the airways in the lungs) is a possibility.

Self-help: Take aspirin or an aspirin substitute, drink fluids and stay in a warm, humidified environment. Call your physician if you have difficulty breathing, or if you are no better in 48 hours.

Chronic bronchitis (persistent inflammation of the airways in the lungs) may be the cause of the wheezing, especially if you smoke and have had similar periods of wheezing in the past. Consult your physician.

Treatment: Your physician will advise you to give up smoking, if you are a smoker, as this is likely to make the problem worse. After tests have been done, such as a *chest X ray* (p. 73), he or she may prescribe *antibiotics*. An aerosol inhaler may help you if you suffer from breathlessness.

NO ↓

Do you wheeze a little most days?

YES →

Do you cough up gray or greenish-yellow phlegm most days?

YES →

NO / NO

Consult your physician if you are unable to make a diagnosis from this chart.

FIRST AID FOR ASTHMA

A severe attack of asthma, in which the person is fighting for breath and/or becomes pale and clammy with a blue tinge to the tongue or lips, is an emergency and admission to the hospital is essential. Call an ambulance or go to the emergency room of your local hospital immediately. Most people with asthma already have drugs or an inhaling apparatus, both of which should be administered. If one dose of inhalant does not quickly relieve the wheezing, it should be repeated only once.

In all cases, help the asthmatic to find the most comfortable position while you are waiting for medical help. The best position is sitting up, leaning forward on the back of a chair, and taking some of the weight on the arms (right). Plenty of fresh air will also help. A sudden severe attack of asthma can be very frightening for the family as well as the asthmatic. However, anxiety can make the attack worse, so only one other person should remain with the asthmatic and this person should be calm until help is provided.

35 Coughing

A cough may produce phlegm or be "dry." It is the body's response to any foreign body, congestion or irritation in the lungs or the throat (for instance, as a result of a cold, smoking or an allergy). Sometimes, however, coughing signals a more serious disease in the respiratory tract and requires medical attention.

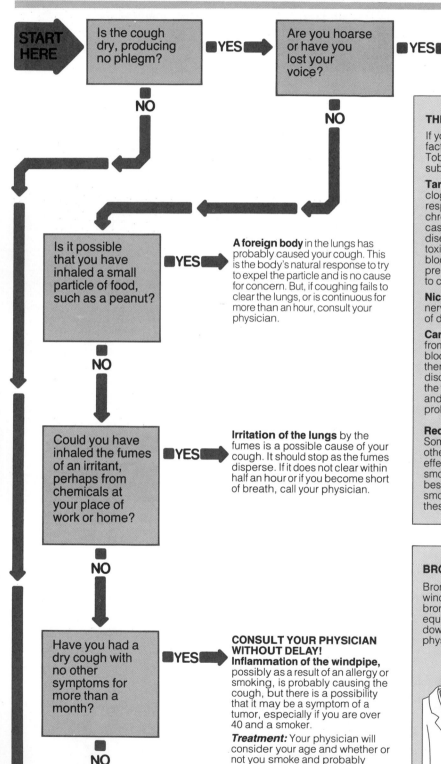

START HERE

Is the cough dry, producing no phlegm?

YES ➡ **Are you hoarse or have you lost your voice?**

YES ➡ Go to chart **33**
Hoarseness or loss of voice

NO | **NO**

Is it possible that you have inhaled a small particle of food, such as a peanut?

YES ➡ **A foreign body** in the lungs has probably caused your cough. This is the body's natural response to try to expel the particle and is no cause for concern. But, if coughing fails to clear the lungs, or is continuous for more than an hour, consult your physician.

NO

Could you have inhaled the fumes of an irritant, perhaps from chemicals at your place of work or home?

YES ➡ **Irritation of the lungs** by the fumes is a possible cause of your cough. It should stop as the fumes disperse. If it does not clear within half an hour or if you become short of breath, call your physician.

NO

Have you had a dry cough with no other symptoms for more than a month?

YES ➡ **CONSULT YOUR PHYSICIAN WITHOUT DELAY!**
Inflammation of the windpipe, possibly as a result of an allergy or smoking, is probably causing the cough, but there is a possibility that it may be a symptom of a tumor, especially if you are over 40 and a smoker.

Treatment: Your physician will consider your age and whether or not you smoke and probably arrange for you to undergo such tests as a *chest X ray* (opposite) and *bronchoscopy* (right). This way he or she will be able to diagnose whether the cough is bronchitis from smoking, the result of an allergy or something more serious.

NO

Go to next page

THE DANGERS OF SMOKING

If you smoke, you should be aware of the following facts about the effects that smoking has on your body. Tobacco smoke contains at least three dangerous substances: tar, nicotine and carbon monoxide.

Tar in tobacco smoke collects as a sticky deposit that clogs and irritates the lungs and other parts of the respiratory tract. This can lead to diseases such as chronic bronchitis and emphysema and, in some cases, can cause lung cancer, a life-threatening disease that is almost unknown in nonsmokers. The toxic chemicals in tar are also absorbed into the bloodstream and then excreted in the urine. The presence of such substances in the bladder is known to contribute to the development of bladder cancer.

Nicotine is a highly addictive drug that acts on the nervous system, increasing the heart rate and the risk of developing abnormal heart rhythms.

Carbon monoxide, absorbed into the bloodstream from tobacco smoke, reduces the ability of the red blood cells to carry oxygen to the body cells and therefore exaggerates the effects of any circulatory disorder. In addition, carbon monoxide may encourage the formation of substances that help block the arteries and cause fatal heart attacks and disabling circulation problems in the legs.

Reducing the risks
Some cigarettes contain less tar and nicotine than others. But switching to a low-tar brand is not an effective way of reducing the risks. Most heavy smokers smoke more and inhale more deeply. The best way to avoid smoking-related disease is to give up smoking. If you succeed, the chances of developing these problems diminish with every cigarette-free year.

BRONCHOSCOPY

Bronchoscopy is a technique for examining the windpipe and lungs using a device known as a bronchoscope. This consists of a special tube equipped with lighting. The narrow tube is passed down the windpipe and into the lungs, allowing the physician to see any abnormalities.

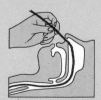

The bronchoscope is gently passed through the nose, down the windpipe and into the lungs.

Continued from previous page

Has the cough started within the past week?

YES → **Is your temperature 100°F (38°C) or above?**

102 — 39
101 —
100 — 38

YES → **Are you short of breath?**

NO ↓

Acute bronchitis (infection of the airways in the lungs) is a possibility.

Self-help: Take aspirin or an aspirin substitute and cough medicine following the instructions on the labels. Stay in a humid environment but it is not necessary to go to bed. Call your physician if you have difficulty breathing, or if you are no better in 48 hours.

YES ↓

NO ↓ (temperature)

Do you have a runny nose AND/OR a sore throat?

YES → **A common cold,** a viral infection of the nasal passages, has probably caused these symptoms.
Self-help: For advice on the treatment of colds, see p. 68.

NO ↓

CALL YOUR PHYSICIAN NOW!
Pneumonia is a possibility. This is an infection of the lungs that can be dangerous, especially for the elderly and those in poor health.

Treatment: Your physician will probably recommend that you take aspirin or an aspirin substitute to reduce your fever and relieve any discomfort. He or she may prescribe *antibiotics* and, in a severe case, may advise admission to a hospital.

Are you short of breath, even when you have not been exercising?

YES → Go to chart **36** **Difficulty breathing**

NO ↓

Chronic bronchitis, persistent inflammation of the airways to the lungs, may be the cause of the cough, especially if you smoke and have had similar periods of persistent coughing in the past. Consult your physician.

Treatment: Your physician may prescribe *antibiotics* in the form of tablets or capsules. An aerosol inhaler may help you if you are suffering from shortness of breath. However, the problem is likely to get worse over the years unless you stop smoking.

Do you cough up thick, gray or greenish-yellow phlegm most days?

YES →

NO ↓

CONSULT YOUR PHYSICIAN WITHOUT DELAY!
A serious lung disorder, such as tuberculosis or lung cancer, may cause persistent coughing although a simpler explanation, such as an allergy or chronic bronchitis, is more likely.

Treatment: Your physician will probably arrange for tests to find out which underlying disorder is causing the symptoms. You may be asked to give blood and phlegm samples for analysis. A *chest X ray* (below) and *bronchoscopy* (opposite) may also be necessary.

Have you had your cough for several weeks or months AND has it been getting more severe?

YES →

NO ↓

Consult your physician if you are unable to make a diagnosis from this chart.

CHEST X RAY

A chest X ray is an effective way of examining the lungs and is used by chest specialists as their main diagnostic test. It can show infections, tumors, other lung disorders, fluid or air in the chest cavity, and damage to the rib cage.

This chest X ray shows a condition called pericardial effusion, in which fluid collects around the heart.

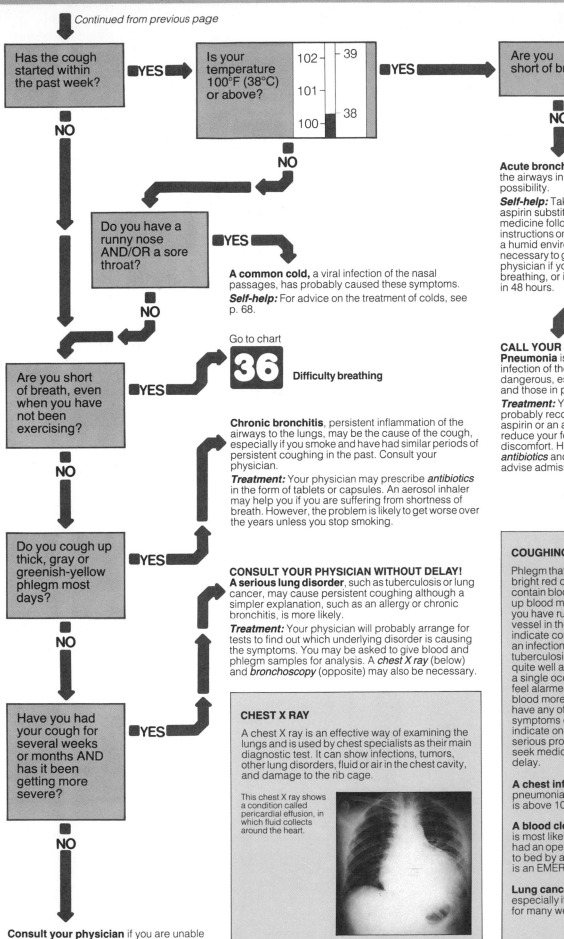

COUGHING UP BLOOD

Phlegm that is colored or streaked bright red or rusty brown may contain blood. Although coughing up blood may simply mean that you have ruptured a small blood vessel in the lung, it may also indicate congestion of the lungs, an infection such as pneumonia or tuberculosis, or a tumor. If you feel quite well and cough up blood on a single occasion, you need not feel alarmed; but coughing up blood more than once, or if you have any of the additional symptoms described, may indicate one of the following serious problems and you should seek medical advice without delay.

A chest infection, such as pneumonia – if your temperature is above 102°F (39°C).

A blood clot in the lung – which is most likely if you have recently had an operation or been confined to bed by an injury or illness. This is an EMERGENCY.

Lung cancer or tuberculosis – especially if you have had a cough for many weeks or months.

36 Difficulty breathing

If you have the feeling that you cannot get enough air or are breathless to the extent that you are breathing rapidly or "puffing," either at rest or after gentle exercise, this suggests the possibility of a problem affecting the heart or the respiratory system. The sudden onset of difficult breathing while eating is more likely to be caused by

choking, and you should immediately carry out first aid as described in the box opposite. Because of the possibility of a disorder that may threaten the supply of oxygen to the body, it is important to seek medical advice promptly if you notice any of the symptoms mentioned in this diagnostic chart.

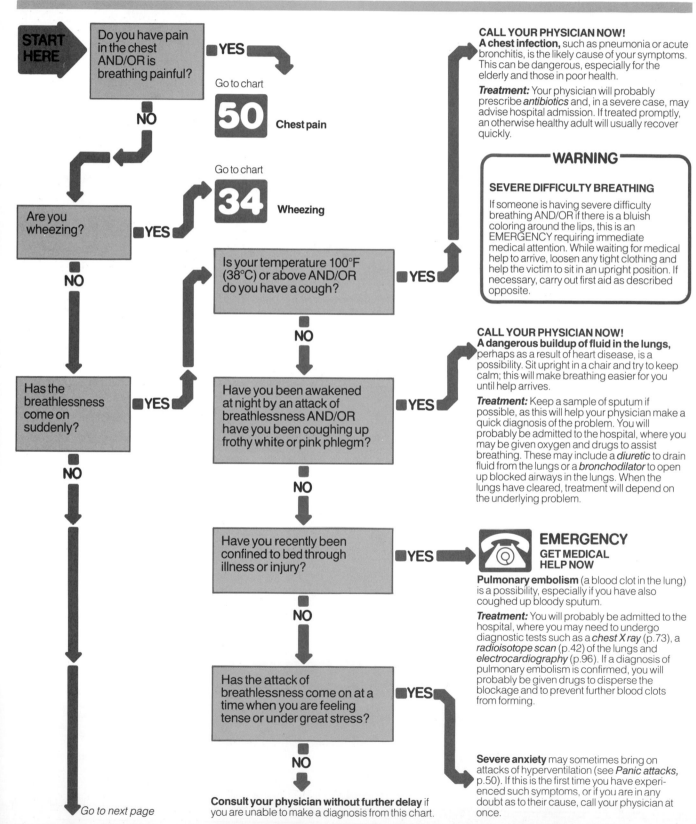

START HERE

Do you have pain in the chest AND/OR is breathing painful?
YES → Go to chart **50** Chest pain
NO

Are you wheezing?
YES → Go to chart **34** Wheezing
NO

Has the breathlessness come on suddenly?
NO

Is your temperature 100°F (38°C) or above AND/OR do you have a cough?
YES
NO

Have you been awakened at night by an attack of breathlessness AND/OR have you been coughing up frothy white or pink phlegm?
YES
NO

Have you recently been confined to bed through illness or injury?
YES
NO

Has the attack of breathlessness come on at a time when you are feeling tense or under great stress?
YES
NO

Go to next page

Consult your physician without further delay if you are unable to make a diagnosis from this chart.

CALL YOUR PHYSICIAN NOW!
A chest infection, such as pneumonia or acute bronchitis, is the likely cause of your symptoms. This can be dangerous, especially for the elderly and those in poor health.
Treatment: Your physician will probably prescribe *antibiotics* and, in a severe case, may advise hospital admission. If treated promptly, an otherwise healthy adult will usually recover quickly.

WARNING

SEVERE DIFFICULTY BREATHING

If someone is having severe difficulty breathing AND/OR if there is a bluish coloring around the lips, this is an EMERGENCY requiring immediate medical attention. While waiting for medical help to arrive, loosen any tight clothing and help the victim to sit in an upright position. If necessary, carry out first aid as described opposite.

CALL YOUR PHYSICIAN NOW!
A dangerous buildup of fluid in the lungs, perhaps as a result of heart disease, is a possibility. Sit upright in a chair and try to keep calm; this will make breathing easier for you until help arrives.
Treatment: Keep a sample of sputum if possible, as this will help your physician make a quick diagnosis of the problem. You will probably be admitted to the hospital, where you may be given oxygen and drugs to assist breathing. These may include a *diuretic* to drain fluid from the lungs or a *bronchodilator* to open up blocked airways in the lungs. When the lungs have cleared, treatment will depend on the underlying problem.

EMERGENCY
GET MEDICAL HELP NOW
Pulmonary embolism (a blood clot in the lung) is a possibility, especially if you have also coughed up bloody sputum.
Treatment: You will probably be admitted to the hospital, where you may need to undergo diagnostic tests such as a *chest X ray* (p.73), a *radioisotope scan* (p.42) of the lungs and *electrocardiography* (p.96). If a diagnosis of pulmonary embolism is confirmed, you will probably be given drugs to disperse the blockage and to prevent further blood clots from forming.

Severe anxiety may sometimes bring on attacks of hyperventilation (see *Panic attacks,* p.50). If this is the first time you have experienced such symptoms, or if you are in any doubt as to their cause, call your physician at once.

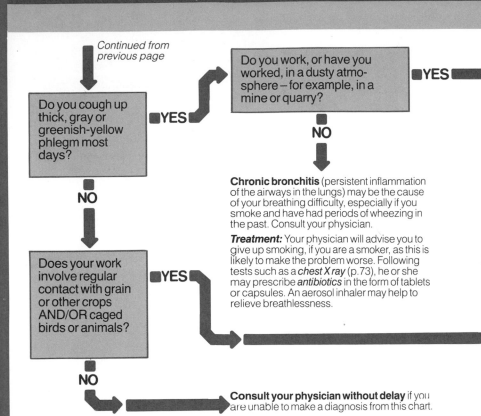

Continued from previous page

Do you cough up thick, gray or greenish-yellow phlegm most days?

NO

Does your work involve regular contact with grain or other crops AND/OR caged birds or animals?

NO

YES

Do you work, or have you worked, in a dusty atmosphere – for example, in a mine or quarry?

NO

YES

Pneumoconiosis (a reaction to coal dust in the lungs) or another dust disease is a possibility. Consult your physician.
Treatment: A *chest X ray* (p. 73) may indicate how seriously your lungs have been affected. Your physician may advise you to change your job and, if you are a smoker, to give up smoking.

Chronic bronchitis (persistent inflammation of the airways in the lungs) may be the cause of your breathing difficulty, especially if you smoke and have had periods of wheezing in the past. Consult your physician.
Treatment: Your physician will advise you to give up smoking, if you are a smoker, as this is likely to make the problem worse. Following tests such as a *chest X ray* (p.73), he or she may prescribe *antibiotics* in the form of tablets or capsules. An aerosol inhaler may help to relieve breathlessness.

Histoplasmosis (a fungal infection of the lungs), farmer's lung (an allergic reaction to inhaled particles in moldy grain or hay), or bird-breeder's lung (a reaction to inhaled dust containing bird proteins) can cause breathless attacks often accompanied by coughing. Consult your physician.
Treatment: Your physician will probably arrange for you to have diagnostic tests including a *chest X ray* (p. 73) and skin tests for allergic sensitivity. If you are found to have histoplasmosis, you will be given treatment with antifungal drugs. If your breathlessness is due to allergy, you will probably be advised to avoid further exposure to the substance causing the reaction by changing your job or by wearing a protective mask at work. You may also be given drugs to reduce inflammation of the lung.

Consult your physician without delay if you are unable to make a diagnosis from this chart.

FIRST AID FOR STOPPED BREATHING

If someone stops breathing, carry out first aid as described below before summoning emergency medical help.

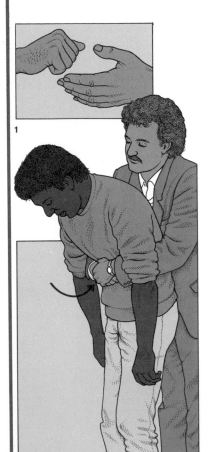

1

Suspected choking
When severe breathing difficulty comes on while eating, and if the victim is unable to cough up the obstruction, carry out the following steps:

1 Hold the victim up from behind in a standing position, pressing one fist (with thumb inward) against the waist. Hold your other hand over the fist and thrust hard in and up under the rib cage. If this does not clear the blockage, repeat 3 more times.

2 If this does not clear the obstruction, lay the victim on his or her back. Tilt the head back (chin up), open the mouth and sweep deeply into the mouth with hooked finger (you may need to remove dentures).

2

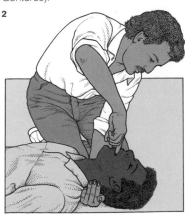

3 If obstruction is still not dislodged, repeat steps 1 and 2.

4 If breathing does not restart following removal of the blockage, carry out mouth-to-mouth resuscitation (right).

Mouth-to-mouth resuscitation
If a person has actually stopped breathing (whether as a result of an accident such as near drowning or electric shock, or from a medical condition such as a suspected heart attack), immediately start mouth-to-mouth resuscitation.

1 Lay the victim face upward. Support the back of the neck and tip the head well back. Clear the mouth with your finger to remove any blockage from the windpipe.

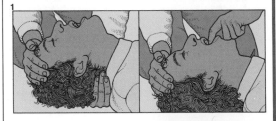

2 Pinch the nose shut, take a deep breath and seal your mouth around the mouth. Blow strongly into the lungs 4 times.

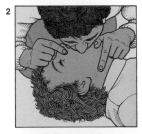

3 Continue to give a breath every 5 seconds. After each breath remove your mouth. Listen for air leaving the lungs and watch the chest fall. Continue until medical help arrives or until the victim is able to breathe on his own.

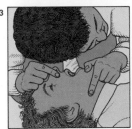

37 Toothache

Teeth are just as much living structures as any other part of the body, despite their tough appearance. They are constantly under threat from our diet because of the high level of sugar we consume. Bacteria act on sugar to produce acids that attack enamel, the tooth's protective layer. When this happens, bacterial destruction (decay) spreads down the root canal to the nerve, causing inflammation and pain. Any pain in one tooth or from teeth and gums in general, whether it is a dull throb or a sharp twinge, should be brought to your dentist's attention.

START HERE →

Do you have one or more of the following symptoms?
- continuous pain
- a tooth that feels long or high
- a tooth that feels loose
- a fever

■YES■ →

NO

Do you have repeated bouts of throbbing pain OR is the tooth extremely sensitive to both hot and cold stimuli AND does the pain continue for several minutes after the stimulus is removed?

■YES■

NO

Has the dentist filled one or more of your teeth within the past few weeks?

■YES■ → **Does the tooth hurt only when you bite on it?**

NO

NO

Does the pain only occur when you are eating something cold or sweet (ice cream or chocolate) AND does the pain go away after a few seconds?

■YES■

NO

CONSULT YOUR DENTIST WITHOUT DELAY!

A tooth abcess is possible. This is formed when pus builds up in the bone and tissue near a tooth that has had a very deep filling or cavity, or one that has been injured.

Treatment: Two forms of treatment are common – root canal treatment or extraction. If the dentist feels the tooth can be saved, a root canal may be performed. The dentist will make an opening in the tooth to release the pus and relieve the pressure. Sometimes an emergency incision is made in the gum to relieve the swollen area. The diseased tissue is then removed from inside the tooth. Later, a permanent filling is placed in the root canal and the tooth is sealed and crowned. About six months later, an X ray will be needed to ensure that the bone and tissue have grown back to normal around the root of the tooth. Extraction of an abscessed tooth may be suggested as an alternative to a root canal. A bridge or partial denture will be needed to keep other teeth from shifting.

Advanced dental decay, a very deep filling or an injury may have irreversibly inflamed the pulp (nerve) in the center of the tooth.
Treatment: The dentist will remove the decay and/or old filling. If the nerve is exposed, a root canal or extraction may be needed. If the pulp is not visibly exposed, the dentist may try to soothe the inflamed pulp with a temporary, medicated filling. After a few weeks, the tooth will be re-evaluated for possible root canal treatment, extraction, or permanent filling.

After a filling, especially a deep one, it is normal to have some sensitivity, especially to cold water or air. This sensitivity will be sharp, but will last for only a few seconds and then subside. If the sensitivity increases in intensity or duration, or if the tooth becomes sensitive to heat, consult your dentist for the possibility of irreversible pulp (nerve) damage.

Decay under an old filling, a cracked tooth or filling, or exposure of the root surface due to improper toothbrushing or gum disease may be the cause of the pain. Consult your dentist.
Treatment: Your dentist may recommend replacing an old filling or remove any decay. If the problem is sensitivity, the dentist may recommend a special desensitizing toothpaste, protective fluoride applications or bonding to seal the sensitive root area.

An uneven or "high" filling can cause discomfort. Your dentist will adjust the filling if necessary.

Does the tooth hurt only when you bite or chew on it?

■YES■

NO

Dental decay may have caused a hole (or cavity) to form in your tooth. Consult your dentist.
Treatment: Your dentist will probably clean out the affected tooth and put in a filling.

A cracked filling or a cracked or fractured tooth is probably the cause of the pain. Consult your dentist.
Treatment: You may need to have the affected tooth crowned (capped) or have a root canal if the pain becomes more severe. The tooth may need to be extracted if the crack is too deep into the tooth. Pain may also be caused by acute sinus problems that make the upper back teeth ache and tender to bite on. If this is the case, you may need to see a physician for further treatment.

CARE OF YOUR TEETH

Brushing
Several tooth brushing techniques are acceptable as long as you manage to remove all traces of food and plaque from the back, front, and biting surfaces of your teeth. If you use a toothbrush with a small head you will be able to get at the difficult areas more easily. The toothbrush should have soft, rounded bristles unless your dentist suggests another type of brush.

Dental floss
Daily use of dental floss helps to remove debris and plaque from between your teeth and under your gums. Your dentist or hygienist will teach you how to floss your teeth correctly.

Diet
Sugary foods are the main cause of tooth decay, so try to keep your consumption of sweet foods to a minimum. If you need to eat snacks during the day, they should consist of cheese or nuts. If you find it hard to do without sweet foods, confine them to mealtimes and finish the meal with cheese, as this tends to neutralize acid formation.

38 Difficulty swallowing

Difficulty swallowing is most often the result of an infection causing soreness, swelling and the production of excess mucus at the back of the throat. Difficulty or pain when swallowing that is not related to a sore throat may be a sign of a more serious disorder affecting the esophagus. Consult your physician.

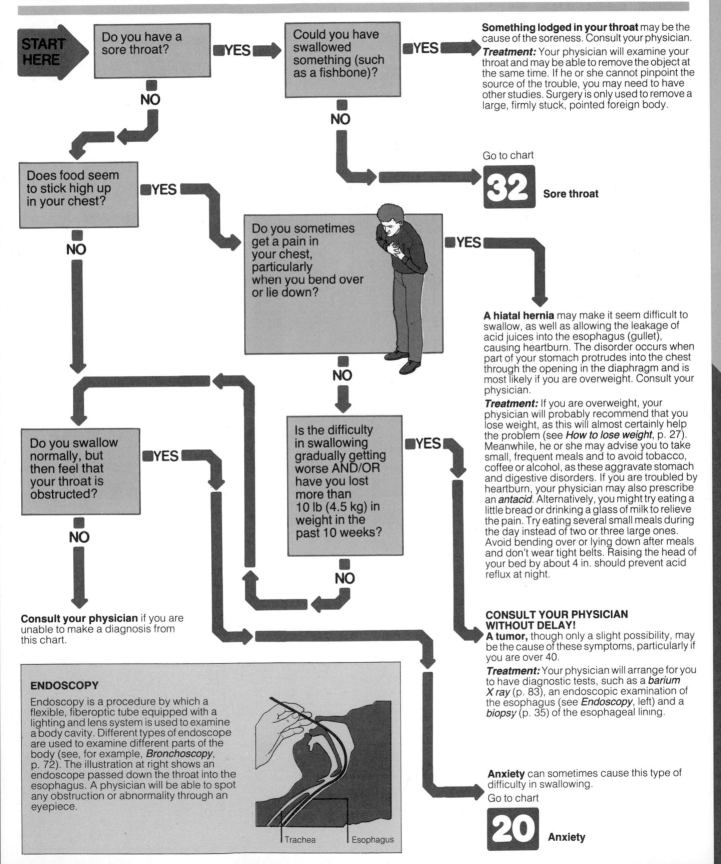

START HERE

Do you have a sore throat? — **YES** → **Could you have swallowed something (such as a fishbone)?** — **YES** →

Something lodged in your throat may be the cause of the soreness. Consult your physician.

Treatment: Your physician will examine your throat and may be able to remove the object at the same time. If he or she cannot pinpoint the source of the trouble, you may need to have other studies. Surgery is only used to remove a large, firmly stuck, pointed foreign body.

↓ **NO**

↓ **NO**

Go to chart

32 Sore throat

Does food seem to stick high up in your chest? — **YES** →

Do you sometimes get a pain in your chest, particularly when you bend over or lie down? — **YES** →

↓ **NO**

↓ **NO**

A hiatal hernia may make it seem difficult to swallow, as well as allowing the leakage of acid juices into the esophagus (gullet), causing heartburn. The disorder occurs when part of your stomach protrudes into the chest through the opening in the diaphragm and is most likely if you are overweight. Consult your physician.

Treatment: If you are overweight, your physician will probably recommend that you lose weight, as this will almost certainly help the problem (see *How to lose weight*, p. 27). Meanwhile, he or she may advise you to take small, frequent meals and to avoid tobacco, coffee or alcohol, as these aggravate stomach and digestive disorders. If you are troubled by heartburn, your physician may also prescribe an *antacid*. Alternatively, you might try eating a little bread or drinking a glass of milk to relieve the pain. Try eating several small meals during the day instead of two or three large ones. Avoid bending over or lying down after meals and don't wear tight belts. Raising the head of your bed by about 4 in. should prevent acid reflux at night.

Do you swallow normally, but then feel that your throat is obstructed? — **YES** →

Is the difficulty in swallowing gradually getting worse AND/OR have you lost more than 10 lb (4.5 kg) in weight in the past 10 weeks? — **YES** →

↓ **NO**

↓ **NO**

Consult your physician if you are unable to make a diagnosis from this chart.

CONSULT YOUR PHYSICIAN WITHOUT DELAY!
A tumor, though only a slight possibility, may be the cause of these symptoms, particularly if you are over 40.

Treatment: Your physician will arrange for you to have diagnostic tests, such as a *barium X ray* (p. 83), an endoscopic examination of the esophagus (see *Endoscopy*, left) and a *biopsy* (p. 35) of the esophageal lining.

ENDOSCOPY

Endoscopy is a procedure by which a flexible, fiberoptic tube equipped with a lighting and lens system is used to examine a body cavity. Different types of endoscope are used to examine different parts of the body (see, for example, *Bronchoscopy*, p. 72). The illustration at right shows an endoscope passed down the throat into the esophagus. A physician will be able to spot any obstruction or abnormality through an eyepiece.

Trachea | Esophagus

Anxiety can sometimes cause this type of difficulty in swallowing.
Go to chart

20 Anxiety

39 Sore mouth or tongue

Most painful areas on the lips or tongue or around the teeth are symptoms of minor conditions. You will be able to tell the mild from the serious by the length of time they take to heal. Any condition lasting longer than 3 weeks should be seen by your physician or dentist. It is important to keep the delicate mucous membrane that lines the mouth healthy by maintaining good oral hygiene at all times (see Care of your teeth, p.76).

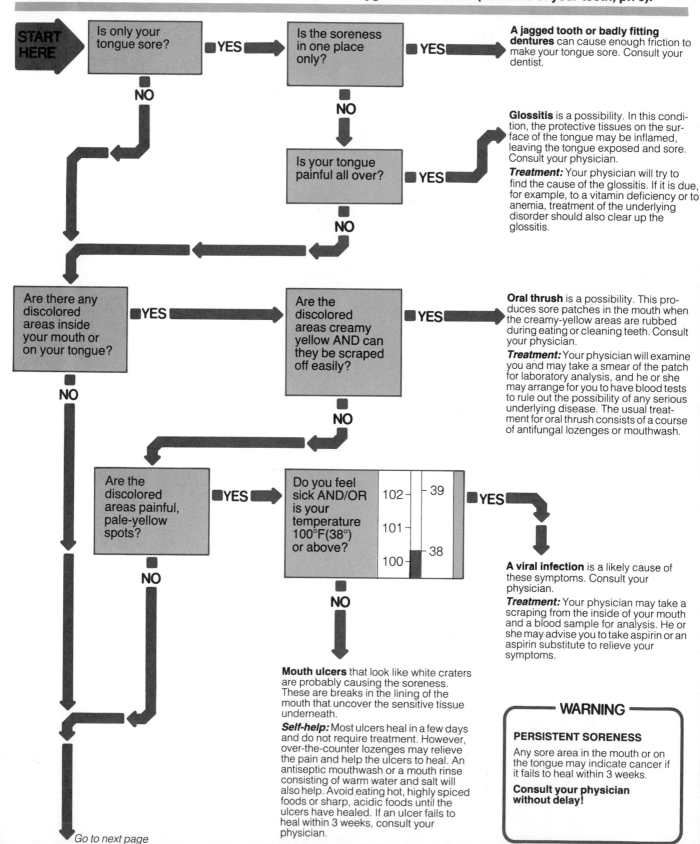

START HERE

Is only your tongue sore?

YES → **Is the soreness in one place only?**

YES → **A jagged tooth or badly fitting dentures** can cause enough friction to make your tongue sore. Consult your dentist.

NO ↓

Is your tongue painful all over?

YES → **Glossitis** is a possibility. In this condition, the protective tissues on the surface of the tongue may be inflamed, leaving the tongue exposed and sore. Consult your physician.
Treatment: Your physician will try to find the cause of the glossitis. If it is due, for example, to a vitamin deficiency or to anemia, treatment of the underlying disorder should also clear up the glossitis.

NO

Are there any discolored areas inside your mouth or on your tongue?

YES → **Are the discolored areas creamy yellow AND can they be scraped off easily?**

YES → **Oral thrush** is a possibility. This produces sore patches in the mouth when the creamy-yellow areas are rubbed during eating or cleaning teeth. Consult your physician.
Treatment: Your physician will examine you and may take a smear of the patch for laboratory analysis, and he or she may arrange for you to have blood tests to rule out the possibility of any serious underlying disease. The usual treatment for oral thrush consists of a course of antifungal lozenges or mouthwash.

NO ↓

NO

Are the discolored areas painful, pale-yellow spots?

YES → **Do you feel sick AND/OR is your temperature 100°F(38°) or above?**

102 — 39
101
100 — 38

YES → **A viral infection** is a likely cause of these symptoms. Consult your physician.
Treatment: Your physician may take a scraping from the inside of your mouth and a blood sample for analysis. He or she may advise you to take aspirin or an aspirin substitute to relieve your symptoms.

NO ↓

NO ↓

Mouth ulcers that look like white craters are probably causing the soreness. These are breaks in the lining of the mouth that uncover the sensitive tissue underneath.
Self-help: Most ulcers heal in a few days and do not require treatment. However, over-the-counter lozenges may relieve the pain and help the ulcers to heal. An antiseptic mouthwash or a mouth rinse consisting of warm water and salt will also help. Avoid eating hot, highly spiced foods or sharp, acidic foods until the ulcers have healed. If an ulcer fails to heal within 3 weeks, consult your physician.

Go to next page

WARNING

PERSISTENT SORENESS

Any sore area in the mouth or on the tongue may indicate cancer if it fails to heal within 3 weeks.

Consult your physician without delay!

Continued from previous page

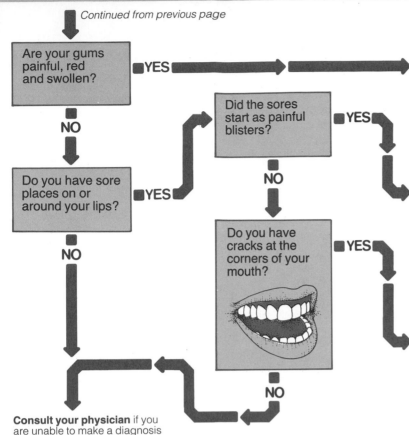

Are your gums painful, red and swollen?

YES →

NO ↓

Do you have sore places on or around your lips?

YES →

NO ↓

Did the sores start as painful blisters?

YES →

NO ↓

Do you have cracks at the corners of your mouth?

YES →

NO ↓

Consult your physician if you are unable to make a diagnosis from this chart.

Inflammation of the gums, usually as a result of inadequate cleaning of the teeth, is the most likely cause of these symptoms. Consult your dentist.

Treatment: Your dentist may recommend an antibacterial mouthwash or an antibiotic. He or she will also scrape away food deposits and calculus (a hard, chalky material that sometimes builds up) from your teeth. The dentist will also show you the most effective way to clean your teeth so that you can prevent the trouble from recurring (see *Care of your teeth*, p. 76).

Cold sores are the likely cause of these symptoms. They are the result of a virus in the body becoming reactivated by a cold, or exposure to strong sunshine or cold weather.

Self-help: Mild cases of cold sores clear up on their own. However, there are over-the-counter preparations that may relieve symptoms. If you are troubled by severe, recurrent cold sores, your physician may prescribe a cream for you to apply when the sore is in its early stages to inhibit its development.

Ill-fitting dentures may be the cause of such soreness. Occasionally, however, cracking at the corners of the mouth may also be a sign of a vitamin deficiency. If you wear dentures, consult your dentist. Otherwise, consult your physician.

Treatment: If dentures are the problem, your dentist may adjust your old baseplate or supply a new set. He or she may also prescribe lozenges to relieve the soreness. If there is a possibility of a vitamin deficiency, your physician will ask you about your diet and examine you to eliminate the possibility of an underlying disease. He or she may prescribe vitamin supplements.

BAD BREATH

You are unlikely to notice that you have bad breath unless it is pointed out to you by a friend. The following are the most common causes of bad breath and are easily remedied:

Sore mouth
Infection or ulceration of the mouth, gums or tongue may cause bad breath. Rinsing out your mouth with an antiseptic mouthwash usually clears up the problem within a few days. If the problem persists, consult your physician.

Inadequately cleaned teeth or dentures
If you do not clean your teeth (or dentures, if you wear them) thoroughly at least twice a day, this may be the cause of your bad breath. Decaying food particles lodge between the teeth or stick to the dentures (see *Care of your teeth*, p.76, and *Caring for your dentures*, right).

Garlic, onions and alcohol
These foods contain volatile substances that, when absorbed into the bloodstream and then released into the lungs, may cause bad breath. Alcohol may also be responsible for bad breath in much the same way. Your breath should return to normal within 24 hours after consuming these foods.

Smoking
Smoking always causes a form of bad breath (see also *The dangers of smoking*, p. 72).

If your bad breath continues for some time, it may be a symptom of something more serious such as a mouth infection or a lung disease,. Consult your physician.

CARING FOR YOUR DENTURES

Always remove your dentures at night and keep them in a glass of water containing a cleansing agent so that they do not dry out and warp. This will also give the gum tissues a regular rest period. Brush your dentures thoroughly every day. Your dentist will show you the best way to do this. It is also important to remember to clean any remaining natural teeth thoroughly, especially where teeth and gums meet. Partial dentures may feel a little tight when inserted in the morning, but this is normal and the feeling disappears in a few minutes. The useful life of dentures varies greatly – from 6 months to 5 years or more – depending on how well your gums and jaws keep their shape. If you have a full set of dentures, you should visit the dentist every 2 years. If you still have some natural teeth, you should go for a checkup every 6 months.

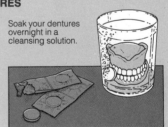

Soak your dentures overnight in a cleansing solution.

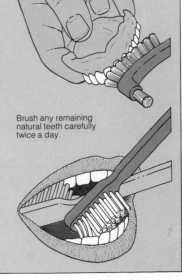

Brush your dentures daily on both sides to remove all food deposits. Rinse throughly before replacing them in your mouth.

Brush any remaining natural teeth carefully twice a day.

40 Vomiting

Vomiting occurs when the muscles around the stomach suddenly contract and "throw up" the contents of the stomach. This is usually the result of irritation of the stomach from infection or overindulgence in rich food or alcohol, but may also occur as a result of disturbance in another part of the digestive tract. Occasionally, a disorder affecting the nerve signals from the brain, or from the balance mechanism in the inner ear (p. 40), can also produce vomiting. Most cases of vomiting can be treated at home, but vomiting that is accompanied by severe abdominal pain, or by severe headache or eye pain, requires urgent medical attention.

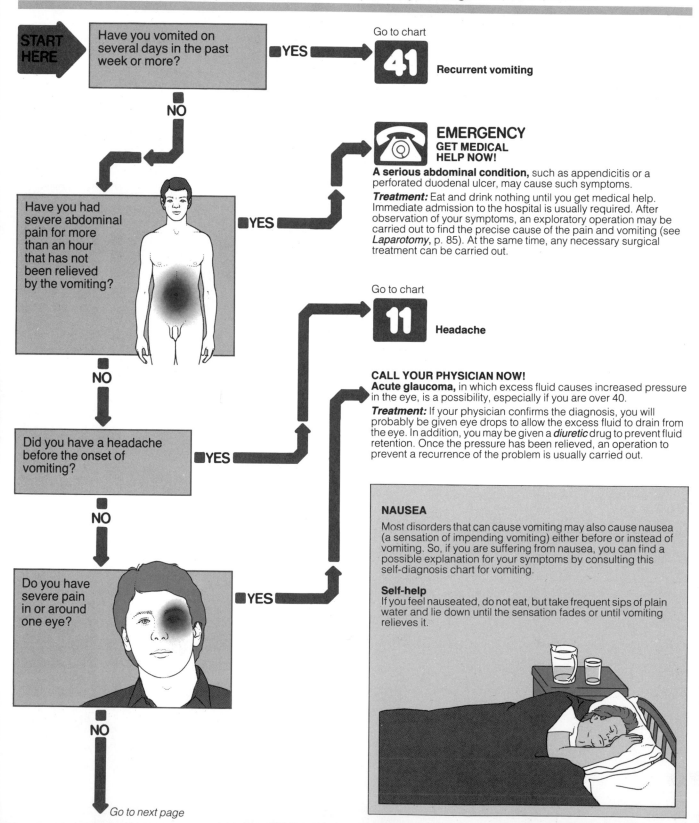

START HERE

Have you vomited on several days in the past week or more?

YES → Go to chart **41** Recurrent vomiting

NO

Have you had severe abdominal pain for more than an hour that has not been relieved by the vomiting?

YES →

EMERGENCY GET MEDICAL HELP NOW!

A serious abdominal condition, such as appendicitis or a perforated duodenal ulcer, may cause such symptoms.

Treatment: Eat and drink nothing until you get medical help. Immediate admission to the hospital is usually required. After observation of your symptoms, an exploratory operation may be carried out to find the precise cause of the pain and vomiting (see *Laparotomy,* p. 85). At the same time, any necessary surgical treatment can be carried out.

NO

Did you have a headache before the onset of vomiting?

YES →

Go to chart **11** Headache

CALL YOUR PHYSICIAN NOW!
Acute glaucoma, in which excess fluid causes increased pressure in the eye, is a possibility, especially if you are over 40.

Treatment: If your physician confirms the diagnosis, you will probably be given eye drops to allow the excess fluid to drain from the eye. In addition, you may be given a *diuretic* drug to prevent fluid retention. Once the pressure has been relieved, an operation to prevent a recurrence of the problem is usually carried out.

NO

Do you have severe pain in or around one eye?

YES →

NO

Go to next page

NAUSEA

Most disorders that can cause vomiting may also cause nausea (a sensation of impending vomiting) either before or instead of vomiting. So, if you are suffering from nausea, you can find a possible explanation for your symptoms by consulting this self-diagnosis chart for vomiting.

Self-help
If you feel nauseated, do not eat, but take frequent sips of plain water and lie down until the sensation fades or until vomiting relieves it.

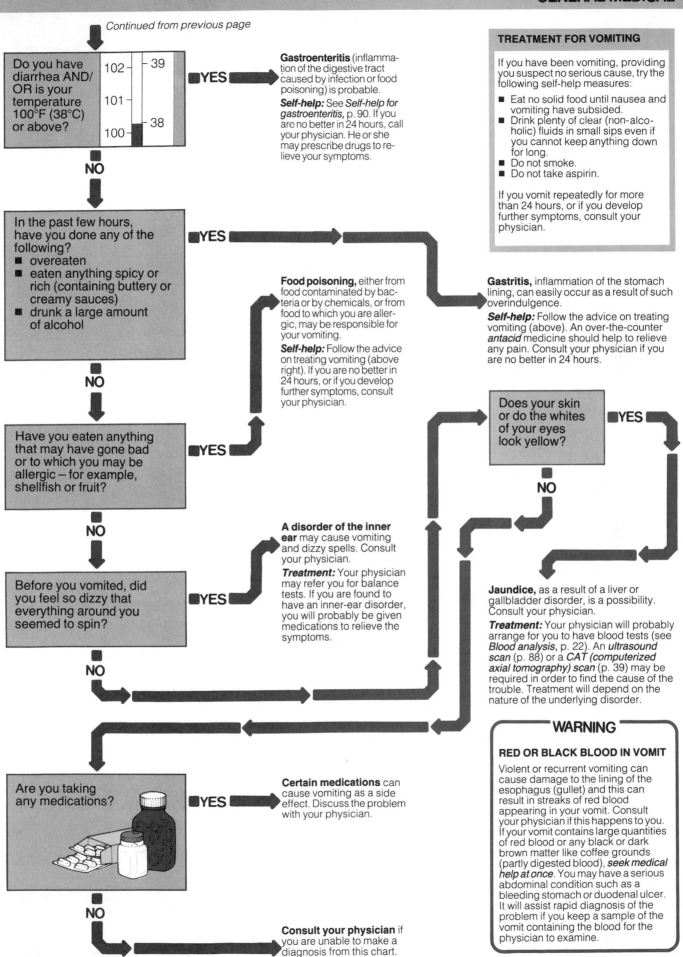

Continued from previous page

Do you have diarrhea AND/OR is your temperature 100°F (38°C) or above?

102 — 39
101
100 — 38

YES → **Gastroenteritis** (inflammation of the digestive tract caused by infection or food poisoning) is probable.
Self-help: See *Self-help for gastroenteritis,* p. 90. If you are no better in 24 hours, call your physician. He or she may prescribe drugs to relieve your symptoms.

NO

In the past few hours, have you done any of the following?
- overeaten
- eaten anything spicy or rich (containing buttery or creamy sauces)
- drunk a large amount of alcohol

YES →

Food poisoning, either from food contaminated by bacteria or by chemicals, or from food to which you are allergic, may be responsible for your vomiting.
Self-help: Follow the advice on treating vomiting (above right). If you are no better in 24 hours, or if you develop further symptoms, consult your physician.

Gastritis, inflammation of the stomach lining, can easily occur as a result of such overindulgence.
Self-help: Follow the advice on treating vomiting (above). An over-the-counter *antacid* medicine should help to relieve any pain. Consult your physician if you are no better in 24 hours.

NO

Have you eaten anything that may have gone bad or to which you may be allergic – for example, shellfish or fruit?

YES

Does your skin or do the whites of your eyes look yellow?

YES

NO

A disorder of the inner ear may cause vomiting and dizzy spells. Consult your physician.
Treatment: Your physician may refer you for balance tests. If you are found to have an inner-ear disorder, you will probably be given medications to relieve the symptoms.

NO

Before you vomited, did you feel so dizzy that everything around you seemed to spin?

YES

Jaundice, as a result of a liver or gallbladder disorder, is a possibility. Consult your physician.
Treatment: Your physician will probably arrange for you to have blood tests (see *Blood analysis,* p. 22). An *ultrasound scan* (p. 88) or a *CAT (computerized axial tomography) scan* (p. 39) may be required in order to find the cause of the trouble. Treatment will depend on the nature of the underlying disorder.

NO

Are you taking any medications?

YES → **Certain medications** can cause vomiting as a side effect. Discuss the problem with your physician.

NO

Consult your physician if you are unable to make a diagnosis from this chart.

TREATMENT FOR VOMITING

If you have been vomiting, providing you suspect no serious cause, try the following self-help measures:
- Eat no solid food until nausea and vomiting have subsided.
- Drink plenty of clear (non-alcoholic) fluids in small sips even if you cannot keep anything down for long.
- Do not smoke.
- Do not take aspirin.

If you vomit repeatedly for more than 24 hours, or if you develop further symptoms, consult your physician.

WARNING

RED OR BLACK BLOOD IN VOMIT

Violent or recurrent vomiting can cause damage to the lining of the esophagus (gullet) and this can result in streaks of red blood appearing in your vomit. Consult your physician if this happens to you. If your vomit contains large quantities of red blood or any black or dark brown matter like coffee grounds (partly digested blood), *seek medical help at once*. You may have a serious abdominal condition such as a bleeding stomach or duodenal ulcer. It will assist rapid diagnosis of the problem if you keep a sample of the vomit containing the blood for the physician to examine.

41 Recurrent vomiting

Consult this chart if you have vomited (or felt nauseated) for several days or more in the past week. Most cases of recurrent vomiting are caused by persistent inflammation of the stomach lining or minor ulceration and are not life-threatening. However, it is important to seek medical advice promptly so that you can obtain effective treatment and eliminate the slight possibility of a more serious underlying disorder.

For isolated attacks of vomiting, see chart 40, Vomiting

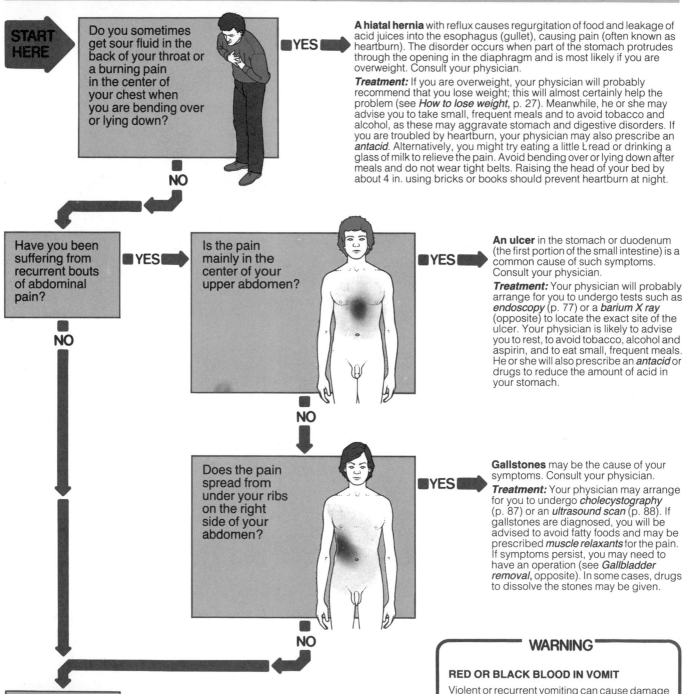

START HERE

Do you sometimes get sour fluid in the back of your throat or a burning pain in the center of your chest when you are bending over or lying down?

YES

A hiatal hernia with reflux causes regurgitation of food and leakage of acid juices into the esophagus (gullet), causing pain (often known as heartburn). The disorder occurs when part of the stomach protrudes through the opening in the diaphragm and is most likely if you are overweight. Consult your physician.

Treatment: If you are overweight, your physician will probably recommend that you lose weight; this will almost certainly help the problem (see *How to lose weight*, p. 27). Meanwhile, he or she may advise you to take small, frequent meals and to avoid tobacco and alcohol, as these may aggravate stomach and digestive disorders. If you are troubled by heartburn, your physician may also prescribe an *antacid*. Alternatively, you might try eating a little bread or drinking a glass of milk to relieve the pain. Avoid bending over or lying down after meals and do not wear tight belts. Raising the head of your bed by about 4 in. using bricks or books should prevent heartburn at night.

NO

Have you been suffering from recurrent bouts of abdominal pain?

YES

Is the pain mainly in the center of your upper abdomen?

YES

An ulcer in the stomach or duodenum (the first portion of the small intestine) is a common cause of such symptoms. Consult your physician.

Treatment: Your physician will probably arrange for you to undergo tests such as *endoscopy* (p. 77) or a *barium X ray* (opposite) to locate the exact site of the ulcer. Your physician is likely to advise you to rest, to avoid tobacco, alcohol and aspirin, and to eat small, frequent meals. He or she will also prescribe an *antacid* or drugs to reduce the amount of acid in your stomach.

NO

NO

Does the pain spread from under your ribs on the right side of your abdomen?

YES

Gallstones may be the cause of your symptoms. Consult your physician.

Treatment: Your physician may arrange for you to undergo *cholecystography* (p. 87) or an *ultrasound scan* (p. 88). If gallstones are diagnosed, you will be advised to avoid fatty foods and may be prescribed *muscle relaxants* for the pain. If symptoms persist, you may need to have an operation (see *Gallbladder removal*, opposite). In some cases, drugs to dissolve the stones may be given.

NO

Does your skin or do your eyes look yellow?

YES

Jaundice may be caused by a disorder of the liver or gallbladder that also causes vomiting. Consult your physician.

Treatment: Your physician will probably arrange for you to have blood tests (see *Blood analysis*, p. 22) and possibly an *ultrasound scan* (p. 88) or a *CAT (computerized axial tomography) scan* (p. 39) to find the cause of the trouble. Treatment will depend on the underlying disorder.

NO

Go to next page

WARNING

RED OR BLACK BLOOD IN VOMIT

Violent or recurrent vomiting can cause damage to the lining of the esophagus (gullet) and this can result in streaks of red blood appearing in your vomit. Consult your physician if this happens to you. If your vomit contains large quantities of red blood or any black or dark brown matter (partly digested blood), you should *seek medical help at once*; you may have a serious abdominal condition such as a bleeding stomach or duodenal ulcer. To assist diagnosis, keep the vomit containing the blood for the physician to examine.

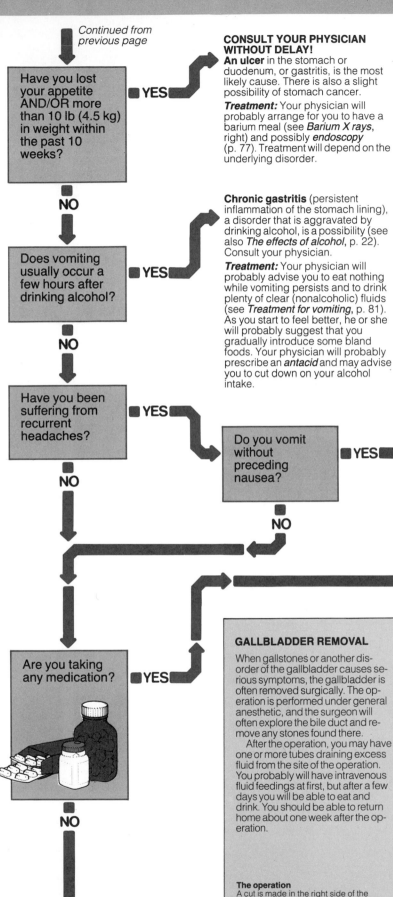

Continued from previous page

Have you lost your appetite AND/OR more than 10 lb (4.5 kg) in weight within the past 10 weeks?

YES →

CONSULT YOUR PHYSICIAN WITHOUT DELAY!
An ulcer in the stomach or duodenum, or gastritis, is the most likely cause. There is also a slight possibility of stomach cancer.

Treatment: Your physician will probably arrange for you to have a barium meal (see *Barium X rays,* right) and possibly *endoscopy* (p. 77). Treatment will depend on the underlying disorder.

NO ↓

Does vomiting usually occur a few hours after drinking alcohol?

YES →

Chronic gastritis (persistent inflammation of the stomach lining), a disorder that is aggravated by drinking alcohol, is a possibility (see also *The effects of alcohol,* p. 22). Consult your physician.

Treatment: Your physician will probably advise you to eat nothing while vomiting persists and to drink plenty of clear (nonalcoholic) fluids (see *Treatment for vomiting,* p. 81). As you start to feel better, he or she will probably suggest that you gradually introduce some bland foods. Your physician will probably prescribe an *antacid* and may advise you to cut down on your alcohol intake.

NO ↓

Have you been suffering from recurrent headaches?

YES →

Do you vomit without preceding nausea?

YES →

CONSULT YOUR PHYSICIAN WITHOUT DELAY!
Pressure on the brain as a result of bleeding or a tumor is possible.

Treatment: Your physician will probably arrange for tests such as a *CAT scan* (p. 39). Treatment usually consists of either surgery or drugs to reduce the pressure and relieve symptoms.

NO ↓

NO ↓

Certain drugs can cause nausea and vomiting as a side effect. Discuss the problem with your physician.

Are you taking any medication?

YES →

NO ↓

Consult your physician If you are unable to make a diagnosis from this chart.

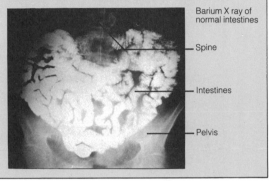

BARIUM X RAYS

Barium sulfate is a metallic compound that is visible on X-ray pictures. In medicine it is used to reveal areas of the digestive tract that need investigation. If you need to have an X ray of the esophagus (gullet), stomach or small intestine, you will probably be given barium in the form of a drink (a barium *swallow* or *meal*). X rays will then be taken when the liquid reaches the relevant part of the digestive tract (after about 10 minutes for the esophagus, after 2 to 3 hours for the small intestine). If the large intestine (colon and rectum) is being examined, barium will be given in the form of an *enema* and the X rays will be taken immediately. Normally, you will be told to eat nothing after midnight on the day before your barium meal or enema. If you are having an enema, you may also be given a laxative.

Barium X ray of normal intestines

— Spine
— Intestines
— Pelvis

GALLBLADDER REMOVAL

When gallstones or another disorder of the gallbladder causes serious symptoms, the gallbladder is often removed surgically. The operation is performed under general anesthetic, and the surgeon will often explore the bile duct and remove any stones found there.

After the operation, you may have one or more tubes draining excess fluid from the site of the operation. You probably will have intravenous fluid feedings at first, but after a few days you will be able to eat and drink. You should be able to return home about one week after the operation.

The operation
A cut is made in the right side of the abdomen (right). The gallbladder is then removed by cutting the cystic duct near where it joins the bile duct as shown in the diagram (above right). After the operation, bile drains straight into the intestine instead of first collecting in the gallbladder.

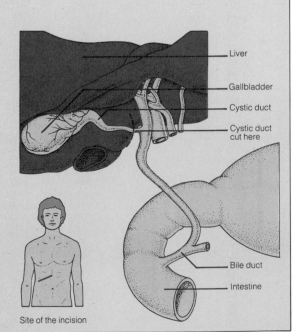

— Liver
— Gallbladder
— Cystic duct
— Cystic duct cut here
— Bile duct
— Intestine

Site of the incision

42 Abdominal pain

Pain between the bottom of the rib cage and the groin can be a sign of a wide number of different disorders of the digestive tract, urinary tract or reproductive organs. Most cases of abdominal pain are due to minor digestive upsets, but severe and persistent pain may have a serious underlying cause and should always receive prompt medical attention (see Severe abdominal pain, below).

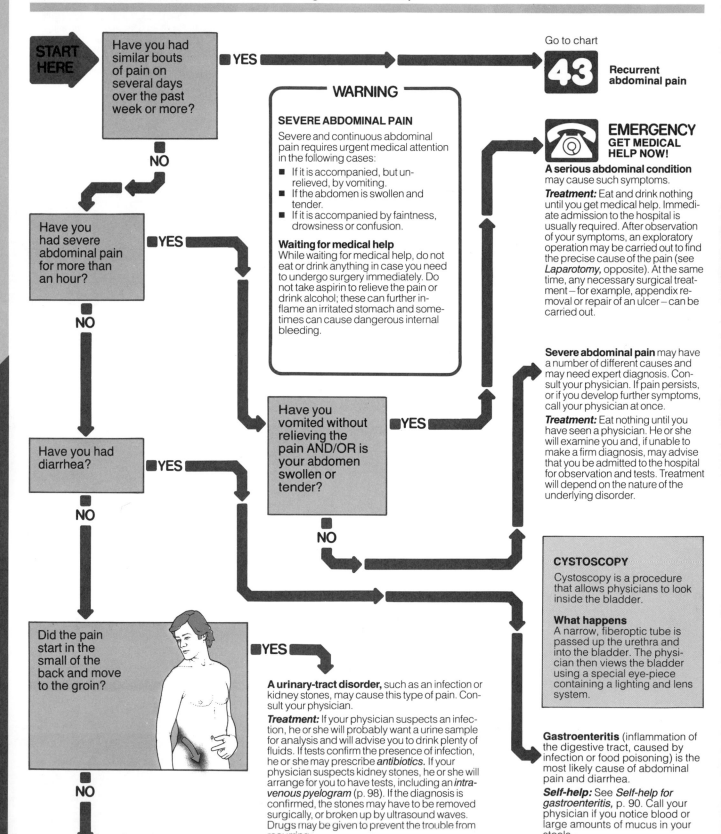

START HERE

Have you had similar bouts of pain on several days over the past week or more?

YES → Go to chart **43** Recurrent abdominal pain

NO

Have you had severe abdominal pain for more than an hour?

YES →

NO

Have you had diarrhea?

YES →

NO

Did the pain start in the small of the back and move to the groin?

NO → Go to next page

Have you vomited without relieving the pain AND/OR is your abdomen swollen or tender?

YES →

NO →

WARNING

SEVERE ABDOMINAL PAIN

Severe and continuous abdominal pain requires urgent medical attention in the following cases:

- If it is accompanied, but unrelieved, by vomiting.
- If the abdomen is swollen and tender.
- If it is accompanied by faintness, drowsiness or confusion.

Waiting for medical help

While waiting for medical help, do not eat or drink anything in case you need to undergo surgery immediately. Do not take aspirin to relieve the pain or drink alcohol; these can further inflame an irritated stomach and sometimes can cause dangerous internal bleeding.

EMERGENCY GET MEDICAL HELP NOW!

A serious abdominal condition may cause such symptoms.

Treatment: Eat and drink nothing until you get medical help. Immediate admission to the hospital is usually required. After observation of your symptoms, an exploratory operation may be carried out to find the precise cause of the pain (see *Laparotomy,* opposite). At the same time, any necessary surgical treatment – for example, appendix removal or repair of an ulcer – can be carried out.

Severe abdominal pain may have a number of different causes and may need expert diagnosis. Consult your physician. If pain persists, or if you develop further symptoms, call your physician at once.

Treatment: Eat nothing until you have seen a physician. He or she will examine you and, if unable to make a firm diagnosis, may advise that you be admitted to the hospital for observation and tests. Treatment will depend on the nature of the underlying disorder.

CYSTOSCOPY

Cystoscopy is a procedure that allows physicians to look inside the bladder.

What happens

A narrow, fiberoptic tube is passed up the urethra and into the bladder. The physician then views the bladder using a special eye-piece containing a lighting and lens system.

A urinary-tract disorder, such as an infection or kidney stones, may cause this type of pain. Consult your physician.

Treatment: If your physician suspects an infection, he or she will probably want a urine sample for analysis and will advise you to drink plenty of fluids. If tests confirm the presence of infection, he or she may prescribe *antibiotics.* If your physician suspects kidney stones, he or she will arrange for you to have tests, including an *intravenous pyelogram* (p. 98). If the diagnosis is confirmed, the stones may have to be removed surgically, or broken up by ultrasound waves. Drugs may be given to prevent the trouble from recurring.

Gastroenteritis (inflammation of the digestive tract, caused by infection or food poisoning) is the most likely cause of abdominal pain and diarrhea.

Self-help: See *Self-help for gastroenteritis,* p. 90. Call your physician if you notice blood or large amounts of mucus in your stools.

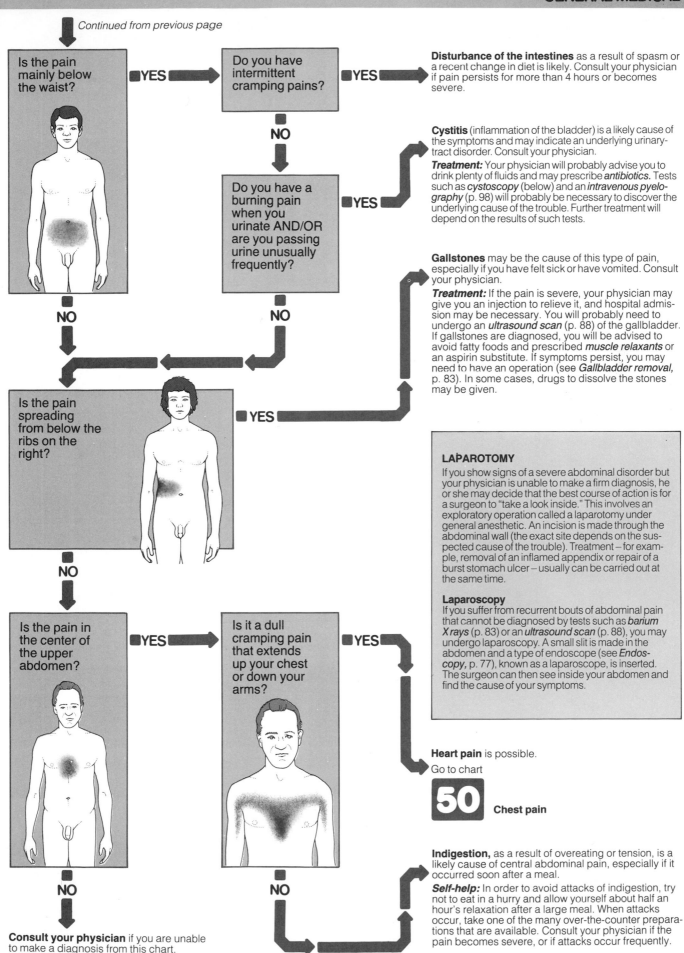

Continued from previous page

Is the pain mainly below the waist?

■YES■ →

Do you have intermittent cramping pains?

■YES■ →

Disturbance of the intestines as a result of spasm or a recent change in diet is likely. Consult your physician if pain persists for more than 4 hours or becomes severe.

NO

Do you have a burning pain when you urinate AND/OR are you passing urine unusually frequently?

■YES■ →

Cystitis (inflammation of the bladder) is a likely cause of the symptoms and may indicate an underlying urinary-tract disorder. Consult your physician.
Treatment: Your physician will probably advise you to drink plenty of fluids and may prescribe *antibiotics.* Tests such as *cystoscopy* (below) and an *intravenous pyelography* (p. 98) will probably be necessary to discover the underlying cause of the trouble. Further treatment will depend on the results of such tests.

NO

NO

Is the pain spreading from below the ribs on the right?

■YES■ →

Gallstones may be the cause of this type of pain, especially if you have felt sick or have vomited. Consult your physician.
Treatment: If the pain is severe, your physician may give you an injection to relieve it, and hospital admission may be necessary. You will probably need to undergo an *ultrasound scan* (p. 88) of the gallbladder. If gallstones are diagnosed, you will be advised to avoid fatty foods and prescribed *muscle relaxants* or an aspirin substitute. If symptoms persist, you may need to have an operation (see *Gallbladder removal*, p. 83). In some cases, drugs to dissolve the stones may be given.

NO

LAPAROTOMY

If you show signs of a severe abdominal disorder but your physician is unable to make a firm diagnosis, he or she may decide that the best course of action is for a surgeon to "take a look inside." This involves an exploratory operation called a laparotomy under general anesthetic. An incision is made through the abdominal wall (the exact site depends on the suspected cause of the trouble). Treatment – for example, removal of an inflamed appendix or repair of a burst stomach ulcer – usually can be carried out at the same time.

Laparoscopy

If you suffer from recurrent bouts of abdominal pain that cannot be diagnosed by tests such as *barium X rays* (p. 83) or an *ultrasound scan* (p. 88), you may undergo laparoscopy. A small slit is made in the abdomen and a type of endoscope (see *Endoscopy,* p. 77), known as a laparoscope, is inserted. The surgeon can then see inside your abdomen and find the cause of your symptoms.

Is the pain in the center of the upper abdomen?

■YES■ →

Is it a dull cramping pain that extends up your chest or down your arms?

■YES■ →

Heart pain is possible.
Go to chart

50 **Chest pain**

NO

NO

Indigestion, as a result of overeating or tension, is a likely cause of central abdominal pain, especially if it occurred soon after a meal.
Self-help: In order to avoid attacks of indigestion, try not to eat in a hurry and allow yourself about half an hour's relaxation after a large meal. When attacks occur, take one of the many over-the-counter preparations that are available. Consult your physician if the pain becomes severe, or if attacks occur frequently.

Consult your physician if you are unable to make a diagnosis from this chart.

43 Recurrent abdominal pain

Consult this chart if you have pain in the abdomen (between the bottom of the rib cage and the groin) of a similar type on several days in the course of a week or more. Most cases of recurrent abdominal pain are the result of long-standing digestive problems that can be remedied by drugs prescribed by your physician, possibly combined with a change in eating habits. However, early diagnosis is important to eliminate the slight possibility of serious underlying disease of the stomach, bowel or other abdominal organs.

For isolated attacks of abdominal pain, see chart 42, Abdominal pain.

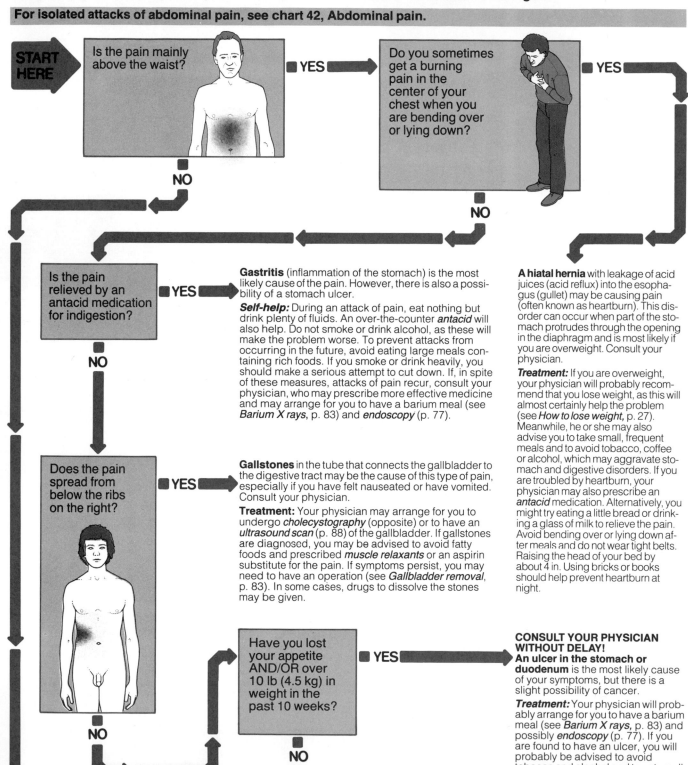

START HERE

Is the pain mainly above the waist?

YES →

Do you sometimes get a burning pain in the center of your chest when you are bending over or lying down?

YES →

↓ **NO**

↓ **NO**

Is the pain relieved by an antacid medication for indigestion?

YES →

Gastritis (inflammation of the stomach) is the most likely cause of the pain. However, there is also a possibility of a stomach ulcer.

Self-help: During an attack of pain, eat nothing but drink plenty of fluids. An over-the-counter *antacid* will also help. Do not smoke or drink alcohol, as these will make the problem worse. To prevent attacks from occurring in the future, avoid eating large meals containing rich foods. If you smoke or drink heavily, you should make a serious attempt to cut down. If, in spite of these measures, attacks of pain recur, consult your physician, who may prescribe more effective medicine and may arrange for you to have a barium meal (see *Barium X rays*, p. 83) and *endoscopy* (p. 77).

A hiatal hernia with leakage of acid juices (acid reflux) into the esophagus (gullet) may be causing pain (often known as heartburn). This disorder can occur when part of the stomach protrudes through the opening in the diaphragm and is most likely if you are overweight. Consult your physician.

Treatment: If you are overweight, your physician will probably recommend that you lose weight, as this will almost certainly help the problem (see *How to lose weight,* p. 27). Meanwhile, he or she may also advise you to take small, frequent meals and to avoid tobacco, coffee or alcohol, which may aggravate stomach and digestive disorders. If you are troubled by heartburn, your physician may also prescribe an *antacid* medication. Alternatively, you might try eating a little bread or drinking a glass of milk to relieve the pain. Avoid bending over or lying down after meals and do not wear tight belts. Raising the head of your bed by about 4 in. Using bricks or books should help prevent heartburn at night.

↓ **NO**

Does the pain spread from below the ribs on the right?

YES →

Gallstones in the tube that connects the gallbladder to the digestive tract may be the cause of this type of pain, especially if you have felt nauseated or have vomited. Consult your physician.

Treatment: Your physician may arrange for you to undergo *cholecystography* (opposite) or to have an *ultrasound scan* (p. 88) of the gallbladder. If gallstones are diagnosed, you may be advised to avoid fatty foods and prescribed *muscle relaxants* or an aspirin substitute for the pain. If symptoms persist, you may need to have an operation (see *Gallbladder removal*, p. 83). In some cases, drugs to dissolve the stones may be given.

↓ **NO**

Have you lost your appetite AND/OR over 10 lb (4.5 kg) in weight in the past 10 weeks?

YES →

CONSULT YOUR PHYSICIAN WITHOUT DELAY!
An ulcer in the stomach or duodenum is the most likely cause of your symptoms, but there is a slight possibility of cancer.

Treatment: Your physician will probably arrange for you to have a barium meal (see *Barium X rays,* p. 83) and possibly *endoscopy* (p. 77). If you are found to have an ulcer, you will probably be advised to avoid tobacco and alcohol and to eat small, frequent meals. Your physician will also prescribe an *antacid* or other medications to reduce the amount of acid in your stomach. Stomach cancer is usually treated surgically.

↓ **NO**

Go to next page

Continued from previous page

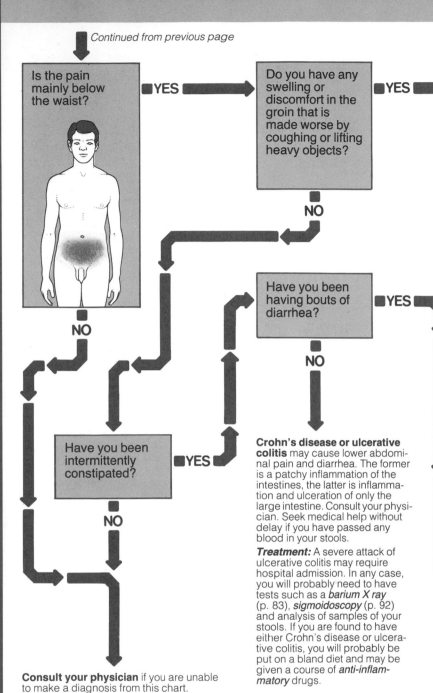

Is the pain mainly below the waist?

→ **YES** → **Do you have any swelling or discomfort in the groin that is made worse by coughing or lifting heavy objects?**

→ **YES** →

A hernia (see *What is a hernia?* below) may be the cause of such pain. Consult your physician.

Treatment: Your physician will examine you to confirm the diagnosis. If you have a hernia, it may be necessary for you to have a minor operation to repair the abdominal wall.

NO (from swelling question)

Have you been having bouts of diarrhea?

→ **YES** →

NO

Crohn's disease or ulcerative colitis may cause lower abdominal pain and diarrhea. The former is a patchy inflammation of the intestines, the latter is inflammation and ulceration of only the large intestine. Consult your physician. Seek medical help without delay if you have passed any blood in your stools.

Treatment: A severe attack of ulcerative colitis may require hospital admission. In any case, you will probably need to have tests such as a *barium X ray* (p. 83), *sigmoidoscopy* (p. 92) and analysis of samples of your stools. If you are found to have either Crohn's disease or ulcerative colitis, you will probably be put on a bland diet and may be given a course of *anti-inflammatory* drugs.

NO (from pain below waist)

Have you been intermittently constipated?

→ **YES** →

NO

Consult your physician if you are unable to make a diagnosis from this chart.

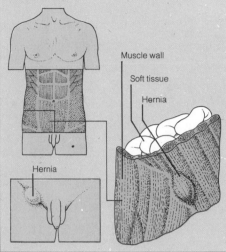

WHAT IS A HERNIA?

A hernia occurs when soft tissue in the abdomen bulges through a weak area in the abdominal wall. Hernias may occur in various places. In men, one of the most common sites is the groin, where the abdominal organs either push aside the weak muscles of the groin or protrude down the inguinal canal (the tube from which the testes descend before birth).

Muscle wall

Soft tissue

Hernia

Hernia

CONSULT YOUR PHYSICIAN WITHOUT DELAY!
Irritable colon (see below) or diverticular disease (in which swellings develop on the walls of the large intestine) may be the cause of your symptoms. However, the slight possibility of bowel cancer also needs to be ruled out.

Treatment: To make an exact diagnosis, your physician may need to arrange for tests such as a barium enema (see *Barium X rays,* p. 83) and *endoscopy* (p. 77). The long-term treatment for both irritable colon and diverticular disease is based on a high-fiber diet (p. 91). Your physician may also prescribe drugs to relieve your symptoms.

CHOLECYSTOGRAPHY

This is a special procedure for diagnosing disorders of the gallbladder and bile duct. A substance visible on X rays is taken as a tablet and photographed as it passes through the gallbladder and bile duct. The X-ray pictures produced are called cholecystograms.

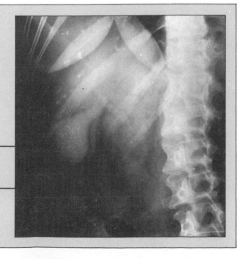

Gallbladder

Gallstones

A cholecystogram showing a gallbladder filled with gallstones.

IRRITABLE COLON

Many people who suffer from recurrent cramping pains in the lower abdomen with or without intermittent diarrhea and/or constipation have no serious underlying disorder and are diagnosed as having an irritable colon (or irritable bowel syndrome). It is thought that the disorder is caused by abnormally strong and irregular muscle contractions in the bowel. This may be due to sensitivity to the passage of matter through the intestines, but it may also be linked to psychological stress (see *What is stress?* p. 51). A large proportion of those with this complaint are anxious, and attacks seem to be made worse by worry. Most sufferers learn to live with the problem without specific treatment. A high-fiber diet (p. 91) often relieves the symptoms. Those who suffer from severe pain may be prescribed *antispasmodic* drugs.

44 Swollen abdomen

A generalized swelling over the whole abdomen (the area between the bottom of the rib cage and the groin) suggests that there is something wrong with your digestive organs. If your abdomen is painful as well as swollen, this is an emergency and you should seek medical advice immediately.

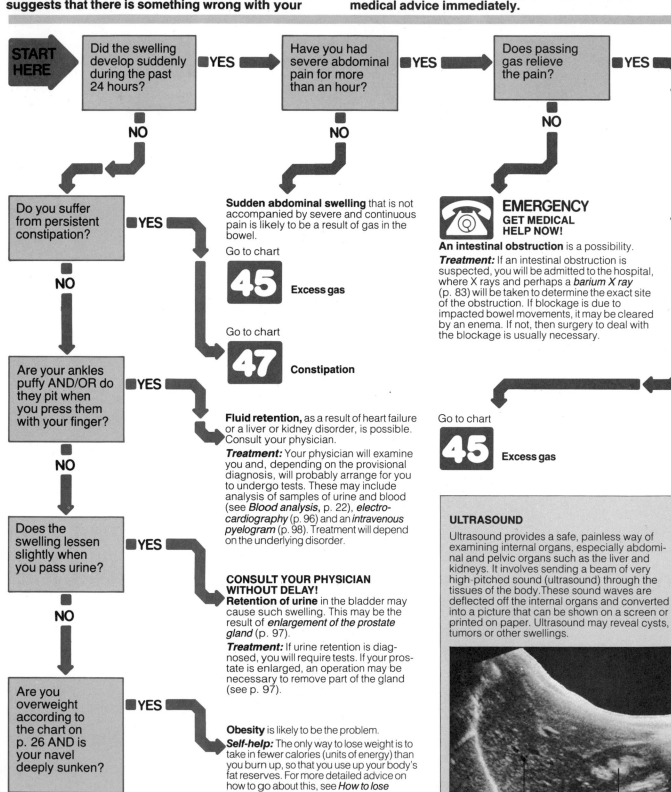

START HERE

Did the swelling develop suddenly during the past 24 hours?

→ **YES** → **Have you had severe abdominal pain for more than an hour?**

→ **YES** → **Does passing gas relieve the pain?**

→ **YES** →

NO ↓ (from first box)

NO ↓ (from second box)

NO ↓ (from third box)

Do you suffer from persistent constipation?

YES →

Sudden abdominal swelling that is not accompanied by severe and continuous pain is likely to be a result of gas in the bowel.

Go to chart

45 Excess gas

Go to chart

47 Constipation

NO ↓

Are your ankles puffy AND/OR do they pit when you press them with your finger?

YES →

Fluid retention, as a result of heart failure or a liver or kidney disorder, is possible. Consult your physician.

Treatment: Your physician will examine you and, depending on the provisional diagnosis, will probably arrange for you to undergo tests. These may include analysis of samples of urine and blood (see *Blood analysis*, p. 22), *electrocardiography* (p. 96) and an *intravenous pyelogram* (p. 98). Treatment will depend on the underlying disorder.

NO ↓

Does the swelling lessen slightly when you pass urine?

YES →

CONSULT YOUR PHYSICIAN WITHOUT DELAY!
Retention of urine in the bladder may cause such swelling. This may be the result of *enlargement of the prostate gland* (p. 97).

Treatment: If urine retention is diagnosed, you will require tests. If your prostate is enlarged, an operation may be necessary to remove part of the gland (see p. 97).

NO ↓

Are you overweight according to the chart on p. 26 AND is your navel deeply sunken?

YES →

Obesity is likely to be the problem.
Self-help: The only way to lose weight is to take in fewer calories (units of energy) than you burn up, so that you use up your body's fat reserves. For more detailed advice on how to go about this, see *How to lose weight,* p. 27.

NO ↓

Consult your physician if you are unable to make a diagnosis from this chart and your abdomen remains swollen for more than 48 hours.

EMERGENCY GET MEDICAL HELP NOW!

An intestinal obstruction is a possibility.
Treatment: If an intestinal obstruction is suspected, you will be admitted to the hospital, where X rays and perhaps a *barium X ray* (p. 83) will be taken to determine the exact site of the obstruction. If blockage is due to impacted bowel movements, it may be cleared by an enema. If not, then surgery to deal with the blockage is usually necessary.

Go to chart

45 Excess gas

ULTRASOUND

Ultrasound provides a safe, painless way of examining internal organs, especially abdominal and pelvic organs such as the liver and kidneys. It involves sending a beam of very high-pitched sound (ultrasound) through the tissues of the body. These sound waves are deflected off the internal organs and converted into a picture that can be shown on a screen or printed on paper. Ultrasound may reveal cysts, tumors or other swellings.

Liver   Kidney

This ultrasound scan shows a patient's healthy liver and kidney

45 Excess gas

Excess gas in the digestive system may cause an uncomfortable, distended feeling in the abdomen and may produce rumbling noises in the intestines. Expulsion of gas, either through the mouth or the anus, generally relieves these symptoms. Although it may be embarrassing, passing gas is rarely a sign of an under-

lying disease. In most cases, it is caused by swallowing air or by certain foods not being properly broken down by the digestive juices, leaving a residue that ferments, producing gas in the intestines. Different foods affect different people in different ways – though onions, cabbage and beans are common causes of gas.

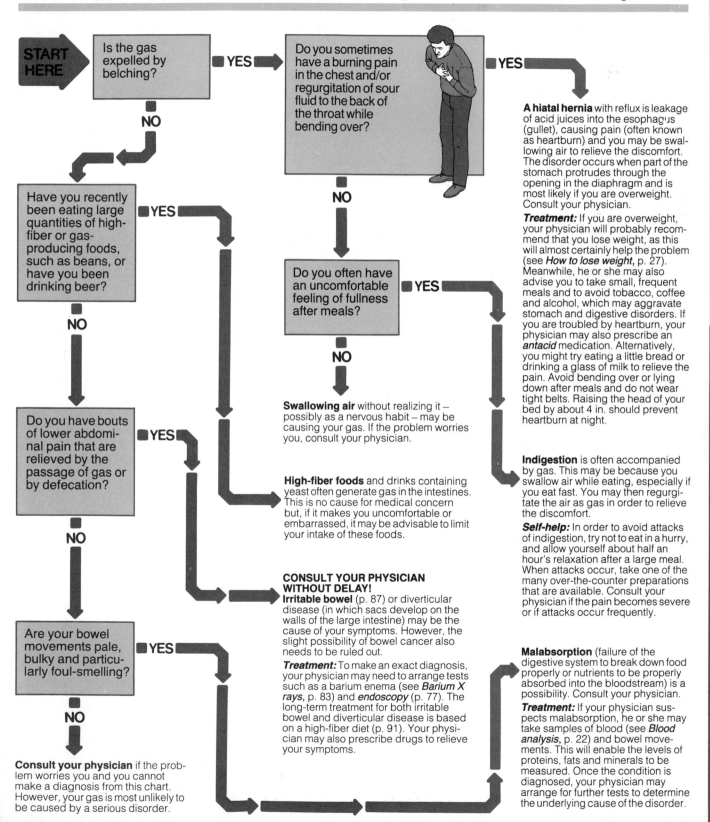

START HERE

Is the gas expelled by belching?
YES → Do you sometimes have a burning pain in the chest and/or regurgitation of sour fluid to the back of the throat while bending over? **YES** →

A hiatal hernia with reflux is leakage of acid juices into the esophagus (gullet), causing pain (often known as heartburn) and you may be swallowing air to relieve the discomfort. The disorder occurs when part of the stomach protrudes through the opening in the diaphragm and is most likely if you are overweight. Consult your physician.

Treatment: If you are overweight, your physician will probably recommend that you lose weight, as this will almost certainly help the problem (see *How to lose weight*, p. 27). Meanwhile, he or she may also advise you to take small, frequent meals and to avoid tobacco, coffee and alcohol, which may aggravate stomach and digestive disorders. If you are troubled by heartburn, your physician may also prescribe an *antacid* medication. Alternatively, you might try eating a little bread or drinking a glass of milk to relieve the pain. Avoid bending over or lying down after meals and do not wear tight belts. Raising the head of your bed by about 4 in. should prevent heartburn at night.

NO

Have you recently been eating large quantities of high-fiber or gas-producing foods, such as beans, or have you been drinking beer? **YES** →

NO

Do you have bouts of lower abdominal pain that are relieved by the passage of gas or by defecation? **YES** →

NO

Do you often have an uncomfortable feeling of fullness after meals? **YES** →

NO

Swallowing air without realizing it – possibly as a nervous habit – may be causing your gas. If the problem worries you, consult your physician.

High-fiber foods and drinks containing yeast often generate gas in the intestines. This is no cause for medical concern but, if it makes you uncomfortable or embarrassed, it may be advisable to limit your intake of these foods.

Indigestion is often accompanied by gas. This may be because you swallow air while eating, especially if you eat fast. You may then regurgitate the air as gas in order to relieve the discomfort.

Self-help: In order to avoid attacks of indigestion, try not to eat in a hurry, and allow yourself about half an hour's relaxation after a large meal. When attacks occur, take one of the many over-the-counter preparations that are available. Consult your physician if the pain becomes severe or if attacks occur frequently.

CONSULT YOUR PHYSICIAN WITHOUT DELAY!
Irritable bowel (p. 87) or diverticular disease (in which sacs develop on the walls of the large intestine) may be the cause of your symptoms. However, the slight possibility of bowel cancer also needs to be ruled out.

Treatment: To make an exact diagnosis, your physician may need to arrange tests such as a barium enema (see *Barium X rays*, p. 83) and *endoscopy* (p. 77). The long-term treatment for both irritable bowel and diverticular disease is based on a high-fiber diet (p. 91). Your physician may also prescribe drugs to relieve your symptoms.

Malabsorption (failure of the digestive system to break down food properly or nutrients to be properly absorbed into the bloodstream) is a possibility. Consult your physician.

Treatment: If your physician suspects malabsorption, he or she may take samples of blood (see *Blood analysis*, p. 22) and bowel movements. This will enable the levels of proteins, fats and minerals to be measured. Once the condition is diagnosed, your physician may arrange for further tests to determine the underlying cause of the disorder.

Are your bowel movements pale, bulky and particularly foul-smelling? **YES** →

NO

Consult your physician if the problem worries you and you cannot make a diagnosis from this chart. However, your gas is most unlikely to be caused by a serious disorder.

46 Diarrhea

Diarrhea is the passing of unusually loose and frequent bowel movements. It is rarely a dangerous symptom, but it may cause discomfort and is often accompanied by cramping pains in the lower abdomen. In this coun-

try, most attacks of diarrhea are the result of infections. No special treatment, other than ensuring that you drink plenty of fluids, is usually needed. However, if diarrhea persists, report it to your physician.

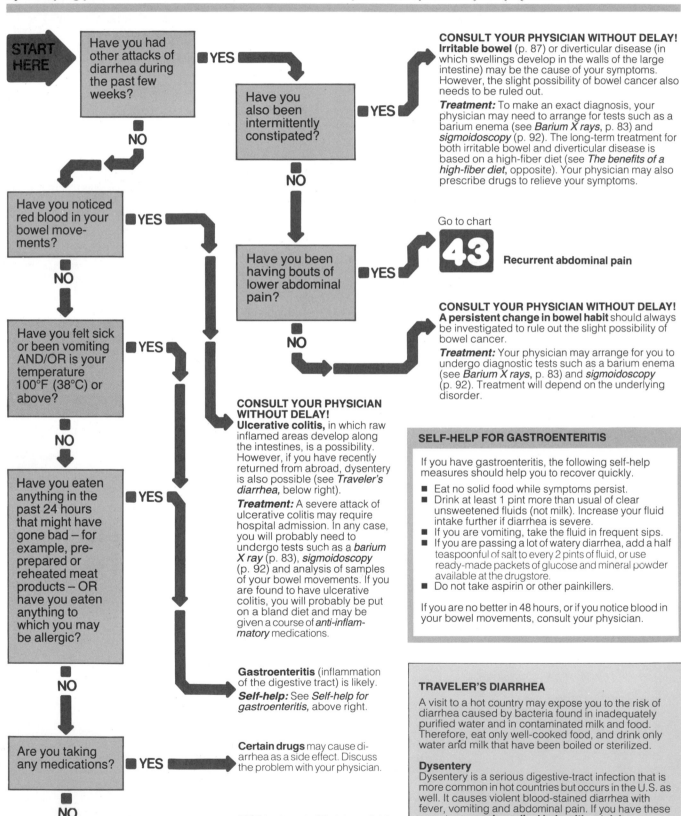

START HERE

Have you had other attacks of diarrhea during the past few weeks? — YES → **Have you also been intermittently constipated?** — YES →

NO ↓

Have you been having bouts of lower abdominal pain? — YES → Go to chart **43** **Recurrent abdominal pain**

CONSULT YOUR PHYSICIAN WITHOUT DELAY!
Irritable bowel (p. 87) or diverticular disease (in which swellings develop in the walls of the large intestine) may be the cause of your symptoms. However, the slight possibility of bowel cancer also needs to be ruled out.

Treatment: To make an exact diagnosis, your physician may need to arrange for tests such as a barium enema (see *Barium X rays*, p. 83) and *sigmoidoscopy* (p. 92). The long-term treatment for both irritable bowel and diverticular disease is based on a high-fiber diet (see *The benefits of a high-fiber diet*, opposite). Your physician may also prescribe drugs to relieve your symptoms.

CONSULT YOUR PHYSICIAN WITHOUT DELAY!
A persistent change in bowel habit should always be investigated to rule out the slight possibility of bowel cancer.

Treatment: Your physician may arrange for you to undergo diagnostic tests such as a barium enema (see *Barium X rays*, p. 83) and *sigmoidoscopy* (p. 92). Treatment will depend on the underlying disorder.

Have you noticed red blood in your bowel movements? — YES →

NO ↓

Have you felt sick or been vomiting AND/OR is your temperature 100°F (38°C) or above? — YES →

NO ↓

Have you eaten anything in the past 24 hours that might have gone bad – for example, pre-prepared or reheated meat products – OR have you eaten anything to which you may be allergic? — YES →

NO ↓

CONSULT YOUR PHYSICIAN WITHOUT DELAY!
Ulcerative colitis, in which raw inflamed areas develop along the intestines, is a possibility. However, if you have recently returned from abroad, dysentery is also possible (see *Traveler's diarrhea,* below right).

Treatment: A severe attack of ulcerative colitis may require hospital admission. In any case, you will probably need to undergo tests such as a *barium X ray* (p. 83), *sigmoidoscopy* (p. 92) and analysis of samples of your bowel movements. If you are found to have ulcerative colitis, you will probably be put on a bland diet and may be given a course of *anti-inflammatory* medications.

Gastroenteritis (inflammation of the digestive tract) is likely.
Self-help: See *Self-help for gastroenteritis,* above right.

Are you taking any medications? — YES → **Certain drugs** may cause diarrhea as a side effect. Discuss the problem with your physician.

NO ↓

Mild gastroenteritis (above right) is the most likely cause of diarrhea with no other symptoms.

SELF-HELP FOR GASTROENTERITIS

If you have gastroenteritis, the following self-help measures should help you to recover quickly.

- Eat no solid food while symptoms persist.
- Drink at least 1 pint more than usual of clear unsweetened fluids (not milk). Increase your fluid intake further if diarrhea is severe.
- If you are vomiting, take the fluid in frequent sips.
- If you are passing a lot of watery diarrhea, add a half teaspoonful of salt to every 2 pints of fluid, or use ready-made packets of glucose and mineral powder available at the drugstore.
- Do not take aspirin or other painkillers.

If you are no better in 48 hours, or if you notice blood in your bowel movements, consult your physician.

TRAVELER'S DIARRHEA

A visit to a hot country may expose you to the risk of diarrhea caused by bacteria found in inadequately purified water and in contaminated milk and food. Therefore, eat only well-cooked food, and drink only water and milk that have been boiled or sterilized.

Dysentery
Dysentery is a serious digestive-tract infection that is more common in hot countries but occurs in the U.S. as well. It causes violent blood-stained diarrhea with fever, vomiting and abdominal pain. If you have these symptoms, **seek medical help without delay.**

47 Constipation

Bowel habits vary between persons – some have one or more bowel movements a day, while others regularly move their bowels only once or twice a week. These variations are normal, especially if this is your pattern. **Constipation occurs when stools are hard, difficult to pass or more infrequently passed than usual.**

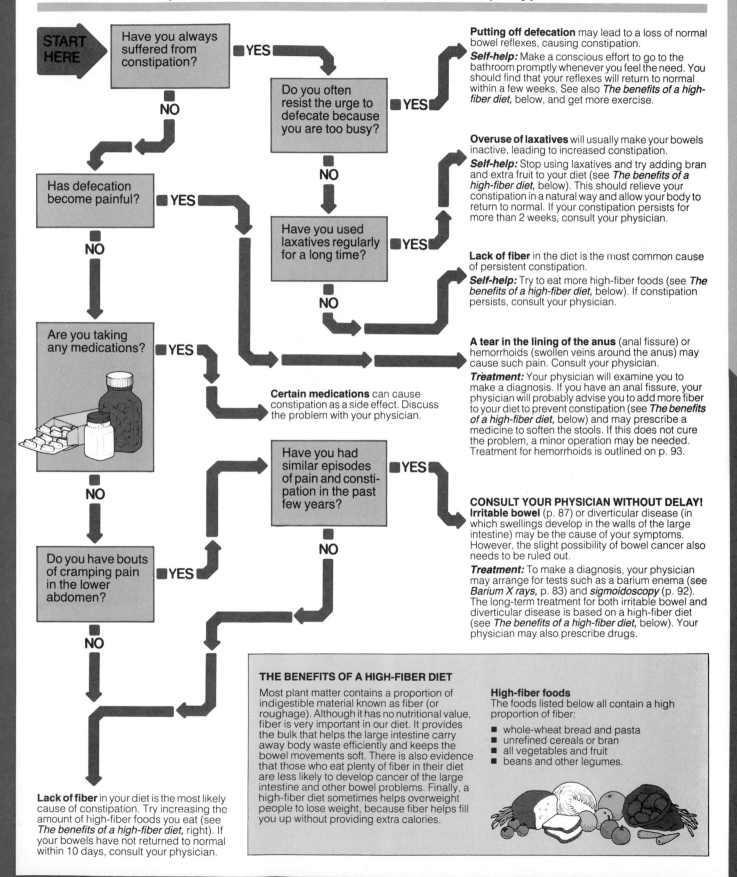

START HERE

Have you always suffered from constipation?

NO

Has defecation become painful?

NO

Are you taking any medications?

NO

Do you have bouts of cramping pain in the lower abdomen?

NO

YES → **Do you often resist the urge to defecate because you are too busy?**

NO

Have you used laxatives regularly for a long time?

NO

YES → **Have you had similar episodes of pain and constipation in the past few years?**

NO

YES

YES

YES

YES

Putting off defecation may lead to a loss of normal bowel reflexes, causing constipation.
Self-help: Make a conscious effort to go to the bathroom promptly whenever you feel the need. You should find that your reflexes will return to normal within a few weeks. See also *The benefits of a high-fiber diet,* below, and get more exercise.

Overuse of laxatives will usually make your bowels inactive, leading to increased constipation.
Self-help: Stop using laxatives and try adding bran and extra fruit to your diet (see *The benefits of a high-fiber diet,* below). This should relieve your constipation in a natural way and allow your body to return to normal. If your constipation persists for more than 2 weeks, consult your physician.

Lack of fiber in the diet is the most common cause of persistent constipation.
Self-help: Try to eat more high-fiber foods (see *The benefits of a high-fiber diet,* below). If constipation persists, consult your physician.

Certain medications can cause constipation as a side effect. Discuss the problem with your physician.

A tear in the lining of the anus (anal fissure) or hemorrhoids (swollen veins around the anus) may cause such pain. Consult your physician.
Treatment: Your physician will examine you to make a diagnosis. If you have an anal fissure, your physician will probably advise you to add more fiber to your diet to prevent constipation (see *The benefits of a high-fiber diet,* below) and may prescribe a medicine to soften the stools. If this does not cure the problem, a minor operation may be needed. Treatment for hemorrhoids is outlined on p. 93.

CONSULT YOUR PHYSICIAN WITHOUT DELAY!
Irritable bowel (p. 87) or diverticular disease (in which swellings develop in the walls of the large intestine) may be the cause of your symptoms. However, the slight possibility of bowel cancer also needs to be ruled out.
Treatment: To make a diagnosis, your physician may arrange for tests such as a barium enema (see *Barium X rays,* p. 83) and *sigmoidoscopy* (p. 92). The long-term treatment for both irritable bowel and diverticular disease is based on a high-fiber diet (see *The benefits of a high-fiber diet,* below). Your physician may also prescribe drugs.

Lack of fiber in your diet is the most likely cause of constipation. Try increasing the amount of high-fiber foods you eat (see *The benefits of a high-fiber diet,* right). If your bowels have not returned to normal within 10 days, consult your physician.

THE BENEFITS OF A HIGH-FIBER DIET

Most plant matter contains a proportion of indigestible material known as fiber (or roughage). Although it has no nutritional value, fiber is very important in our diet. It provides the bulk that helps the large intestine carry away body waste efficiently and keeps the bowel movements soft. There is also evidence that those who eat plenty of fiber in their diet are less likely to develop cancer of the large intestine and other bowel problems. Finally, a high-fiber diet sometimes helps overweight people to lose weight, because fiber helps fill you up without providing extra calories.

High-fiber foods
The foods listed below all contain a high proportion of fiber:

- whole-wheat bread and pasta
- unrefined cereals or bran
- all vegetables and fruit
- beans and other legumes.

48 Abnormal-looking bowel movements

Most minor changes in the color, shape and consistency of your bowel movements are due to a recent change in diet. But if the stools are black or significantly lighter than usual, or if they are streaked with blood, this may indicate something more serious and you should consult your physician.

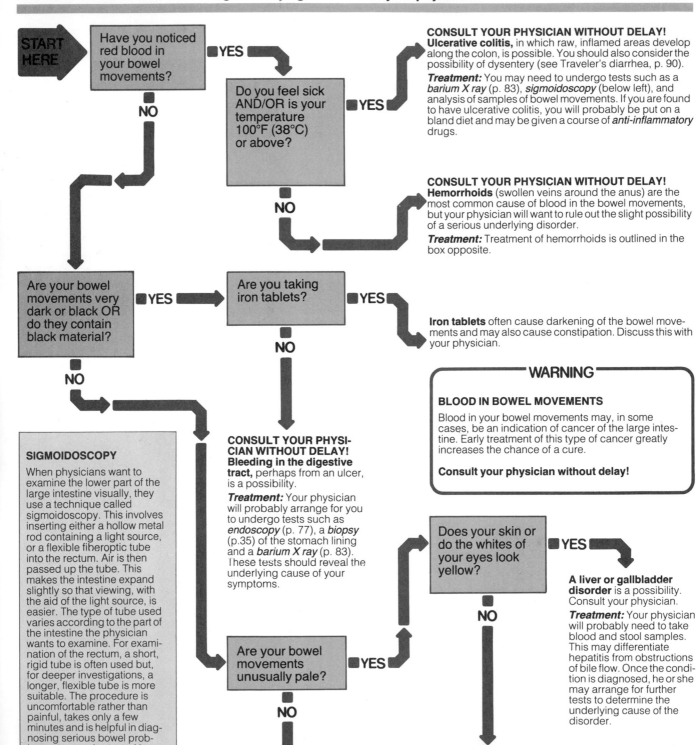

START HERE

Have you noticed red blood in your bowel movements?

YES → **Do you feel sick AND/OR is your temperature 100°F (38°C) or above?**

YES → **CONSULT YOUR PHYSICIAN WITHOUT DELAY!**
Ulcerative colitis, in which raw, inflamed areas develop along the colon, is possible. You should also consider the possibility of dysentery (see Traveler's diarrhea, p. 90).

Treatment: You may need to undergo tests such as a *barium X ray* (p. 83), *sigmoidoscopy* (below left), and analysis of samples of bowel movements. If you are found to have ulcerative colitis, you will probably be put on a bland diet and may be given a course of *anti-inflammatory* drugs.

(from "Do you feel sick...") **NO** →

CONSULT YOUR PHYSICIAN WITHOUT DELAY!
Hemorrhoids (swollen veins around the anus) are the most common cause of blood in the bowel movements, but your physician will want to rule out the slight possibility of a serious underlying disorder.

Treatment: Treatment of hemorrhoids is outlined in the box opposite.

(from "Have you noticed red blood...") **NO** →

Are your bowel movements very dark or black OR do they contain black material?

YES → **Are you taking iron tablets?**

YES → **Iron tablets** often cause darkening of the bowel movements and may also cause constipation. Discuss this with your physician.

(from "Are your bowel movements very dark...") **NO** →

SIGMOIDOSCOPY

When physicians want to examine the lower part of the large intestine visually, they use a technique called sigmoidoscopy. This involves inserting either a hollow metal rod containing a light source, or a flexible fiberoptic tube into the rectum. Air is then passed up the tube. This makes the intestine expand slightly so that viewing, with the aid of the light source, is easier. The type of tube used varies according to the part of the intestine the physician wants to examine. For examination of the rectum, a short, rigid tube is often used but, for deeper investigations, a longer, flexible tube is more suitable. The procedure is uncomfortable rather than painful, takes only a few minutes and is helpful in diagnosing serious bowel problems at an early stage. Your physician may suggest that you have an enema before the investigation.

(from "Are you taking iron tablets?") **NO** →

CONSULT YOUR PHYSICIAN WITHOUT DELAY!
Bleeding in the digestive tract, perhaps from an ulcer, is a possibility.

Treatment: Your physician will probably arrange for you to undergo tests such as *endoscopy* (p. 77), a *biopsy* (p.35) of the stomach lining and a *barium X ray* (p. 83). These tests should reveal the underlying cause of your symptoms.

WARNING

BLOOD IN BOWEL MOVEMENTS

Blood in your bowel movements may, in some cases, be an indication of cancer of the large intestine. Early treatment of this type of cancer greatly increases the chance of a cure.

Consult your physician without delay!

Does your skin or do the whites of your eyes look yellow?

YES → **A liver or gallbladder disorder** is a possibility. Consult your physician.

Treatment: Your physician will probably need to take blood and stool samples. This may differentiate hepatitis from obstructions of bile flow. Once the condition is diagnosed, he or she may arrange for further tests to determine the underlying cause of the disorder.

Are your bowel movements unusually pale?

YES → (to "Does your skin...")

(from "Does your skin...") **NO** →

Malabsorption exists when your digestive system fails to break down food properly or its nutrients fail to be properly absorbed into the bloodstream. However, pale bowel movements may also occur normally for a few days after a bout of diarrhea and/or vomiting. Consult your physician.

Treatment: If malabsorption is suspected, your physician may ask for samples of blood (see *Blood analysis,* p. 22) and bowel movements. This will enable the levels of proteins, fats and minerals to be measured. Once the condition is diagnosed, he or she may arrange for further tests to determine the underlying cause of the disorder.

(from "Are your bowel movements unusually pale?") **NO** →

Consult your physician if you are unable to make a diagnosis from this chart.

49 Anal problems

The anus is a short tube that leads from the last part of the digestive tract (rectum) to the outside. The anus is closed by a ring of muscles (or sphincter). The most common disorder affecting this area is swelling of the veins around the anus (hemorrhoids). This is often related to painful constipation.

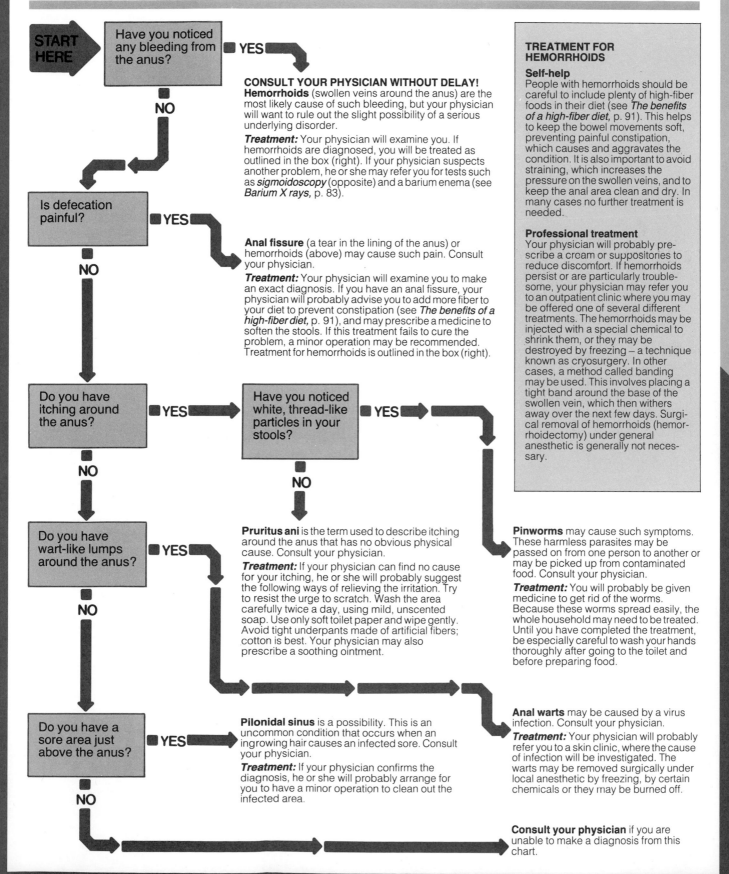

START HERE

Have you noticed any bleeding from the anus?

YES →

CONSULT YOUR PHYSICIAN WITHOUT DELAY!
Hemorrhoids (swollen veins around the anus) are the most likely cause of such bleeding, but your physician will want to rule out the slight possibility of a serious underlying disorder.

Treatment: Your physician will examine you. If hemorrhoids are diagnosed, you will be treated as outlined in the box (right). If your physician suspects another problem, he or she may refer you for tests such as *sigmoidoscopy* (opposite) and a barium enema (see *Barium X rays,* p. 83).

NO ↓

Is defecation painful?

YES →

Anal fissure (a tear in the lining of the anus) or hemorrhoids (above) may cause such pain. Consult your physician.

Treatment: Your physician will examine you to make an exact diagnosis. If you have an anal fissure, your physician will probably advise you to add more fiber to your diet to prevent constipation (see *The benefits of a high-fiber diet,* p. 91), and may prescribe a medicine to soften the stools. If this treatment fails to cure the problem, a minor operation may be recommended. Treatment for hemorrhoids is outlined in the box (right).

NO ↓

Do you have itching around the anus?

YES →

Have you noticed white, thread-like particles in your stools?

YES →

NO ↓

Pruritus ani is the term used to describe itching around the anus that has no obvious physical cause. Consult your physician.

Treatment: If your physician can find no cause for your itching, he or she will probably suggest the following ways of relieving the irritation. Try to resist the urge to scratch. Wash the area carefully twice a day, using mild, unscented soap. Use only soft toilet paper and wipe gently. Avoid tight underpants made of artificial fibers; cotton is best. Your physician may also prescribe a soothing ointment.

NO ↓

Do you have wart-like lumps around the anus?

YES →

NO ↓

Do you have a sore area just above the anus?

YES →

Pilonidal sinus is a possibility. This is an uncommon condition that occurs when an ingrowing hair causes an infected sore. Consult your physician.

Treatment: If your physician confirms the diagnosis, he or she will probably arrange for you to have a minor operation to clean out the infected area.

NO ↓

Pinworms may cause such symptoms. These harmless parasites may be passed on from one person to another or may be picked up from contaminated food. Consult your physician.

Treatment: You will probably be given medicine to get rid of the worms. Because these worms spread easily, the whole household may need to be treated. Until you have completed the treatment, be especially careful to wash your hands thoroughly after going to the toilet and before preparing food.

Anal warts may be caused by a virus infection. Consult your physician.

Treatment: Your physician will probably refer you to a skin clinic, where the cause of infection will be investigated. The warts may be removed surgically under local anesthetic by freezing, by certain chemicals or they may be burned off.

Consult your physician if you are unable to make a diagnosis from this chart.

TREATMENT FOR HEMORRHOIDS

Self-help
People with hemorrhoids should be careful to include plenty of high-fiber foods in their diet (see *The benefits of a high-fiber diet,* p. 91). This helps to keep the bowel movements soft, preventing painful constipation, which causes and aggravates the condition. It is also important to avoid straining, which increases the pressure on the swollen veins, and to keep the anal area clean and dry. In many cases no further treatment is needed.

Professional treatment
Your physician will probably prescribe a cream or suppositories to reduce discomfort. If hemorrhoids persist or are particularly troublesome, your physician may refer you to an outpatient clinic where you may be offered one of several different treatments. The hemorrhoids may be injected with a special chemical to shrink them, or they may be destroyed by freezing – a technique known as cryosurgery. In other cases, a method called banding may be used. This involves placing a tight band around the base of the swollen vein, which then withers away over the next few days. Surgical removal of hemorrhoids (hemorrhoidectomy) under general anesthetic is generally not necessary.

50 Chest pain

Pain in the chest (anywhere between the neck and the bottom of the rib cage) may be dull and persistent, sharp and stabbing, or crushing. Although it may be alarming, most chest pain does not have a serious cause. However, severe, crushing, central chest pain, or pain that is associated with breathlessness or irregular heartbeat, may be a sign of a serious disorder of the heart or lungs and may warrant emergency treatment.

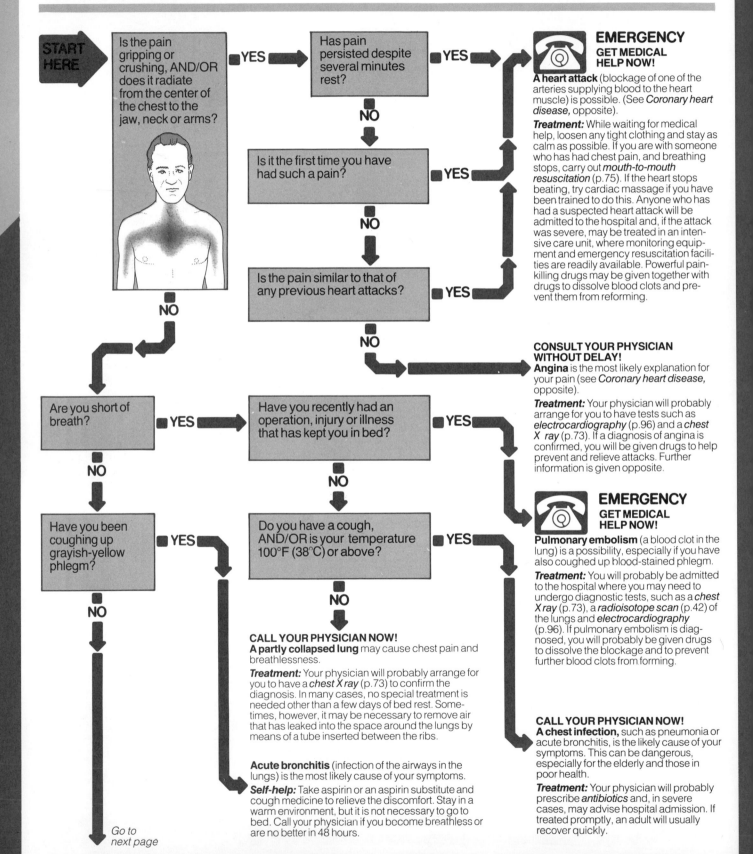

START HERE

Is the pain gripping or crushing, AND/OR does it radiate from the center of the chest to the jaw, neck or arms?

YES → **Has pain persisted despite several minutes rest?**

YES → **EMERGENCY GET MEDICAL HELP NOW!**

NO ↓

Is it the first time you have had such a pain?

YES → EMERGENCY

NO ↓

Is the pain similar to that of any previous heart attacks?

YES → EMERGENCY

NO ↓

EMERGENCY
GET MEDICAL HELP NOW!

A heart attack (blockage of one of the arteries supplying blood to the heart muscle) is possible. (See *Coronary heart disease,* opposite).

Treatment: While waiting for medical help, loosen any tight clothing and stay as calm as possible. If you are with someone who has had chest pain, and breathing stops, carry out *mouth-to-mouth resuscitation* (p.75). If the heart stops beating, try cardiac massage if you have been trained to do this. Anyone who has had a suspected heart attack will be admitted to the hospital and, if the attack was severe, may be treated in an intensive care unit, where monitoring equipment and emergency resuscitation facilities are readily available. Powerful pain-killing drugs may be given together with drugs to dissolve blood clots and prevent them from reforming.

CONSULT YOUR PHYSICIAN WITHOUT DELAY!

Angina is the most likely explanation for your pain (see *Coronary heart disease,* opposite).

Treatment: Your physician will probably arrange for you to have tests such as *electrocardiography* (p.96) and a *chest X ray* (p.73). If a diagnosis of angina is confirmed, you will be given drugs to help prevent and relieve attacks. Further information is given opposite.

Is the pain gripping... NO ↓

Are you short of breath?

YES → **Have you recently had an operation, injury or illness that has kept you in bed?**

YES → EMERGENCY

NO ↓

Have you been coughing up grayish-yellow phlegm?

YES → ↓

NO ↓

Do you have a cough, AND/OR is your temperature 100°F (38°C) or above?

YES → CALL YOUR PHYSICIAN NOW!

NO ↓

CALL YOUR PHYSICIAN NOW!
A partly collapsed lung may cause chest pain and breathlessness.

Treatment: Your physician will probably arrange for you to have a *chest X ray* (p.73) to confirm the diagnosis. In many cases, no special treatment is needed other than a few days of bed rest. Sometimes, however, it may be necessary to remove air that has leaked into the space around the lungs by means of a tube inserted between the ribs.

Acute bronchitis (infection of the airways in the lungs) is the most likely cause of your symptoms.

Self-help: Take aspirin or an aspirin substitute and cough medicine to relieve the discomfort. Stay in a warm environment, but it is not necessary to go to bed. Call your physician if you become breathless or are no better in 48 hours.

EMERGENCY
GET MEDICAL HELP NOW!

Pulmonary embolism (a blood clot in the lung) is a possibility, especially if you have also coughed up blood-stained phlegm.

Treatment: You will probably be admitted to the hospital where you may need to undergo diagnostic tests, such as a *chest X ray* (p.73), a *radioisotope scan* (p.42) of the lungs and *electrocardiography* (p.96). If pulmonary embolism is diagnosed, you will probably be given drugs to dissolve the blockage and to prevent further blood clots from forming.

CALL YOUR PHYSICIAN NOW!
A chest infection, such as pneumonia or acute bronchitis, is the likely cause of your symptoms. This can be dangerous, especially for the elderly and those in poor health.

Treatment: Your physician will probably prescribe *antibiotics* and, in severe cases, may advise hospital admission. If treated promptly, an adult will usually recover quickly.

Go to next page

Continued from previous page

Is there a burning pain in the center of the chest that gets worse when you bend over or lie down?

YES

A hiatal hernia may accompany leakage of acid juices (reflux) into the esophagus, causing pain (heartburn). The disorder occurs when part of the stomach protrudes through the opening in the diaphragm and is more likely if you are overweight. However, reflux may occur in the absence of hiatal hernia. Consult your physician.
Treatment: See *Hiatal hernia,* p. 86.

NO

Do you have a pain in the middle of the chest that came on soon after eating?

YES

Indigestion is the most likely explanation for such pain. This may occur as a result of overeating or tension.
Self-help: In order to avoid attacks of indigestion, try not to eat in a hurry and allow yourself about half an hour's relaxation after a large meal. When attacks occur, take one of the many over-the-counter preparations that are available. Consult your physician if pain becomes severe, or if attacks occur frequently.

NO

Is the pain on one side only?

YES

NO

Consult your physician without delay if you are unable to make a diagnosis from this chart.

Have you recently had a chest injury or a severe cough?

YES

NO

Is the painful region tender to the touch?

YES

A pulled muscle or injury to the ligaments and cartilages of the rib cage are the most likely causes of your pain.
Self-help: Try not to strain the muscle further while you are feeling pain. A painkiller, such as aspirin or an aspirin substitute, will give relief, but, if pain persists for more than 48 hours, consult your physician, who may arrange for you to have a *chest X ray* (p.73) to rule out the possibility of a broken rib.

NO

Do you have a burning pain in the skin that is unaffected by breathing?

YES

Shingles, a virus infection of the nerves, is a possibility. The appearance of a blistery rash along the site of the pain a few days after the onset of pain will confirm the diagnosis. Consult your physician.
Treatment: Your physician will probably prescribe a painkiller and a soothing ointment to put on the skin. He or she may also prescribe an *antiviral* agent to hasten healing.

NO

Consult your physician without delay if you are unable to make a diagnosis from this chart.

CORONARY HEART DISEASE

Coronary heart disease occurs when fatty deposits, or plaques, called atheroma, build up on the inside walls of the arteries that supply oxygenated blood to the heart muscle. This causes them to become narrowed and disturbs the flow of blood.

Coronary heart disease may cause chest pain (angina). This can occur after exertion or emotional stress, when the increased oxygen needs of the heart cannot be supplied through the narrowed coronary arteries. However, many people with coronary heart disease have no symptoms. Often their first indication of the disease is when they experience a heart attack, which occurs when a blood clot or buildup of atheroma blocks a coronary artery, cutting off the blood supply to part of the heart muscle. This can be fatal and, even if it is not, usually results in some permanent damage to the heart muscle.

What is the treatment?
If you are found to have coronary heart disease, you will probably be advised to change any aspects of your life-style that seem to be contributing to the disease (see *Preventing coronary heart disease,* right). You will probably be given medication to reduce the likelihood of angina attacks and others to take if attacks do occur. If you are found to have high blood pressure, this may also need drug treatment.

Coronary artery bypass surgery
If your coronary arteries are found to be dangerously narrowed, you may be advised to have an operation in which the diseased sections of the coronary arteries are bypassed using healthy veins from the leg or an artery in the chest wall. This is a major operation, but the prospects for an active life and relief of chest pain are good.

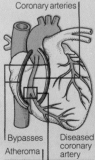

Coronary arteries

Bypasses | Diseased coronary artery
Atheroma

If surgery is necessary, the diseased sections of the coronary arteries containing atheroma are bypassed, usually with multiple bypass sections.

Preventing coronary heart disease
There are many factors that are known to increase the risk of developing coronary heart disease – notably, the tendency for the disease to run in families. But anyone who has a family history of heart disease can reduce the risk of developing serious problems by avoiding the factors listed below.

- **Smoking** Smokers are at least twice as likely to die of a heart attack than nonsmokers. This is because substances in tobacco smoke increase the level of atheroma-forming fats in the bloodstream.

- **Obesity** Overweight people tend to eat higher-than-average amounts of fat, increasing the risk of atheroma buildup. Carrying too much weight places an increased strain on the heart, making it less able to withstand any restriction of its blood supply.

- **Too much fat in the diet** The tendency for atheroma to form in the arteries seems to be related to the level of certain types of fat in the bloodstream, which in turn is related partly to heredity and partly to the amount of fat in the diet. Cutting down on all types of fat should help to reduce your risk of developing coronary heart disease.

- **Lack of exercise** Regular strenuous exercise increases the efficiency of the heart, so that it needs less oxygen to function well. If you gradually increase your physical fitness, your heart will be under less strain should its blood supply be reduced by coronary heart disease.

51 Palpitations

Palpitations is a term used to describe unusually rapid, strong or irregular beating of the heart. It is normal for the heart rate to speed up during strenuous exercise and to feel your heart "thumping" for some minutes after. This is no cause for concern. Consult this chart if you have palpitations unconnected with physical exertion. In most cases such palpitations are caused by consumption of nicotine or caffeine, or by anxiety. However, in a small proportion of cases, they are a symptom of an underlying illness. Palpitations that recur on several days or that are connected with pain or breathlessness should always be brought to your physician's attention.

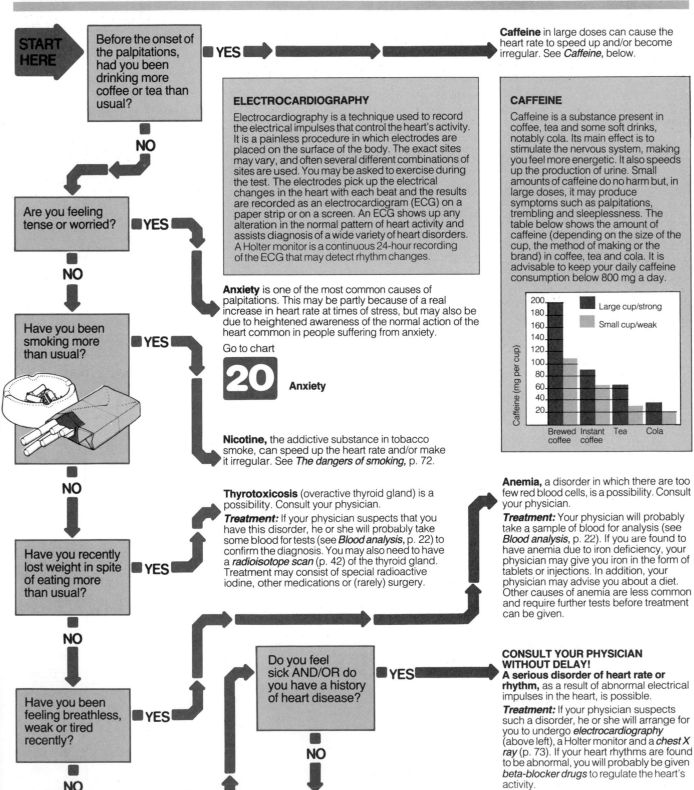

START HERE

Before the onset of the palpitations, had you been drinking more coffee or tea than usual?

YES → **Caffeine** in large doses can cause the heart rate to speed up and/or become irregular. See *Caffeine*, below.

NO

Are you feeling tense or worried?

YES → **Anxiety** is one of the most common causes of palpitations. This may be partly because of a real increase in heart rate at times of stress, but may also be due to heightened awareness of the normal action of the heart common in people suffering from anxiety.

Go to chart

20 Anxiety

NO

Have you been smoking more than usual?

YES → **Nicotine,** the addictive substance in tobacco smoke, can speed up the heart rate and/or make it irregular. See *The dangers of smoking,* p. 72.

NO

Have you recently lost weight in spite of eating more than usual?

YES → **Thyrotoxicosis** (overactive thyroid gland) is a possibility. Consult your physician.

Treatment: If your physician suspects that you have this disorder, he or she will probably take some blood for tests (see *Blood analysis*, p. 22) to confirm the diagnosis. You may also need to have a *radioisotope scan* (p. 42) of the thyroid gland. Treatment may consist of special radioactive iodine, other medications or (rarely) surgery.

NO

Have you been feeling breathless, weak or tired recently?

YES → **Anemia,** a disorder in which there are too few red blood cells, is a possibility. Consult your physician.

Treatment: Your physician will probably take a sample of blood for analysis (see *Blood analysis*, p. 22). If you are found to have anemia due to iron deficiency, your physician may give you iron in the form of tablets or injections. In addition, your physician may advise you about a diet. Other causes of anemia are less common and require further tests before treatment can be given.

NO

Do you feel sick AND/OR do you have a history of heart disease?

YES → **CONSULT YOUR PHYSICIAN WITHOUT DELAY!**
A serious disorder of heart rate or rhythm, as a result of abnormal electrical impulses in the heart, is possible.

Treatment: If your physician suspects such a disorder, he or she will arrange for you to undergo *electrocardiography* (above left), a Holter monitor and a *chest X ray* (p. 73). If your heart rhythms are found to be abnormal, you will probably be given *beta-blocker drugs* to regulate the heart's activity.

NO

Consult your physician if you are unable to make a diagnosis from this chart.

ELECTROCARDIOGRAPHY

Electrocardiography is a technique used to record the electrical impulses that control the heart's activity. It is a painless procedure in which electrodes are placed on the surface of the body. The exact sites may vary, and often several different combinations of sites are used. You may be asked to exercise during the test. The electrodes pick up the electrical changes in the heart with each beat and the results are recorded as an electrocardiogram (ECG) on a paper strip or on a screen. An ECG shows up any alteration in the normal pattern of heart activity and assists diagnosis of a wide variety of heart disorders. A Holter monitor is a continuous 24-hour recording of the ECG that may detect rhythm changes.

CAFFEINE

Caffeine is a substance present in coffee, tea and some soft drinks, notably cola. Its main effect is to stimulate the nervous system, making you feel more energetic. It also speeds up the production of urine. Small amounts of caffeine do no harm but, in large doses, it may produce symptoms such as palpitations, trembling and sleeplessness. The table below shows the amount of caffeine (depending on the size of the cup, the method of making or the brand) in coffee, tea and cola. It is advisable to keep your daily caffeine consumption below 800 mg a day.

Caffeine (mg per cup) — axis marks: 20, 40, 60, 80, 100, 120, 140, 160, 180, 200

■ Large cup/strong
□ Small cup/weak

Categories: Brewed coffee, Instant coffee, Tea, Cola

52 General urinary problems

Consult this chart if you notice a change in your urinary habits – for instance, a difference in the number of times you pass urine daily, or if you have difficulty passing or controlling your passage of urine.

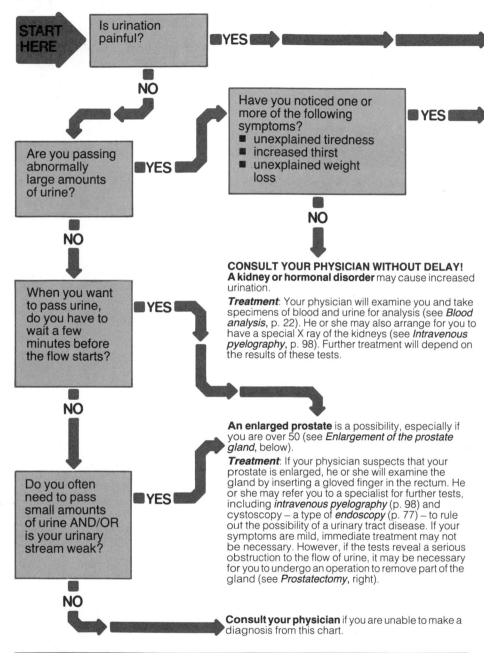

START HERE

Is urination painful?

YES ➡ Go to chart **53** Painful urination

NO

Are you passing abnormally large amounts of urine?

YES ➡ **Have you noticed one or more of the following symptoms?**
- unexplained tiredness
- increased thirst
- unexplained weight loss

YES ➡ **Diabetes mellitus** is a possibility. This disorder is caused by insufficient production of the hormone insulin. Consult your physician.

Treatment: If tests on blood (see *Blood analysis*, p. 22) and urine confirm the diagnosis, you may need treatment with drugs or with regular injections of insulin. Your physician will also advise you on diet.

NO

NO (from Have you noticed symptoms)

CONSULT YOUR PHYSICIAN WITHOUT DELAY!
A kidney or hormonal disorder may cause increased urination.

Treatment: Your physician will examine you and take specimens of blood and urine for analysis (see *Blood analysis*, p. 22). He or she may also arrange for you to have a special X ray of the kidneys (see *Intravenous pyelography*, p. 98). Further treatment will depend on the results of these tests.

When you want to pass urine, do you have to wait a few minutes before the flow starts?

YES ➡

NO

An enlarged prostate is a possibility, especially if you are over 50 (see *Enlargement of the prostate gland*, below).

Treatment: If your physician suspects that your prostate is enlarged, he or she will examine the gland by inserting a gloved finger in the rectum. He or she may refer you to a specialist for further tests, including *intravenous pyelography* (p. 98) and cystoscopy – a type of *endoscopy* (p. 77) – to rule out the possibility of a urinary tract disease. If your symptoms are mild, immediate treatment may not be necessary. However, if the tests reveal a serious obstruction to the flow of urine, it may be necessary for you to undergo an operation to remove part of the gland (see *Prostatectomy*, right).

Do you often need to pass small amounts of urine AND/OR is your urinary stream weak?

YES ➡

NO

Consult your physician if you are unable to make a diagnosis from this chart.

WARNING

INABILITY TO PASS URINE

If you find that you are unable to pass any urine, even though you feel the urge to urinate, you may have a blocked urethra. This requires urgent medical attention to prevent damage to the bladder and kidneys. Try taking a warm bath, which may enable you to pass some urine.

SUDDEN LOSS OF BLADDER CONTROL

Sudden inability to control urination may be a sign of damage to the spinal cord or nervous system, especially if you have recently had a back injury or have experienced weakness in your legs.

Seek medical help at once!

PROSTATECTOMY

When the prostate gland becomes so enlarged that it seriously interferes with the flow of urine, an operation to remove part or all of the gland is usually necessary. This is known as prostatectomy. There are two main alternative types of operation available. The choice of method depends on the details of the case. Both methods successfully relieve urinary symptoms of an enlarged prostate, but occasionally impotence or sterility may result. Your physician will discuss these risks with you. Both methods require a general anesthetic.

Traditional surgery
In a traditional prostatectomy, access to the gland is gained through an incision in the lower abdomen. The surgeon can then remove tissue from the gland as necessary.

Transurethral resection
In this form of prostatectomy, a tube is passed up the urethra from the penis to the prostate. This tube is fitted with a lens system and a cutting tool so that the surgeon can see the gland and cut away as much tissue as necessary.

ENLARGEMENT OF THE PROSTATE GLAND

Nearly every man over the age of 50 has some degree of enlargement of the prostate, although this rarely becomes troublesome before the age of 55. It is a natural effect of aging. As the gland becomes larger, it tends to distort the urethra (the tube that carries the urine away from the bladder), making the flow of urine weak and, in some cases, blocking it altogether.

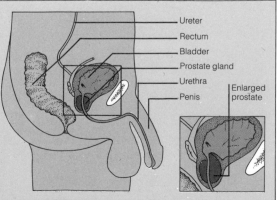

Ureter
Rectum
Bladder
Prostate gland
Urethra
Penis
Enlarged prostate

53 Painful urination

Consult this chart if you feel pain or discomfort when passing urine. This may be a symptom of infection or inflammation, or may follow injury to the urinary tract, and you should consult your physician without delay.

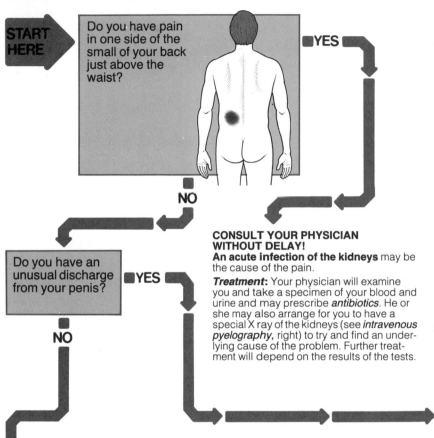

START HERE

Do you have pain in one side of the small of your back just above the waist?

YES

NO

Do you have an unusual discharge from your penis?

YES

NO

CONSULT YOUR PHYSICIAN WITHOUT DELAY!
An acute infection of the kidneys may be the cause of the pain.

Treatment: Your physician will examine you and take a specimen of your blood and urine and may prescribe *antibiotics*. He or she may also arrange for you to have a special X ray of the kidneys (see *intravenous pyelography,* right) to try and find an underlying cause of the problem. Further treatment will depend on the results of the tests.

An infection that may have been transmitted sexually may cause pain during urination and also discharge from the penis. See *Sexually transmitted diseases* (opposite) and consult your physician.

INTRAVENOUS PYELOGRAPHY

Intravenous pyelography provides the physician with a series of X-ray pictures of the urinary tract. A special dye that shows up on X-ray pictures is injected into your bloodstream. It travels through your body until it reaches your kidneys, where it is excreted through the ureters and into the bladder. This process takes an hour or more, and X-ray pictures are taken at regular intervals.

An intravenous pyelogram of a normal urinary tract

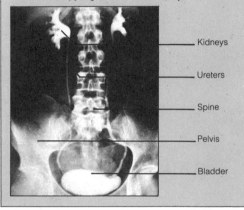

Kidneys
Ureters
Spine
Pelvis
Bladder

ABNORMAL-LOOKING URINE

Color of urine	Possible causes	What action is necessary
Pink, red or smoky	There is a chance that you may have blood in the urine, possibly caused by infection, inflammation or a growth in the urinary tract. However, natural or artificial food colorings can also pass into the urine.	Consult your physician without delay. He or she may need to take samples of urine and blood for analysis (see *Blood analysis*, p. 22) in order to make a firm diagnosis. Treatment will depend on the underlying problem.
Dark yellow or orange	If you have not been drinking much fluid, your urine has become concentrated. Loss of fluid caused by diarrhea, vomiting or sweating can also make your urine more concentrated and therefore darker than normal. Certain substances in senna-based laxatives and in rhubarb can also darken your urine temporarily.	This is no cause for concern; as soon as you compensate for any loss of fluid by drinking, your urine will return to its normal color. Substances in laxatives and rhubarb will pass through your system within 24 hours.
Clear and dark brown	Jaundice caused by a disorder of the liver (most commonly hepatitis) or gallbladder is a possibility, especially if your bowel movements are very pale and your skin or the whites of your eyes look yellow.	Consult your physician, who will need to take samples of urine and blood for analysis (see *Blood analysis,* p. 22) in order to make a firm diagnosis. Treatment will depend on the underlying problem.
Green or blue	Artificial coloring in food or medicine is almost certainly the cause of this.	This is no cause for concern, as the coloring will pass through your system without harmful effects.

Go to next page

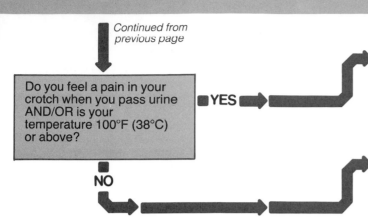

Continued from previous page

Do you feel a pain in your crotch when you pass urine AND/OR is your temperature 100°F (38°C) or above?

▶ YES ▶

NO

Prostatitis (inflammation of the prostate gland, usually caused by an infection) is a possibility. Consult your physician.
Treatment: Your physician will probably feel your prostate gland to find out if it is swollen and tender by inserting a finger into your rectum. You will be asked to provide a urine sample so that it can be analyzed. If the diagnosis is confirmed, your physician will probably advise you to rest and he or she may prescribe *antibiotics* to clear the infection.

A urinary tract infection is the most likely cause of painful urination with no other symptoms. Consult your physician.
Treatment: If your physician suspects infection, he or she may take a sample of urine for analysis. In some cases, further tests such as *intravenous pyelography* (opposite) are necessary. Treatment for infection in the urinary tract is likely to consist of *antibiotics*. You will also be advised to drink plenty of fluids.

SEXUALLY TRANSMITTED DISEASES (STDs)

Infections passed from one person to another during sexual contact (including anal and oral sex) are known as sexually transmitted (venereal) diseases. If you think you have caught a sexually transmitted disease, consult your physician or go to a clinic that specializes in treating such diseases, where you will be treated in the strictest confidence. It is important to seek medical advice promptly because of the risk of passing the infection to someone else. Also, an infection may be less easy to eradicate if there is any delay in starting treatment. If you are found to have a sexually transmitted disease, you will be asked to inform any recent sexual partners so that they too may seek treatment. You should avoid sexual contact until treatment has cleared up your symptoms.

Disease	Incubation period*	Symptoms	Treatment
Gonorrhea	2 to 10 days	Discomfort when passing urine and perhaps a slight discharge of pus from the tip of the penis.	The physician will take a sample of the discharge from the infected urethra for laboratory examination. The usual treatment consists of *antibiotics*.
Nonspecific urethritis	1 to 5 weeks	A slight tingling at the base of the penis – sometimes only felt when urinating first thing in the morning. The tingling may be accompanied by a discharge.	The physician will take a sample of urethral discharge for laboratory examination. The usual treatment is a course of *antibiotics*.
Syphilis	9 to 90 days	In the first stage, a highly infectious, painless sore called a chancre develops on the penis (or in the anus if you have had anal intercourse). This disappears after a few weeks. In the second stage, a rash that does not itch appears all over the body, including the palms and soles. There may also be painless swelling of the lymph glands and infectious wart-like lumps around the anus and maybe the armpits.	The disease is diagnosed by blood tests and samples taken from any sores. The usual treatment is a course of *antibiotic* injections. You will need to have periodic blood tests for 1 to 2 years after treatment to ensure that the disease has not reappeared.
Herpes genitalis	7 days or less	There is usually an itching feeling on the shaft of the penis followed by the appearance of a crop of small, painful blisters. Sometimes these also appear on the thighs and buttocks. The blisters burst after 24 hours, leaving small, red, moist, painful ulcers, which sometimes form a hard crust. The glands in the groin may become enlarged and painful, accompanied by feeling sick and a raised temperature. Outbreaks of blisters are likely to recur.	There is no total cure for this disorder. Your physician may prescribe an *antiviral* drug or ointment to make the ulcers less sore and speed healing. You will be advised to avoid sexual contact while you have an attack so that you do not transmit the infection to your partner. It is not known if someone with herpes is capable of infecting others between attacks, since virus shedding may continue.
Pubic lice (crabs)		Many people have no symptoms while others experience itching in the pubic region, particularly at night. You may be able to see the lice; they are brown and about 1/16 in. long.	Your physician will give you a lotion that kills lice and their eggs. At the same time he or she will ensure that you do not have any other sexually transmitted disease.
Acquired immune deficiency syndrome (AIDS)	Varies greatly. May take many months or years to develop	This disorder affects the body's natural defense system, so that it is unable to protect the body against infections and some forms of cancer. Symptoms of AIDS include frequent infections, a constant feeling of tiredness, loss of weight, swollen glands (in the front and back of the neck, behind the ears, under the arms, at the elbows, and in the groin) and skin blotches or rashes.	You will probably need to spend time in the hospital undergoing tests and treatment. Treatment may consist of *antibiotics* and/or *anticancer* drugs. Research into cures and a vaccine for this disease is continuing.

*Time between contact with the disease and appearance of symptoms

54 Back pain

Your backbone (or spine) extends from the base of your skull to the buttocks. It consists of the spinal column, which is made up of more than 30 separate bones called vertebrae stacked on top of one another. In between each pair of vertebrae is an elastic disc. The vertebrae and discs are held together by ligaments. Along the length of the spinal column is a space containing the spinal cord and the nerves that run from it to the rest of the body. Most people suffer from mild back pain from time to time, the exact cause of which may be difficult to diagnose. It is usually a sign that you have damaged one or more joints, ligaments or discs by overstretching or twisting your back into an awkward position. Severe pain, however, may be the result of pressure on the nerves from malalignment of the bones or discs in the back. Consult your physician.

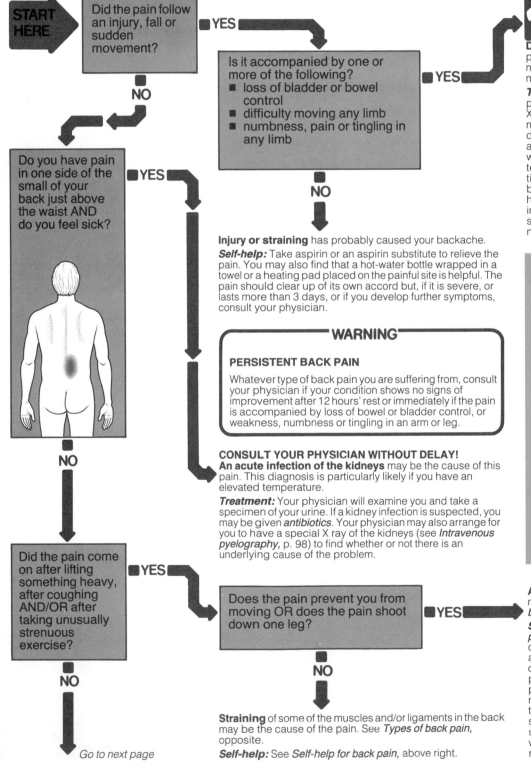

START HERE

Did the pain follow an injury, fall or sudden movement?

YES →

Is it accompanied by one or more of the following?
- loss of bladder or bowel control
- difficulty moving any limb
- numbness, pain or tingling in any limb

YES →

NO ↓

Do you have pain in one side of the small of your back just above the waist AND do you feel sick?

YES →

NO ↓

NO ↓

Did the pain come on after lifting something heavy, after coughing AND/OR after taking unusually strenuous exercise?

YES →

NO ↓

Go to next page

NO ↓

Injury or straining has probably caused your backache.

Self-help: Take aspirin or an aspirin substitute to relieve the pain. You may also find that a hot-water bottle wrapped in a towel or a heating pad placed on the painful site is helpful. The pain should clear up of its own accord but, if it is severe, or lasts more than 3 days, or if you develop further symptoms, consult your physician.

---WARNING---

PERSISTENT BACK PAIN

Whatever type of back pain you are suffering from, consult your physician if your condition shows no signs of improvement after 12 hours' rest or immediately if the pain is accompanied by loss of bowel or bladder control, or weakness, numbness or tingling in an arm or leg.

CONSULT YOUR PHYSICIAN WITHOUT DELAY!
An acute infection of the kidneys may be the cause of this pain. This diagnosis is particularly likely if you have an elevated temperature.

Treatment: Your physician will examine you and take a specimen of your urine. If a kidney infection is suspected, you may be given *antibiotics*. Your physician may also arrange for you to have a special X ray of the kidneys (see *Intravenous pyelography,* p. 98) to find whether or not there is an underlying cause of the problem.

Does the pain prevent you from moving OR does the pain shoot down one leg?

YES →

NO ↓

Straining of some of the muscles and/or ligaments in the back may be the cause of the pain. See *Types of back pain,* opposite.

Self-help: See *Self-help for back pain,* above right.

EMERGENCY
GET MEDICAL HELP NOW!

Damage to the spinal cord is possible. While waiting for medical help to arrive, do not move. Keep warm and stay calm.

Treatment: In the hospital, a physical examination and spine X rays (see *Bone X rays,* p. 103) may be carried out in order to determine the site and extent of any damage. Further treatment will depend on the results of these tests and the physician's observations. In some cases, resting in bed will be sufficient to allow healing. If there is little or no improvement, or if damage is severe, surgery may be necessary.

SELF-HELP FOR BACK PAIN

If you are suffering from back pain caused by a minor strain or that has no obvious cause, try these measures:

- Take the recommended dose of aspirin or an aspirin substitute.
- Rest on your back (or whichever position is most comfortable) on a firm mattress for as long as pain persists, getting up only when necessary.
- A hot-water bottle or heating pad on the back may help to relieve pain.

If pain becomes severe, or if your condition is no better in 12 hours, consult your physician, who will examine you, and may order X rays and recommend treatment.

A prolapsed (or slipped) disc may cause sciatica (see *Types of back pain,* opposite).

Self-help: See *Self-help for back pain* (above). If pain persists, consult your physician, who may arrange for tests such as an X ray of the spine (see *Bone X rays,* p. 103). If you are found to have a prolapsed disc, your physician may advise rest, manipulation of the spine or that you wear a special corset. In severe cases, surgery or injection of the disc with a special chemical may be recommended.

Continued from previous page

Has your back gradually become stiff as well as painful over a period of months or years? **YES** ➡

Are you over 45? **YES** ➡

Is the pain mainly in the back between the shoulder blades? **YES** ➡

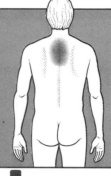

NO ⬇

NO ⬇

NO ⬇

Consult your physician if you are unable to make a diagnosis from this chart and if your back pain has not been relieved within 24 hours.

Ankylosing spondylitis, inflammation of the joints that link the vertebrae so that the spinal column gradually becomes hard and inflexible, may be the cause of this, especially if you are between 20 and 40. Consult your physician.

Treatment: Your physician will examine you and arrange for you to have a blood test (see *Blood analysis,* p. 22) and an X ray of your back and pelvic area (see *Bone X rays,* p. 103). If you are found to have ankylosing spondylitis, you will probably be given *anti-inflammatory* drugs. You will also be taught exercises that will help to keep your back mobile. Such mobility exercises are an essential part of the treatment for this disorder and can be supplemented by other physical activities such as swimming.

Lumbar osteoarthritis, a form of arthritis, is a possible diagnosis. This normally occurs as a result of wear and tear on the spine and is a natural consequence of growing older. Consult your physician.

Treatment: Your physician will examine you and possibly arrange for you to have an X ray (see *Bone X rays,* p. 103) and a blood test (see *Blood analysis,* p. 22) to check that no other disorder is responsible for these symptoms. If the diagnosis is confirmed, you will probably have painkillers prescribed and be advised to do exercises to strengthen the muscles in your back. You may be advised to wear a specially fitted support corset. If you are overweight, your physician will probably advise you to go on a weight-reducing diet (see *How to lose weight,* p. 27).

Cervical osteoarthritis, arthritis of the bones in the neck as a result of wear and tear, may be the cause of this pain. Consult your physician.

Treatment: Your physician will examine you and may arrange for you to have an X ray of the bones in your neck (see *Bone X rays,* p. 103). If he or she thinks that the symptoms are due to this disorder, you may be given a supportive collar to wear to reduce neck mobility. Aspirin or an aspirin substitute can be taken to relieve the discomfort. If these measures fail to help the condition, your physician may send you to an occupational or physical therapist for further treatment.

TYPES OF BACK PAIN

Nonspecific back pain
If back pain has no obvious cause, it is "nonspecific." Such pain is probably the result of strained ligaments or a strained or slightly misplaced vertebral joint that has caused the surrounding muscles to go into spasm. Or it may be fibrositis (stiffness and pain within the muscles). Some people tend to develop nonspecific back pain when they are under stress. Follow the self-help measures opposite.

Low back pain
Low back pain is centered in the small of the back and there is often a tender spot. In severe cases, the sufferer is unable to move his or her back. It is usually brought on by unaccustomed strenuous activity. Follow the self-help measures opposite.

Sciatica
This is pain caused by pressure on one of the nerves where it leaves the spine. It is usually the result of pressure on a nerve from a prolapsed (slipped) disc. A severe pain shoots through the buttocks and along the back of the thigh down toward the ankle. If you cough, sneeze or try to bend your back, the pain becomes worse. Mild sciatica may be relieved by self-help treatment (opposite) but, if it persists or is severe, consult your physician.

Coccygodynia
Coccygodynia is a condition affecting the coccyx, at the base of the spine. It is a localized ache that is made worse when you sit down. It may be caused by a heavy blow on the buttocks or a fall. Sitting on a cushion or resting on your side may help to relieve the pain.

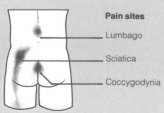

Pain sites

— Lumbago

— Sciatica

— Coccygodynia

MYELOGRAPHY

Myelography is a procedure that is used to diagnose disorders of the spine and spinal cord, such as a prolapsed (or slipped) disc. A solution that is visible on X rays is injected into the fluid-filled space around the spinal cord. The patient is than tilted into various positions so that the movement of the solution inside the spinal column can be recorded by X-ray pictures. Myelography takes about an hour and requires sedation because it may be uncomfortable.

PREVENTING BACKACHE

There are several practical ways in which you can minimize the amount of strain on your back to help prevent backaches. Feeling comfortable in any movement or position is a general guide to whether or not you are putting strain on your back. Below are some suggestions on specific precautions you can take.

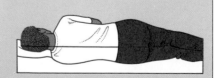

Sitting correctly
When sitting for any length of time, try to keep your back straight and avoid slumping. Choose a chair that has a firm, upright back that will support the length of your spine. You should be able to rest your feet flat on the floor with your knees bent at a right angle.

Posture
To avoid placing unnecessary strain on your back, stand with your head, trunk and legs aligned.

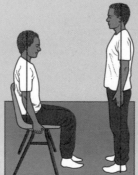

Sleeping
Sleep on a firm mattress or put a board under your mattress. Use a flat pillow to support your head (or use none at all). These measures will support your back and prevent your spine from sagging.

Lifting
When lifting a heavy object, get as close to it as possible. Keep your back straight and bend your knees so that your leg muscles, not the weaker back muscles, take the strain.

55 Painful or stiff neck

A stiff or painful neck is most often the result of a muscle stiffness brought on by sitting in a cold draft, sleeping in an uncomfortable position or doing some form of exercise or activity to which you are not accustomed.

This type of problem should resolve itself within a day or so. If pain and/or stiffness persist, ask your physician for advice. Occasionally, a stiff or painful neck may be a sign of a disorder that requires medical treatment.

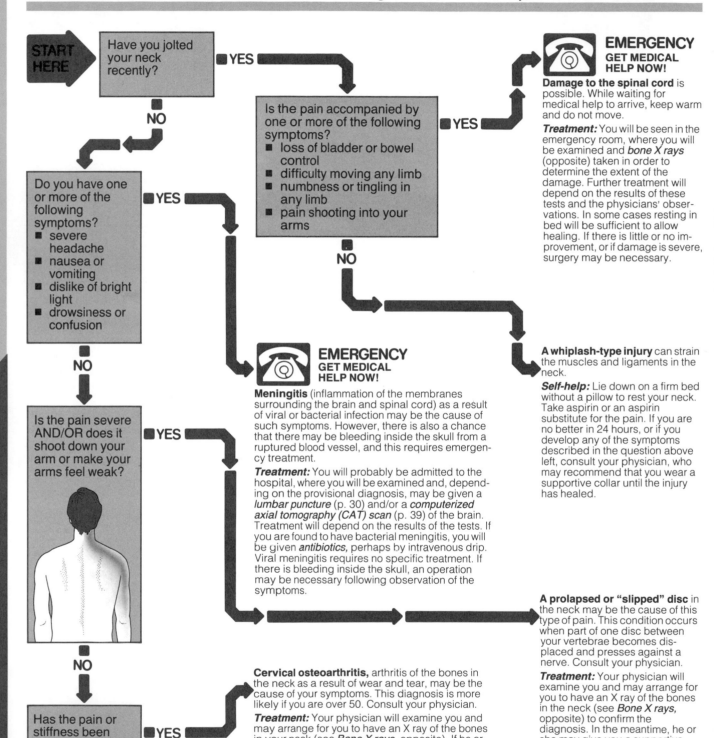

START HERE

Have you jolted your neck recently? — **YES** →

Is the pain accompanied by one or more of the following symptoms?
- loss of bladder or bowel control
- difficulty moving any limb
- numbness or tingling in any limb
- pain shooting into your arms

YES →

NO ↓

NO ↓

Do you have one or more of the following symptoms?
- severe headache
- nausea or vomiting
- dislike of bright light
- drowsiness or confusion

YES →

NO ↓

Is the pain severe AND/OR does it shoot down your arm or make your arms feel weak? — **YES** →

NO ↓

Has the pain or stiffness been getting worse over a period of months? — **YES** →

NO ↓

EMERGENCY
GET MEDICAL HELP NOW!

Damage to the spinal cord is possible. While waiting for medical help to arrive, keep warm and do not move.

Treatment: You will be seen in the emergency room, where you will be examined and *bone X rays* (opposite) taken in order to determine the extent of the damage. Further treatment will depend on the results of these tests and the physicians' observations. In some cases resting in bed will be sufficient to allow healing. If there is little or no improvement, or if damage is severe, surgery may be necessary.

EMERGENCY
GET MEDICAL HELP NOW!

Meningitis (inflammation of the membranes surrounding the brain and spinal cord) as a result of viral or bacterial infection may be the cause of such symptoms. However, there is also a chance that there may be bleeding inside the skull from a ruptured blood vessel, and this requires emergency treatment.

Treatment: You will probably be admitted to the hospital, where you will be examined and, depending on the provisional diagnosis, may be given a *lumbar puncture* (p. 30) and/or a *computerized axial tomography (CAT) scan* (p. 39) of the brain. Treatment will depend on the results of the tests. If you are found to have bacterial meningitis, you will be given *antibiotics,* perhaps by intravenous drip. Viral meningitis requires no specific treatment. If there is bleeding inside the skull, an operation may be necessary following observation of the symptoms.

A whiplash-type injury can strain the muscles and ligaments in the neck.

Self-help: Lie down on a firm bed without a pillow to rest your neck. Take aspirin or an aspirin substitute for the pain. If you are no better in 24 hours, or if you develop any of the symptoms described in the question above left, consult your physician, who may recommend that you wear a supportive collar until the injury has healed.

A prolapsed or "slipped" disc in the neck may be the cause of this type of pain. This condition occurs when part of one disc between your vertebrae becomes displaced and presses against a nerve. Consult your physician.

Treatment: Your physician will examine you and may arrange for you to have an X ray of the bones in the neck (see *Bone X rays,* opposite) to confirm the diagnosis. In the meantime, he or she may give you a supportive collar to wear to reduce neck mobility and to relieve pressure on the nerves of your neck. He or she will probably prescribe painkillers to ease any pain or discomfort that you may feel. In some cases, surgery may be necessary.

Cervical osteoarthritis, arthritis of the bones in the neck as a result of wear and tear, may be the cause of your symptoms. This diagnosis is more likely if you are over 50. Consult your physician.

Treatment: Your physician will examine you and may arrange for you to have an X ray of the bones in your neck (see *Bone X rays,* opposite). If he or she thinks that the symptoms are due to this disorder, you may be given a supportive collar to wear to help relieve the pain by reducing neck mobility and relieving pressure on nearby nerves.

Consult your physician if you are unable to make a diagnosis from this chart.

56 Painful arm

Pain in the arm is almost always the result of injury or straining of the muscles and ligaments that hold the various bones and joints in place. Such injuries are particularly likely to occur after any unaccustomed strenuous physical activity, such as participating in a sport for the first time. The pain should disappear if you rest your arm. If any pain in your arm is recurrent or persistent, consult your physician.

START HERE

Did the pain immediately follow an injury, fall or sudden movement?

 YES

Are you unable to move your arm AND/OR is the pain severe, even when resting?

YES

NO

NO

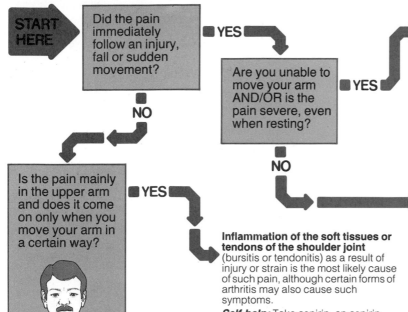

Is the pain mainly in the upper arm and does it come on only when you move your arm in a certain way?

YES

NO

Do you have shooting pains down the length of your arm?

YES

NO

Do you have "pins and needles" in your hand, especially at night?

YES

NO

 EMERGENCY
GET MEDICAL HELP NOW!

A fracture, dislocation or serious injury to the muscles or ligaments may be causing this pain (see *First aid for suspected broken bones and dislocated joints*, p. 107).

Treatment: The limb will be examined and probably X-rayed (see *Bone X rays*, below) to discover the extent of the damage. Depending on the nature of the injury, you may need to wear a plaster cast or a firm bandage. Sometimes an operation is necessary to reposition the bones.

Injury to the soft tissues (muscles, ligaments and cartilages), such as a sprain or strain or bruising of the arm, is probably causing this pain.

Self-help: Follow the advice on treating such injuries given in the box on p. 109. Consult your physician if the pain is severe or is no better the following day (see also *Sports injuries*, p. 105).

Inflammation of the soft tissues or tendons of the shoulder joint (bursitis or tendonitis) as a result of injury or strain is the most likely cause of such pain, although certain forms of arthritis may also cause such symptoms.

Self-help: Take aspirin, an aspirin substitute or an over-the-counter *anti-inflammatory* drug to relieve the pain. Rest the arm while pain persists. Consult your physician if you are no better in 3 days.

CONSULT YOUR PHYSICIAN WITHOUT DELAY!
Displacement of a disc between the bones in the neck (see *Prolapsed disc*, opposite) may cause such pain as a result of pressure on a nerve (see Cervical osteoarthritis, opposite). There is also likely to be some numbness in the hand.

Treatment: If your physician confirms this diagnosis, you may be referred for an X ray (see *Bone X rays*, right) of the neck bones. Your physician will probably prescribe painkillers and may recommend that you wear a supportive collar. In some cases, traction may be necessary.

Carpal tunnel syndrome, a disorder in which a nerve (the median nerve) in the wrist is pinched due to swelling of surrounding tissues, is possible. You may also have a pinched nerve at the elbow (cubital tunnel syndrome). Consult your physician.

Treatment: The condition often clears up of its own accord. Your physician may refer you for tests to confirm the diagnosis and you may be given injections of *steroids* into the wrist. If the condition is particularly painful and persistent, a simple operation will relieve it.

BONE X RAYS

Because X rays pass through soft tissues such as muscle and fat and clearly show up areas of bone, X-ray pictures are often used to diagnose the extent and nature of damage to any bones from injury or disease. This helps physicians decide on the best form of treatment and, in the case of a broken (fractured) bone, whether or not an operation is necessary to reposition the pieces.

This bone X ray shows a fracture in one of the bones in the lower arm. This type of break is difficult to diagnose without an X ray.

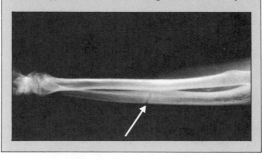

Does the pain mainly affect your joints – for example, your shoulder, elbow or finger joints?

YES

Go to chart

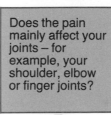 **59** **Painful or swollen joints**

NO

Consult your physician if you are unable to make a diagnosis from this chart and if the pain is severe or persists for more than 24 hours.

57 Painful knee

The knee is one of the principal weight-bearing joints and is subject to much wear and tear. If your work involves a great deal of bending or squatting, the risk of damage to the bones, ligaments and cartilages through overuse and/or injury is increased. Consult this chart if you experience pain in one or both knees.

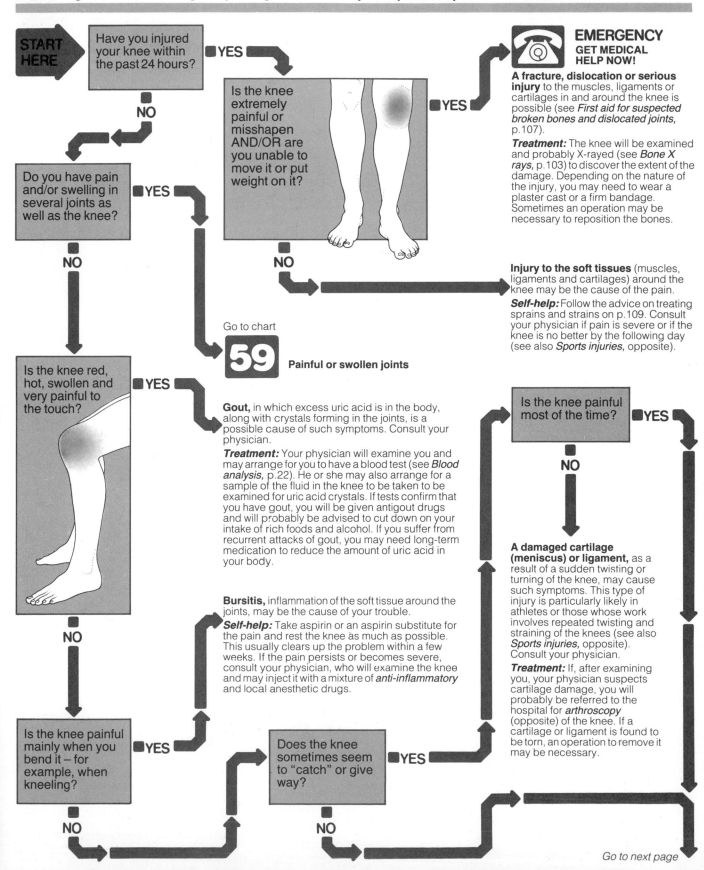

START HERE

Have you injured your knee within the past 24 hours? — **YES** → **Is the knee extremely painful or misshapen AND/OR are you unable to move it or put weight on it?** — **YES** →

EMERGENCY
GET MEDICAL HELP NOW!

A fracture, dislocation or serious injury to the muscles, ligaments or cartilages in and around the knee is possible (see *First aid for suspected broken bones and dislocated joints*, p.107).

Treatment: The knee will be examined and probably X-rayed (see *Bone X rays*, p.103) to discover the extent of the damage. Depending on the nature of the injury, you may need to wear a plaster cast or a firm bandage. Sometimes an operation may be necessary to reposition the bones.

(Is the knee extremely painful...) **NO** →

Injury to the soft tissues (muscles, ligaments and cartilages) around the knee may be the cause of the pain.

Self-help: Follow the advice on treating sprains and strains on p.109. Consult your physician if pain is severe or if the knee is no better by the following day (see also *Sports injuries*, opposite).

Go to chart

59
Painful or swollen joints

Have you injured your knee within the past 24 hours? **NO** → **Do you have pain and/or swelling in several joints as well as the knee?** — **YES** → Go to chart **59**

Gout, in which excess uric acid is in the body, along with crystals forming in the joints, is a possible cause of such symptoms. Consult your physician.

Treatment: Your physician will examine you and may arrange for you to have a blood test (see *Blood analysis*, p.22). He or she may also arrange for a sample of the fluid in the knee to be taken to be examined for uric acid crystals. If tests confirm that you have gout, you will be given antigout drugs and will probably be advised to cut down on your intake of rich foods and alcohol. If you suffer from recurrent attacks of gout, you may need long-term medication to reduce the amount of uric acid in your body.

Do you have pain and/or swelling in several joints as well as the knee? **NO** → **Is the knee red, hot, swollen and very painful to the touch?** — **YES** → *(Gout)*

Bursitis, inflammation of the soft tissue around the joints, may be the cause of your trouble.

Self-help: Take aspirin or an aspirin substitute for the pain and rest the knee as much as possible. This usually clears up the problem within a few weeks. If the pain persists or becomes severe, consult your physician, who will examine the knee and may inject it with a mixture of *anti-inflammatory* and local anesthetic drugs.

Is the knee red, hot, swollen and very painful to the touch? **NO** → **Is the knee painful mainly when you bend it – for example, when kneeling?** — **YES** → *(Bursitis)*

Is the knee painful most of the time? — **YES** →

Is the knee painful most of the time? **NO** →

A damaged cartilage (meniscus) or ligament, as a result of a sudden twisting or turning of the knee, may cause such symptoms. This type of injury is particularly likely in athletes or those whose work involves repeated twisting and straining of the knees (see also *Sports injuries*, opposite). Consult your physician.

Treatment: If, after examining you, your physician suspects cartilage damage, you will probably be referred to the hospital for *arthroscopy* (opposite) of the knee. If a cartilage or ligament is found to be torn, an operation to remove it may be necessary.

Is the knee painful mainly when you bend it – for example, when kneeling? **NO** →

Does the knee sometimes seem to "catch" or give way? — **YES** → *(A damaged cartilage...)*

Does the knee sometimes seem to "catch" or give way? **NO** →

Go to next page

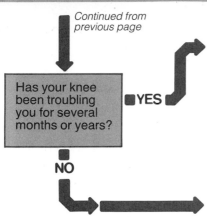

Continued from previous page

Has your knee been troubling you for several months or years?

YES

NO

Osteoarthritis, as a result of injury or wear and tear on the knee, is a possible cause of such pain, especially if you are over 50, or if you have regularly overused the joint at work or participating in sports. Consult your physician.

Treatment: Your physician will examine you and may arrange for you to have a blood test (see *Blood analysis,* p.22) to exclude other possible causes of pain, and you may need to have an X ray (see *Bone X rays,* p.103) of the knee. If these investigations confirm the diagnosis, your physician will prescribe painkillers. If you are overweight, it will help relieve the strain on your knee if you try to lose weight (see *How to lose weight,* p.27). In some cases, physical or occupational therapy and/or heat treatment may be helpful.

Consult your physician if you are unable to make a diagnosis from this chart and your knee is no better after 24 hours' rest.

ARTHROSCOPY

Arthroscopy allows the physician to examine the interior of a joint using an arthroscope. This is a flexible fiberoptic tube with a lighting and lens system that is passed through a small incision into the joint. It is then possible to discover the abnormality by looking through an eyepiece. A local or general anesthetic will be given. Many common knee problems can be surgically corrected using arthroscopy.

SPORTS INJURIES

Sports and other forms of exercise are important for maintaining health and general fitness (see *The benefits of exercise,* p.25), but an overambitious program may lead to injuries and other health problems. Injuries may also be due to inadequate warm-ups before exercise, or failure to use the correct safety equipment or clothing. Some sports by their very nature carry a high risk of injury – for example, boxing – and brain damage and other injuries are common. Other sports, such as football, carry a risk of accidental injury – commonly, pulled muscles and broken bones. Make sure that you are aware of the risks of any exercise activity you undertake so that you can balance these against the likely health benefits, and so that you can take reasonable precautions to prevent injury.

Sensible precautions

If you belong to any of the following categories, consult your physician before taking up any sort of strenuous activity for the first time:

- If you are over 50 years of age, or if you are over 40 and have not exercised regularly since early adulthood.
- If you are a heavy smoker (more than 20 cigarettes a day).
- If you are overweight (see *Weight charts,* p.26).
- If you have a long-term health problem such as high blood pressure, heart disease, diabetes or kidney disease.

Safety equipment

In some sports you can reduce the risk of injury by the use of special safety equipment – for example, eyeguards for racquetball players and helmets for football players and cyclists. Make sure than any equipment you buy is of good quality and meets your individual requirements; if you are unsure what equipment is necessary, seek advice from a sports club or from the appropriate sporting organization.

Clothing

For most sporting activities, choose clothes that are comfortable and that do not restrict your movement. Natural fibers such as cotton are best for shirts, shorts and socks because they allow air to circulate more freely, reducing the likelihood of chafing and blisters. For many activities, especially in cold weather, it is a good idea to start off wearing several layers of clothing that you can remove as necessary as you warm up. Wash your sports gear regularly to reduce the risk of fungal infection. Some sports, such as skiing, require specialized protective clothing and, if you are unsure

what to buy, you should seek advice from an expert.

Shoes

Wearing the correct shoes is essential if you are to avoid minor foot problems such as blisters. Make sure that your sports shoes fit well, allowing room for your feet to expand slightly during exercise.

Warm-up exercises

You can reduce the risk of pulled muscles and torn ligaments by doing some gentle exercises to stretch and loosen the muscles and ligaments before you put them under strain. Repeat the exercises described here for about 15 minutes before each exercise session, and for 5 minutes afterward. These exercises can be practiced at other times to help increase all-around fitness.

Head and neck (1)
Slowly roll your head in a full circle, flexing your neck backward at the back of the circle and bending it forward at the front.

Shoulders and chest (2)
Extend both arms in front of you. Lift them above your head, placing the palms together. Keeping your arms straight, lower them toward your sides, holding them at shoulder height.

Backs of the legs (3)
Stand upright with your feet wide apart and hands on hips. Lean forward, bending at the hips and keeping your back straight. Lower your arms toward the floor in front.

Trunk (4)
Stand up straight with your feet about a shoulder-width apart and with your arms by your sides. Bend sideways from the waist toward the right, allowing your right hand to slide down the leg to below the knee. Straighten up and do a similar bend to the left.

Common injuries

Minor injuries: Chafing (soreness that can result from friction between clothes, equipment and skin) may be prevented by rubbing petroleum jelly into susceptible areas, or by wearing protective bandages. Blisters on the feet are usually the result of poorly fitting shoes. Apply an adhesive bandage to protect against further rubbing.

Strains, sprains and pulled muscles and ligaments: Such injuries are most common in those just starting exercise after a long period of inactivity and those who have not undertaken adequate warm-up exercises. Serious injuries of this type can be very painful and require first aid and professional medical attention (see *First aid for sprains and strains,* p.109). Never attempt to continue exercise after such an injury, as you may do further damage. Aching in the muscles the day after unaccustomed exercise is usual and best treated by keeping mobile. Some people find that a warm bath after exercise helps prevent such pain from developing.

Shin splints: Shin splints are pains along the shin bone that may occur during or after exercise. Shin splints may be the result of a stress fracture, swelling of the muscles, or inflammation of the lining of the bone. If you have pain, apply an ice bag, elevate your leg and rest it as much as possible. Wrapping the leg with an elastic bandage may also help. If after 2 to 3 weeks the pain persists, consult your physician.

Stress fractures: Bones that are constantly under stress may develop hair-line cracks known as stress fractures. Pain may only be slight, so there is a danger that the injury may go unnoticed and that further exercise may increase the damage. If you suspect a stress fracture, consult your physician, who will arrange for you to be X-rayed (see *Bone X rays,* p.103). Rest and bandaging of the affected part is the usual treatment.

Osteoarthritis: The main long-term health problem sometimes associated with regular vigorous exercise is osteoarthritis. It often develops in later life as a result of wear and tear on joints, even in those who do not exercise excessively, but it is more likely to occur at a younger age in professional athletes.

After an injury

After you have been treated for an injury, be careful not to strain the injured part by an overrapid return to your former exercise routine. It may be helpful to follow a program of special exercises to help restore strength to the injured part gradually. If pain or swelling persists or recurs, consult your physician.

58 Painful leg

Pain in the leg is almost always the result of injury or straining of the muscles and ligaments that hold the joints in place. Such injuries are likely if you take part in any unaccustomed activity, such as participating in a **sport for the first time. Such pain should disappear if you rest your leg. However, any pain in your leg that is persistent or recurrent may indicate an underlying disorder, so consult your physician.**

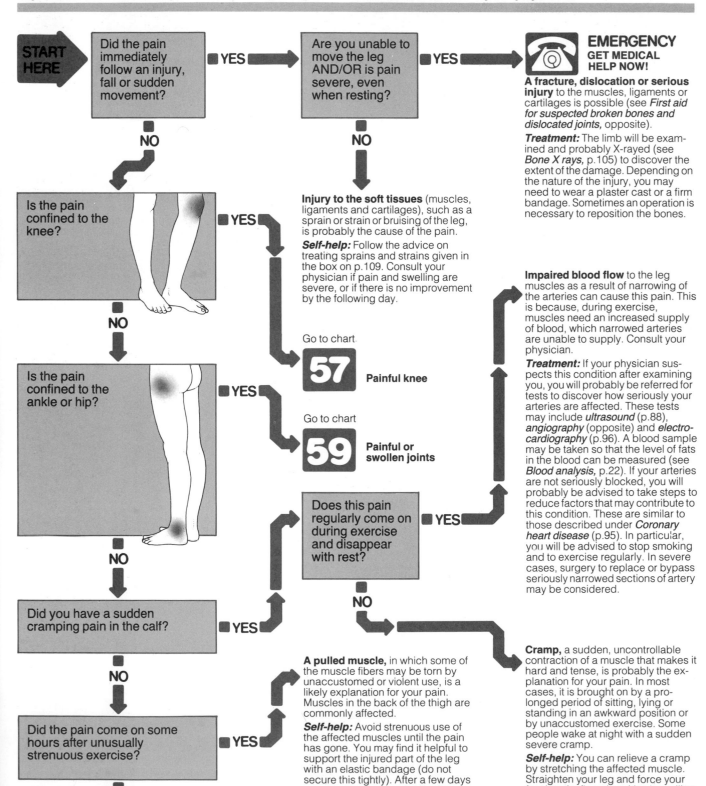

START HERE → Did the pain immediately follow an injury, fall or sudden movement? — **YES** → Are you unable to move the leg AND/OR is pain severe, even when resting? — **YES** → **EMERGENCY GET MEDICAL HELP NOW!**

A fracture, dislocation or serious injury to the muscles, ligaments or cartilages is possible (see *First aid for suspected broken bones and dislocated joints,* opposite).

Treatment: The limb will be examined and probably X-rayed (see *Bone X rays,* p.105) to discover the extent of the damage. Depending on the nature of the injury, you may need to wear a plaster cast or a firm bandage. Sometimes an operation is necessary to reposition the bones.

NO ↓

Is the pain confined to the knee? — **YES** →

NO ↓

Is the pain confined to the ankle or hip? — **YES** →

NO ↓

Did you have a sudden cramping pain in the calf? — **YES** →

NO ↓

Did the pain come on some hours after unusually strenuous exercise? — **YES** →

NO ↓ *Go to next page*

Injury to the soft tissues (muscles, ligaments and cartilages), such as a sprain or strain or bruising of the leg, is probably the cause of the pain.

Self-help: Follow the advice on treating sprains and strains given in the box on p.109. Consult your physician if pain and swelling are severe, or if there is no improvement by the following day.

Go to chart

57 Painful knee

Go to chart

59 Painful or swollen joints

Does this pain regularly come on during exercise and disappear with rest? — **YES** →

NO ↓

Impaired blood flow to the leg muscles as a result of narrowing of the arteries can cause this pain. This is because, during exercise, muscles need an increased supply of blood, which narrowed arteries are unable to supply. Consult your physician.

Treatment: If your physician suspects this condition after examining you, you will probably be referred for tests to discover how seriously your arteries are affected. These tests may include *ultrasound* (p.88), *angiography* (opposite) and *electrocardiography* (p.96). A blood sample may be taken so that the level of fats in the blood can be measured (see *Blood analysis,* p.22). If your arteries are not seriously blocked, you will probably be advised to take steps to reduce factors that may contribute to this condition. These are similar to those described under *Coronary heart disease* (p.95). In particular, you will be advised to stop smoking and to exercise regularly. In severe cases, surgery to replace or bypass seriously narrowed sections of artery may be considered.

A pulled muscle, in which some of the muscle fibers may be torn by unaccustomed or violent use, is a likely explanation for your pain. Muscles in the back of the thigh are commonly affected.

Self-help: Avoid strenuous use of the affected muscles until the pain has gone. You may find it helpful to support the injured part of the leg with an elastic bandage (do not secure this tightly). After a few days you can start to exercise the leg again to prevent stiffness. If pain is severe, or if the leg becomes swollen, consult your physician (see also *Sports injuries,* p.105).

Cramp, a sudden, uncontrollable contraction of a muscle that makes it hard and tense, is probably the explanation for your pain. In most cases, it is brought on by a prolonged period of sitting, lying or standing in an awkward position or by unaccustomed exercise. Some people wake at night with a sudden severe cramp.

Self-help: You can relieve a cramp by stretching the affected muscle. Straighten your leg and force your foot into the flexed position by pulling it back or pushing it against the floor. If you suffer from frequent attacks of cramps, consult your physician.

Continued from previous page

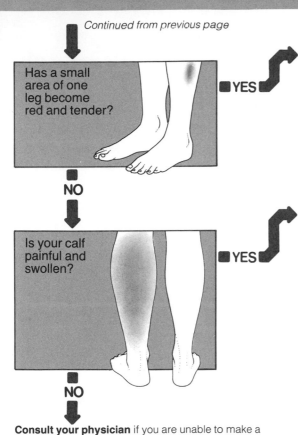

Has a small area of one leg become red and tender?

YES → **Thrombophlebitis** (inflammation of a superficial vein) is the likely cause of such symptoms. Consult your physician.

Treatment: If your physician confirms the diagnosis, he or she will probably prescribe painkillers and, possibly, other medications. A sample of blood may be taken for analysis (see *Blood analysis,* p.22) to find out if there is an underlying reason you have developed this disorder.

NO

Is your calf painful and swollen?

YES → **CONSULT YOUR PHYSICIAN WITHOUT DELAY!**
Deep-vein thrombosis, a condition in which a blood clot (thrombus) blocks a vein in the leg, may be the cause of such symptoms. This disorder is also likely to cause swelling of the ankle. Those who have been immobilized by injury or illness for a long period are particularly susceptible.

Treatment: Your physician will examine you and, if he or she confirms the possibility of deep-vein thrombosis, will probably arrange for you to be admitted to the hospital for blood-flow tests and venography (see *Angiography,* below right), to verify the diagnosis. Treatment for the condition consists of *anticoagulant* drugs to help dissolve and prevent blood clots. These drugs are usually taken for several months.

NO

Consult your physician if you are unable to make a diagnosis from this chart.

VARICOSE VEINS

Varicose veins are swollen leg veins causing poor circulation in the legs, usually as a result of damage to the valves in the veins. The veins in the back of the calf and along the inside of the leg are most commonly affected. Varicose veins are likely to cause aching of the leg and swelling of the ankle, especially after long periods of standing.

Self-help measures
If you think that you may be susceptible to varicose veins, or if you already have swollen veins in the leg, try to keep your weight off your feet as much as possible. Sit with your legs up whenever you can to help the blood to flow back up your leg. If you have to spend long periods standing up, flex your calf muscles occasionally to help blood circulate in your leg. Wear specially prescribed hose. Consult your physician if your varicose veins trouble you, or if the surrounding skin is cracked or sore.

Professional treatment
Your physician may arrange for you to have tests such as venography (see *Angiography,* below). If varicose veins are severe and the self-help measures are not helpful, your physician may recommend surgery to remove the affected veins, or they may be injected with a chemical that seals the vein.

FIRST AID FOR SUSPECTED BROKEN BONES AND DISLOCATED JOINTS

A limb or joint that is very painful or looks misshapen and that will not move following an injury or fall may be broken and/or dislocated. Go to your hospital emergency room. If no help is readily available and/or if you are unable to move, call an ambulance.

General points
- If there is bleeding from the wound, cover it firmly with a clean dressing or cloth.
- Do not try to manipulate the bone or joint back into position yourself; this should only be attempted by a physician.
- While waiting for medical help to arrive, a helper should try to keep the injured person warm and as calm as possible.
- A person with a suspected broken bone or dislocated joint should not eat or drink anything in case a general anesthetic is needed later in order to reset the bone.
- If you have to wait some time for medical attention, immobilize the limb in the most comfortable position, using bandages and splints as described here.

Arm injury
Gently place the injured arm in the most comfortable position across the chest. Some padding, such as a pillow, should be placed between the arm and chest. Support the weight of the arm along its length together with the padding. If the arm cannot be bent, use bandages or tape to secure the arm to the side of the body. A splint (right) may help provide increased support.

Shoulder, collarbone or elbow injury.
Support the weight of the arm in a sling in the most comfortable position.

Leg injury
Secure the injured leg to the undamaged one. If possible, place a well-padded splint (below) between them.

Knee injury
Support the joint in the most comfortable position. If the knee is bent, support it in the bent position. If the knee is unable to bend, support the leg along its length from underneath, using a board or something similar as a splint. Place padding between the knee and the splint and around the heel.

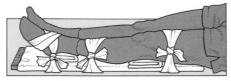

Splints
A splint is a support used to immobilize an injured part of the body (usually an arm or a leg) to reduce pain and the likelihood of further damage. Always secure a splint in at least 2 places not too close to the injury, preferably on either side of it. Use wide lengths of material or tape to do this (not string or rope) and do not secure it too tightly.

ANGIOGRAPHY

Angiography is a procedure that allows physicians to take X-ray pictures of blood vessels that may have become narrowed or blocked. When an artery is under investigation, the procedure is known as arteriography; when it is a vein being examined, it is called venography.

What happens
During angiography, for which you may be sedated, a solution that is visible on X ray is injected into the bloodstream. This is done either by injecting directly into the blood vessel concerned or by means of a fine tube (catheter) inserted through an incision in an accessible blood vessel. The catheter is passed along the blood vessel until it reaches the area where examination is required. The solution is then released and X rays taken.

59 Painful or swollen joints

Joints occur at the junction of two or more bones and usually allow movement between those bones. The degree and type of movement allowed depends on the structure of the joint. Major joints such as the hips, knees and ankles undergo constant wear and tear, so minor degrees of discomfort or stiffness may occur from time to time. However, severe pain, swelling or limitation of movement may be the result of damage to the bones or soft tissues or the joint from injury or may indicate an underlying disorder of the joints or skeletal system. Consult this chart if you suffer to any extent from pain, stiffness and/or swelling in or around a joint.

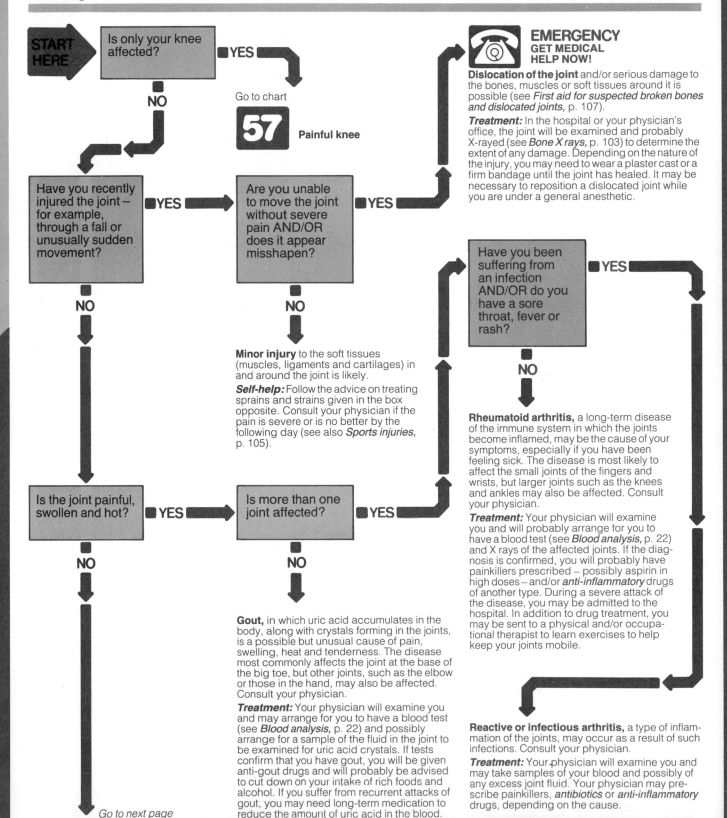

START HERE

Is only your knee affected?

YES → Go to chart **57** **Painful knee**

NO

Have you recently injured the joint – for example, through a fall or unusually sudden movement?

YES → **Are you unable to move the joint without severe pain AND/OR does it appear misshapen?**

NO

EMERGENCY
GET MEDICAL HELP NOW!

Dislocation of the joint and/or serious damage to the bones, muscles or soft tissues around it is possible (see *First aid for suspected broken bones and dislocated joints,* p. 107).

Treatment: In the hospital or your physician's office, the joint will be examined and probably X-rayed (see *Bone X rays,* p. 103) to determine the extent of any damage. Depending on the nature of the injury, you may need to wear a plaster cast or a firm bandage until the joint has healed. It may be necessary to reposition a dislocated joint while you are under a general anesthetic.

YES →

NO

Minor injury to the soft tissues (muscles, ligaments and cartilages) in and around the joint is likely.

Self-help: Follow the advice on treating sprains and strains given in the box opposite. Consult your physician if the pain is severe or is no better by the following day (see also *Sports injuries,* p. 105).

Have you been suffering from an infection AND/OR do you have a sore throat, fever or rash?

YES →

NO

Rheumatoid arthritis, a long-term disease of the immune system in which the joints become inflamed, may be the cause of your symptoms, especially if you have been feeling sick. The disease is most likely to affect the small joints of the fingers and wrists, but larger joints such as the knees and ankles may also be affected. Consult your physician.

Treatment: Your physician will examine you and will probably arrange for you to have a blood test (see *Blood analysis,* p. 22) and X rays of the affected joints. If the diagnosis is confirmed, you will probably have painkillers prescribed – possibly aspirin in high doses – and/or *anti-inflammatory* drugs of another type. During a severe attack of the disease, you may be admitted to the hospital. In addition to drug treatment, you may be sent to a physical and/or occupational therapist to learn exercises to help keep your joints mobile.

Is the joint painful, swollen and hot?

YES → **Is more than one joint affected?**

NO

NO

YES →

Gout, in which uric acid accumulates in the body, along with crystals forming in the joints, is a possible but unusual cause of pain, swelling, heat and tenderness. The disease most commonly affects the joint at the base of the big toe, but other joints, such as the elbow or those in the hand, may also be affected. Consult your physician.

Treatment: Your physician will examine you and may arrange for you to have a blood test (see *Blood analysis,* p. 22) and possibly arrange for a sample of the fluid in the joint to be examined for uric acid crystals. If tests confirm that you have gout, you will be given anti-gout drugs and will probably be advised to cut down on your intake of rich foods and alcohol. If you suffer from recurrent attacks of gout, you may need long-term medication to reduce the amount of uric acid in the blood.

Go to next page

Reactive or infectious arthritis, a type of inflammation of the joints, may occur as a result of such infections. Consult your physician.

Treatment: Your physician will examine you and may take samples of your blood and possibly of any excess joint fluid. Your physician may prescribe painkillers, *antibiotics* or *anti-inflammatory* drugs, depending on the cause.

Continued from previous page

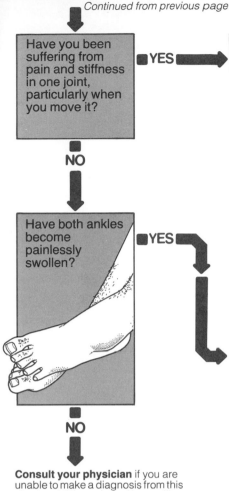

Have you been suffering from pain and stiffness in one joint, particularly when you move it?

YES → Has this come on gradually over a period of months or years?

YES → **Osteoarthritis** (degenerative joint disease) as a result of wear and tear on the joint is a possible cause of such pain, especially if you are over 50 or if you have regularly injured the joint at work or participating in sports. Consult your physician.

Treatment: Your physician may arrange for you to have a blood test (see *Blood analysis,* p. 22) to exclude other possible causes of pain, and you may need to have an X ray of the joint. If these investigations confirm the diagnosis, your physician will probably prescribe painkillers. If you are overweight, it will help if you lose weight (see *How to lose weight,* p.27). Physical and/or occupational therapy (supervised exercises), joint preservation techniques and/or heat treatment may be helpful.

NO ↓

NO ↓

Have both ankles become painlessly swollen?

NO

NO ↓

Bursitis, inflammation of the soft tissue around the joint, may be the cause of your trouble.

Self-help: Take aspirin or an aspirin substitute for the pain, and rest the joint as much as possible. This usually clears up the problem. If pain persists or becomes severe, consult your physician, who will examine the joint and may inject it with a mixture of *adrenocorticosteroids* and local anesthetic drugs.

YES →

Accumulation of fluid in the ankles is the most likely cause of such swelling. This may occur on long journeys, especially by air when you have been seated for many hours, and should subside by the following day. Swelling of the ankles that has no obvious cause and that persists for more than 24 hours is most commonly the result of inefficient veins in the legs and often accompanies *varicose veins* (p. 107). Occasionally, ankle swelling is the result of a heart or kidney condition. Consult your physician about any persistent ankle swelling. Do this without delay if you have noticed additional symptoms such as breathlessness, unusual fatigue or swelling in any other part of the body.

Consult your physician if you are unable to make a diagnosis from this chart and if the pain and/or swelling is severe or persists for more than 48 hours.

FROZEN SHOULDER

Frozen shoulder is a condition that sometimes occurs following a minor injury to the shoulder, or a condition such as bursitis (left). The shoulder becomes stiff and sometimes painful, which leads to a reduction in its range of movement. Disuse leads in turn to further stiffness and further limitation of movement. Frozen shoulder often persists for many months.

Treatment
If you think you have frozen shoulder or if you have recently suffered from a painful shoulder condition, it is important to keep the shoulder mobile by regular, gentle exercise. Take painkillers such as aspirin or an aspirin substitute. Consult your physician, who may prescribe *anti-inflammatory* drugs by mouth or in the form of an injection into the shoulder. Supervised exercises (occupational and physical therapy) may also be recommended.

FIRST AID FOR SPRAINS AND STRAINS

A joint is said to be sprained when it is wrenched or twisted beyond its normal range of movement – in a fall, for example – thus tearing some or all of the ligaments that support it. Ankles are especially prone to this type of injury. The main symptoms, which may be indistinguishable from those of a minor strain, are pain, swelling and bruising. If you are unable to move the injured part, or if it looks misshapen, a broken bone or dislocated joint is possible and you should carry out first aid as described on p. 107. In other cases, try the following first-aid treatment:

1 For the first 24 hours after the injury, cool the injured part (see right).

2 Support an injured joint or limb with a firm, but not overtight bandage (below). An arm or wrist may be more comfortable in a sling (below right).

3 Rest the injured part for a day or so. If it is a foot, leg or ankle that is injured, keep it raised whenever possible.

If you have a badly sprained ankle that is still painful the day after the injury, go to your physician, local hospital emergency room or urgent care center to have the joint firmly bandaged to prevent movement while the joint is healing. In this case, you should make sure that you rest the joint for at least a week.

Cooling an injury
Applying cold to any injury causing pain, swelling and/or bruising will help to reduce swelling and relieve pain. This is best done by use of an ice bag (a cloth bag filled with ice), but you can improvise by using a cloth pad soaked in cold water or an unopened packet of frozen vegetables. After the first 24 hours, you should apply warmth to the affected part to reduce inflammation.

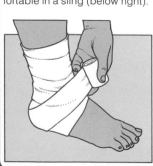

60 Foot problems

Problems with feet rarely indicate any serious underlying disorder or disease. Most foot problems are the result of injury or failure to take good care of the feet (see Caring for your feet, below). Consult this chart if you have any pain, irritation or itching of your feet, or if they become deformed in any way.

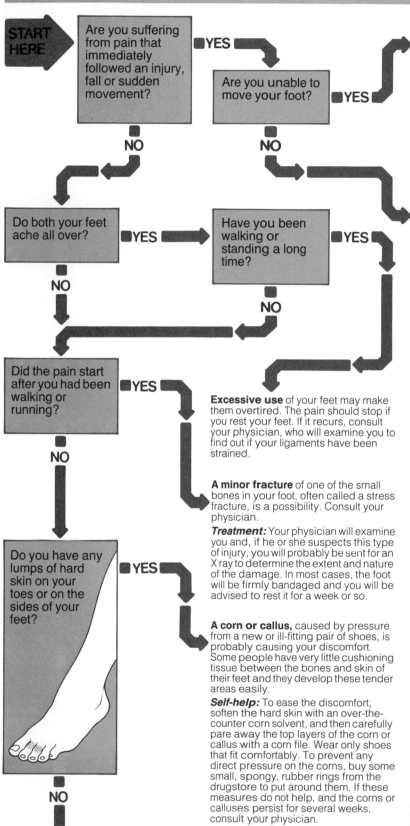

START HERE → Are you suffering from pain that immediately followed an injury, fall or sudden movement? → **YES** → Are you unable to move your foot? → **YES** →

**EMERGENCY
GET MEDICAL
HELP NOW!**

A fracture, dislocation or serious injury to the ligaments or muscles may be causing this pain. Carry out the first-aid measures for suspected broken bones and dislocated joints as described on p.107 until medical help arrives.

Treatment: The foot will be examined and probably X-rayed to discover the extent of the damage. Depending on the nature of the injury, you may need to wear a plaster cast or a firm bandage. Sometimes an operation to reposition the bones is necessary.

Are you suffering from pain that immediately followed an injury, fall or sudden movement? → **NO**

Are you unable to move your foot? → **NO**

A soft tissue injury, such as a sprain, strain or bruising, is probably causing this pain.

Self-help: Follow the advice on treating such injuries given in the box on p.109. Consult your physician if the pain is severe or is no better the following day.

Do both your feet ache all over? → **YES** → Have you been walking or standing a long time? → **YES** →

Do both your feet ache all over? → **NO**

Have you been walking or standing a long time? → **NO**

Did the pain start after you had been walking or running? → **YES** →

Excessive use of your feet may make them overtired. The pain should stop if you rest your feet. If it recurs, consult your physician, who will examine you to find out if your ligaments have been strained.

Did the pain start after you had been walking or running? → **NO**

A minor fracture of one of the small bones in your foot, often called a stress fracture, is a possibility. Consult your physician.

Treatment: Your physician will examine you and, if he or she suspects this type of injury, you will probably be sent for an X ray to determine the extent and nature of the damage. In most cases, the foot will be firmly bandaged and you will be advised to rest it for a week or so.

Do you have any lumps of hard skin on your toes or on the sides of your feet? → **YES** →

A corn or callus, caused by pressure from a new or ill-fitting pair of shoes, is probably causing your discomfort. Some people have very little cushioning tissue between the bones and skin of their feet and they develop these tender areas easily.

Self-help: To ease the discomfort, soften the hard skin with an over-the-counter corn solvent, and then carefully pare away the top layers of the corn or callus with a corn file. Wear only shoes that fit comfortably. To prevent any direct pressure on the corns, buy some small, spongy, rubber rings from the drugstore to put around them. If these measures do not help, and the corns or calluses persist for several weeks, consult your physician.

Do you have any lumps of hard skin on your toes or on the sides of your feet? → **NO** → *Go to next page*

CARING FOR YOUR FEET

Ill-fitting shoes can sometimes lead to distortion of the toes and may lead to the development of painful conditions such as bunions and corns. When buying shoes, ensure that they fit properly, allowing enough space for the toes to spread out.

Fitting shoes
Allow at least ½ in. between the longest toe and the end of the shoe.

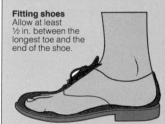
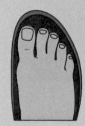

Foot hygiene
Wash your feet daily, drying thoroughly between the toes to reduce the risk of fungal infection (athlete's foot). If your feet are particularly sweaty, wear socks made of natural fibers such as cotton, which absorbs moisture more effectively than man-made fibers. If the skin of your feet is dry or cracked, apply a hand cream to the affected area.

Washing and drying your feet

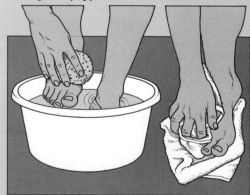

Toenails
Trim your toenails regularly, but do not cut them too short as this may damage the skin underneath. Always cut your toenails straight across.

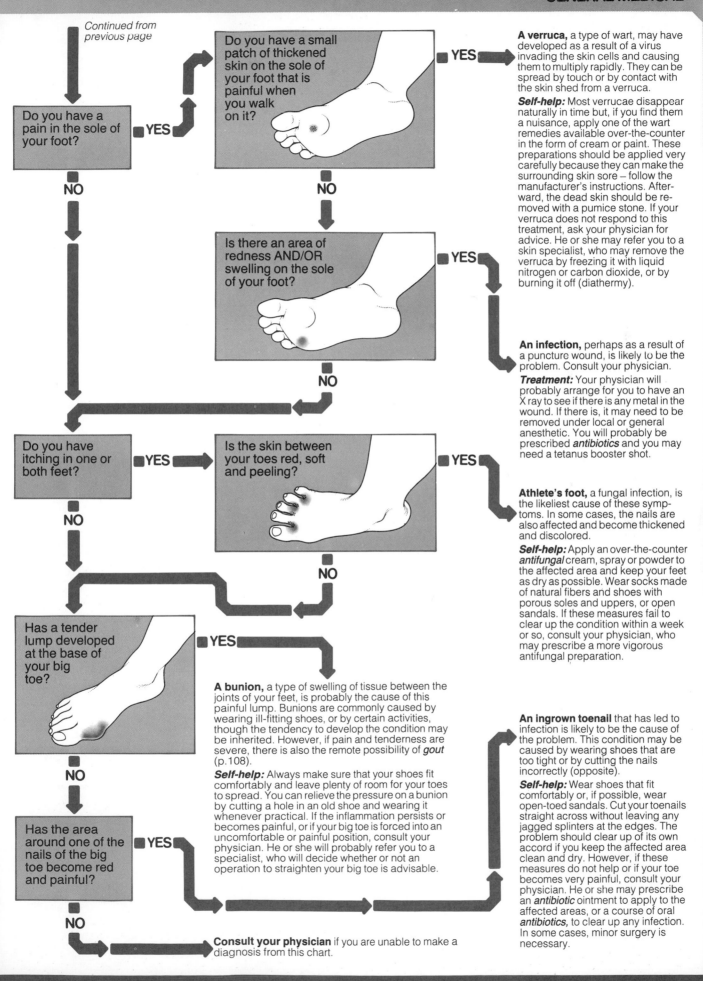

Continued from previous page

Do you have a pain in the sole of your foot?

Do you have a small patch of thickened skin on the sole of your foot that is painful when you walk on it? — YES →

A verruca, a type of wart, may have developed as a result of a virus invading the skin cells and causing them to multiply rapidly. They can be spread by touch or by contact with the skin shed from a verruca.

Self-help: Most verrucae disappear naturally in time but, if you find them a nuisance, apply one of the wart remedies available over-the-counter in the form of cream or paint. These preparations should be applied very carefully because they can make the surrounding skin sore – follow the manufacturer's instructions. Afterward, the dead skin should be removed with a pumice stone. If your verruca does not respond to this treatment, ask your physician for advice. He or she may refer you to a skin specialist, who may remove the verruca by freezing it with liquid nitrogen or carbon dioxide, or by burning it off (diathermy).

NO (from pain in sole) ↓
NO (from thickened skin) ↓

Is there an area of redness AND/OR swelling on the sole of your foot? — YES →

An infection, perhaps as a result of a puncture wound, is likely to be the problem. Consult your physician.

Treatment: Your physician will probably arrange for you to have an X ray to see if there is any metal in the wound. If there is, it may need to be removed under local or general anesthetic. You will probably be prescribed *antibiotics* and you may need a tetanus booster shot.

NO ↓

Do you have itching in one or both feet? — YES →

Is the skin between your toes red, soft and peeling? — YES →

Athlete's foot, a fungal infection, is the likeliest cause of these symptoms. In some cases, the nails are also affected and become thickened and discolored.

Self-help: Apply an over-the-counter *antifungal* cream, spray or powder to the affected area and keep your feet as dry as possible. Wear socks made of natural fibers and shoes with porous soles and uppers, or open sandals. If these measures fail to clear up the condition within a week or so, consult your physician, who may prescribe a more vigorous antifungal preparation.

NO (itching) ↓
NO (skin between toes) ↓

Has a tender lump developed at the base of your big toe? — YES →

A bunion, a type of swelling of tissue between the joints of your feet, is probably the cause of this painful lump. Bunions are commonly caused by wearing ill-fitting shoes, or by certain activities, though the tendency to develop the condition may be inherited. However, if pain and tenderness are severe, there is also the remote possibility of *gout* (p.108).

Self-help: Always make sure that your shoes fit comfortably and leave plenty of room for your toes to spread. You can relieve the pressure on a bunion by cutting a hole in an old shoe and wearing it whenever practical. If the inflammation persists or becomes painful, or if your big toe is forced into an uncomfortable or painful position, consult your physician. He or she will probably refer you to a specialist, who will decide whether or not an operation to straighten your big toe is advisable.

NO ↓

Has the area around one of the nails of the big toe become red and painful? — YES →

An ingrown toenail that has led to infection is likely to be the cause of the problem. This condition may be caused by wearing shoes that are too tight or by cutting the nails incorrectly (opposite).

Self-help: Wear shoes that fit comfortably or, if possible, wear open-toed sandals. Cut your toenails straight across without leaving any jagged splinters at the edges. The problem should clear up of its own accord if you keep the affected area clean and dry. However, if these measures do not help or if your toe becomes very painful, consult your physician. He or she may prescribe an *antibiotic* ointment to apply to the affected areas, or a course of oral *antibiotics,* to clear up any infection. In some cases, minor surgery is necessary.

NO ↓

Consult your physician if you are unable to make a diagnosis from this chart.

61 Painful penis

Pain in the penis or soreness of the overlying skin can signal a variety of different disorders of the penis itself or of the urinary tract. Many painful conditions of the penis are the result of minor injuries – perhaps incurred while participating in sports – or from friction with clothing. Nevertheless, it is important that any pain or change in the appearance of your penis not attributable to an injury of this kind be diagnosed by your physician at an early stage so that treatment, if necessary, can be started as soon as possible.

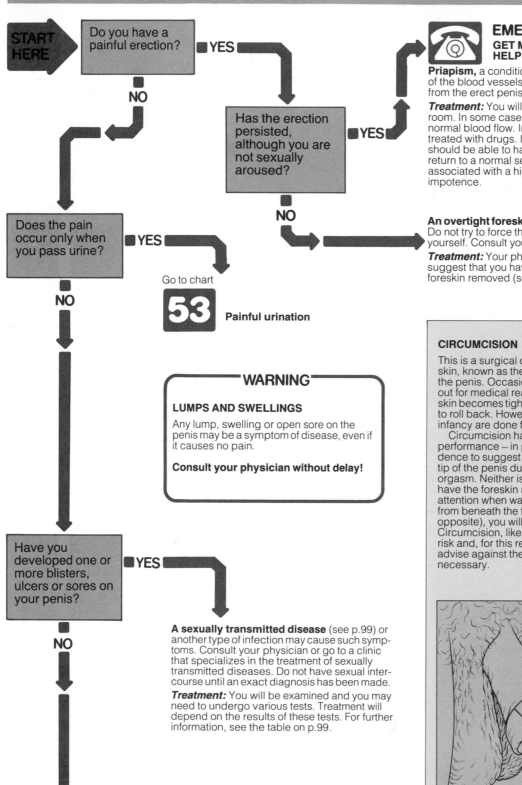

START HERE

Do you have a painful erection?

YES → **Has the erection persisted, although you are not sexually aroused?**

YES → **EMERGENCY GET MEDICAL HELP NOW!**

Priapism, a condition caused by sudden obstruction of the blood vessels so that blood cannot flow away from the erect penis, is possible.

Treatment: You will be examined at the emergency room. In some cases, surgery is necessary to restore normal blood flow. In other cases the condition can be treated with drugs. If priapism is relieved quickly, you should be able to have normal erections again and return to a normal sex life. Prolonged priapism is associated with a high frequency of subsequent impotence.

NO

Does the pain occur only when you pass urine?

YES → Go to chart

53 **Painful urination**

NO → (from "Has the erection persisted")

An overtight foreskin may be the cause of such pain. Do not try to force the foreskin back over the penis yourself. Consult your physician.

Treatment: Your physician will examine you and may suggest that you have a minor operation to have the foreskin removed (see *Circumcision,* below).

---WARNING---

LUMPS AND SWELLINGS

Any lump, swelling or open sore on the penis may be a symptom of disease, even if it causes no pain.

Consult your physician without delay!

Have you developed one or more blisters, ulcers or sores on your penis?

YES →

A sexually transmitted disease (see p.99) or another type of infection may cause such symptoms. Consult your physician or go to a clinic that specializes in the treatment of sexually transmitted diseases. Do not have sexual intercourse until an exact diagnosis has been made.

Treatment: You will be examined and you may need to undergo various tests. Treatment will depend on the results of these tests. For further information, see the table on p.99.

NO

Go to next page

CIRCUMCISION

This is a surgical operation to remove the fold of skin, known as the foreskin, that covers the tip of the penis. Occasionally, the operation is carried out for medical reasons – for example, if the foreskin becomes tight or uncomfortable and is difficult to roll back. However, most circumcisions done in infancy are done for social and religious reasons.

Circumcision has no significant effect on sexual performance – in particular, there is no firm evidence to suggest that it reduces sensitivity at the tip of the penis during intercourse or that it delays orgasm. Neither is it necessarily more hygienic to have the foreskin removed. By paying careful attention when washing to remove all secretions from beneath the foreskin (see *Genital hygiene,* opposite), you will ensure adequate cleanliness. Circumcision, like any operation, carries a small risk and, for this reason, most physicians now advise against the operation unless it is medically necessary.

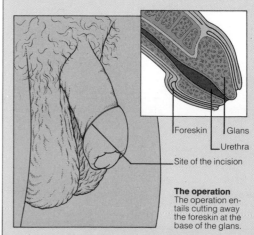

Foreskin   Glans
Urethra
Site of the incision

The operation
The operation entails cutting away the foreskin at the base of the glans.

Continued from previous page

Do you have one or more hard, skin-colored lumps on your penis?

YES → **Anogenital warts,** caused by virus infection, are likely. These often grow quite quickly and can be irritating. They are usually transmitted by sexual contact, but this is not always the case. They may disappear spontaneously, but often recur. Do not attempt to treat this condition yourself with over-the-counter preparations, because the skin of the penis is very sensitive. Consult your physician.

Treatment: Your physician may prescribe a preparation in the form of a cream or paint to apply to the warts. He or she will probably advise you to keep the affected area as clean and dry as possible with regular washing using a mild soap and then gently patting dry. Your physician will also examine you to rule out the possibility of a sexually transmitted disease (p.99) and will also advise you to avoid sexual contact until the warts have disappeared.

NO ↓

Can you see any redness or swelling on the tip (glans) of your penis?

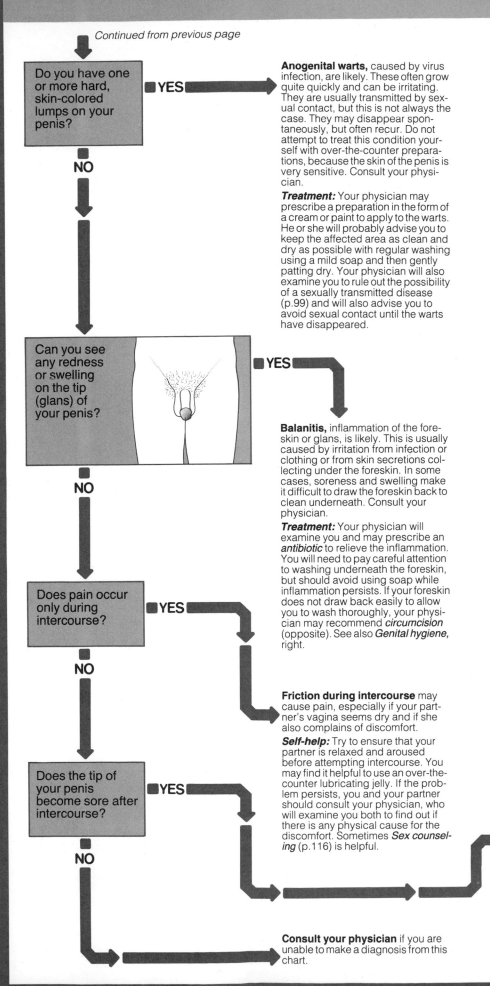

YES → **Balanitis,** inflammation of the foreskin or glans, is likely. This is usually caused by irritation from infection or clothing or from skin secretions collecting under the foreskin. In some cases, soreness and swelling make it difficult to draw the foreskin back to clean underneath. Consult your physician.

Treatment: Your physician will examine you and may prescribe an *antibiotic* to relieve the inflammation. You will need to pay careful attention to washing underneath the foreskin, but should avoid using soap while inflammation persists. If your foreskin does not draw back easily to allow you to wash thoroughly, your physician may recommend *circumcision* (opposite). See also *Genital hygiene,* right.

NO ↓

Does pain occur only during intercourse?

YES → **Friction during intercourse** may cause pain, especially if your partner's vagina seems dry and if she also complains of discomfort.

Self-help: Try to ensure that your partner is relaxed and aroused before attempting intercourse. You may find it helpful to use an over-the-counter lubricating jelly. If the problem persists, you and your partner should consult your physician, who will examine you both to find out if there is any physical cause for the discomfort. Sometimes *Sex counseling* (p.116) is helpful.

NO ↓

Does the tip of your penis become sore after intercourse?

YES → **An allergic reaction** – for example, to a contraceptive cream or douching solution used by your partner – may be the cause of soreness after intercourse. If you use a condom, there is a possibility that you may be allergic to rubber.

Self-help: Soreness should disappear if you avoid contact with whatever you think may be causing the reaction. It may be necessary for you to choose an alternative form of contraception (see p.123). If you can find no obvious cause for the soreness, or if soreness persists, consult your physician.

NO ↓

Consult your physician if you are unable to make a diagnosis from this chart.

BLOOD IN THE SEMEN

Pinkish, reddish or brownish streaks in your semen may be blood. This uncommon condition is known as hemospermia, and may be barely noticeable. It is caused by the rupture of small veins in the upper part of the urethra during an erection. These heal themselves within a few minutes, although the semen may continue to be slightly discolored for a few days afterward.

What should be done?

There is no need to be concerned if you notice blood in your semen. However, if you notice a blood-stained discharge after ejaculation, or if you notice blood in the urine, consult your physician, who will need to investigate the problem.

GENITAL HYGIENE

Minor irritations of the penis can be avoided by paying attention to genital hygiene, especially if you are sexually active. However, there is no need to be overzealous in your approach to this – the genitals need no more attention than the rest of the body. Washing your penis with warm water and mild soap each time you take a bath or shower is sufficient to maintain hygiene. If you have not been circumcised (see *Circumcision,* opposite), be sure to draw back your foreskin to clean the glans (tip) of your penis.

Cleaning under the foreskin

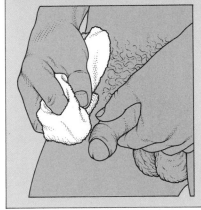

62 Painful or swollen testicles

Consult this chart if you feel any pain or notice a lump or swelling in one or both of your testes, or in the whole area within the scrotum (the supportive bag that contains the testes). It is important to seek your physician's advice because early treatment of an underlying disorder is often necessary to reduce the risk of infertility. Early detection of tumors is also important.

START HERE

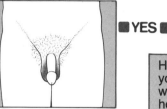 Have you suddenly developed a painful swelling around one or both testes?

YES → Have you injured your genitals within the past 48 hours?

NO ↓

YES →

-- WARNING --

LUMPS AND SWELLINGS

Any lump or swelling in the testes may be a symptom of disease, even if it causes no pain.

Consult your physician without delay!

SELF-EXAMINATION OF THE TESTES

Cancer of the testis, although rare in comparison with other cancers, is one of the most easily treated if diagnosed early. It is therefore a good idea to examine yourself regularly for any abnormalities.

Self-examination technique
About once a month, after you have had a hot bath or shower, when the skin of your scrotum is soft, examine your scrotum and testes following the guidelines below. Look for any change in size, shape or consistency of the testes. After doing this for a while you will get to know this part of your body well enough to detect any changes at an early stage.

1 Examine each testis by placing your index and middle fingers beneath the testis with your thumb on top as illustrated (below).

2 Gently roll each testis beneath your fingers and thumb, backward and forward and then sideways.

If you notice a new lump (whether or not it is painful), any increased sensitivity in the scrotum, or any change in the skin, consult your physician, who will refer you, if necessary, to a urologist for further tests.

Have you recently suffered from mumps?

YES →

NO ↓

 EMERGENCY
GET MEDICAL HELP NOW!

Torsion of the testis (twisting of the testis) is possible. This can happen at any time, even during sleep, and may be accompanied by nausea and vomiting.

Treatment: You will be examined and, if the diagnosis is confirmed, your physician may try to untwist the testis by gently manipulating it. If this is not successful, or if the problem recurs, surgery may be necessary. Sometimes exploratory surgery is needed to make the diagnosis. Often, infections in the scrotal sac mimic torsion.

EMERGENCY
GET MEDICAL HELP NOW!

Internal damage to the testes as a result of the injury may have caused the swelling.

Treatment: You may need to spend some time in the hospital, where any problem can be treated surgically if necessary. If it is necessary for you to have an operation, full recovery normally takes a few weeks.

Orchitis, a fairly common cause of swelling of one or both testes, is probably the cause of this. In rare cases, the disorder may cause infertility (see *Mumps and sterility,* p.124). Consult your physician.

Treatment: Your physician will examine you to rule out the possibility of your having a more serious infection of the lymph glands. He or she will probably prescribe painkillers for you to take to relieve the pain and advise you to rest in bed. It may be helpful to wear a jock strap. The pain and swelling normally subside within 2 weeks without aftereffects.

CONSULT YOUR PHYSICIAN WITHOUT DELAY!
A cyst (fluid-filled sac) may have formed inside the scrotum. Although it can grow quite large before causing any discomfort, it is nevertheless important to see your physician so that he or she can rule out the possibility of a tumor. Such cysts are most common in men over the age of 40, although they can occur at any age.

Treatment: Your physician will examine you and probably refer you to a specialist for tests, including a possible *biopsy* (p.35). If the swelling is caused by a cyst, further treatment is unnecessary unless the cyst grows too big for comfort, in which case it can be removed in a minor operation. If tests reveal a tumor, surgery is the usual treatment.

Is one of your testes enlarged?

YES →

NO ↓

Do you have a generalized, painless swelling of the scrotum?

YES →

NO ↓

Hydrocele, an accumulation of a clear, thin fluid between the inner and outer layers covering the testes, may be causing this swelling. The condition is quite common, especially in elderly men, though it can happen at any age. Consult your physician.

Treatment: Your physician will examine you to decide whether or not treatment is necessary. If the swelling is very large or painful, you may need to have the fluid drawn off by needle under local anesthetic. If the problem recurs, your physician may advise you to have a minor operation to tighten or remove the fibrous sheath so that the fluid can no longer collect there.

Consult your physician if you notice any swelling that is uncomfortable or persists.

2 Sex and fertility symptoms

63 Erection difficulties

Most men fail to get an erection from time to time, despite feeling sexually aroused in other ways, due to any one of a number of reasons including physical factors, psychological factors or a combination of both. Some men can only get an erection while masturbating or during oral sex, but not when they are trying to have sexual intercourse. Others can get an erection with one woman, but fail to do so with another. Consult this chart if you have noticed problems with getting or maintaining an erection.

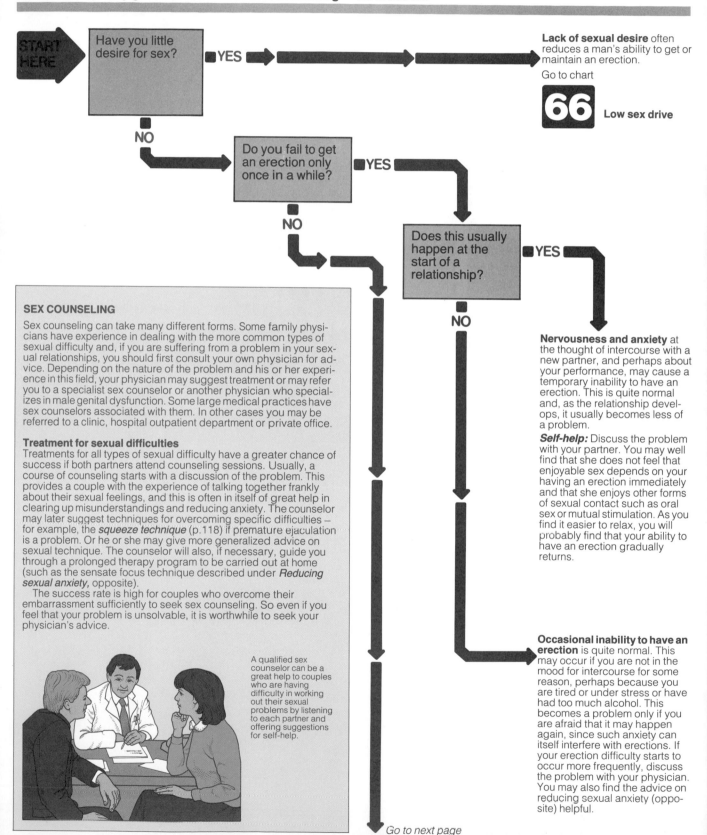

START HERE

Have you little desire for sex?

YES → **Lack of sexual desire** often reduces a man's ability to get or maintain an erection.

Go to chart

66 Low sex drive

NO ↓

Do you fail to get an erection only once in a while?

YES ↓

NO ↓

Does this usually happen at the start of a relationship?

YES → **Nervousness and anxiety** at the thought of intercourse with a new partner, and perhaps about your performance, may cause a temporary inability to have an erection. This is quite normal and, as the relationship develops, it usually becomes less of a problem.

Self-help: Discuss the problem with your partner. You may well find that she does not feel that enjoyable sex depends on your having an erection immediately and that she enjoys other forms of sexual contact such as oral sex or mutual stimulation. As you find it easier to relax, you will probably find that your ability to have an erection gradually returns.

NO ↓

SEX COUNSELING

Sex counseling can take many different forms. Some family physicians have experience in dealing with the more common types of sexual difficulty and, if you are suffering from a problem in your sexual relationships, you should first consult your own physician for advice. Depending on the nature of the problem and his or her experience in this field, your physician may suggest treatment or may refer you to a specialist sex counselor or another physician who specializes in male genital dysfunction. Some large medical practices have sex counselors associated with them. In other cases you may be referred to a clinic, hospital outpatient department or private office.

Treatment for sexual difficulties

Treatments for all types of sexual difficulty have a greater chance of success if both partners attend counseling sessions. Usually, a course of counseling starts with a discussion of the problem. This provides a couple with the experience of talking together frankly about their sexual feelings, and this is often in itself of great help in clearing up misunderstandings and reducing anxiety. The counselor may later suggest techniques for overcoming specific difficulties – for example, the *squeeze technique* (p.118) if premature ejaculation is a problem. Or he or she may give more generalized advice on sexual technique. The counselor will also, if necessary, guide you through a prolonged therapy program to be carried out at home (such as the sensate focus technique described under *Reducing sexual anxiety,* opposite).

The success rate is high for couples who overcome their embarrassment sufficiently to seek sex counseling. So even if you feel that your problem is unsolvable, it is worthwhile to seek your physician's advice.

A qualified sex counselor can be a great help to couples who are having difficulty in working out their sexual problems by listening to each partner and offering suggestions for self-help.

Occasional inability to have an erection is quite normal. This may occur if you are not in the mood for intercourse for some reason, perhaps because you are tired or under stress or have had too much alcohol. This becomes a problem only if you are afraid that it may happen again, since such anxiety can itself interfere with erections. If your erection difficulty starts to occur more frequently, discuss the problem with your physician. You may also find the advice on reducing sexual anxiety (opposite) helpful.

Go to next page

Continued from previous page

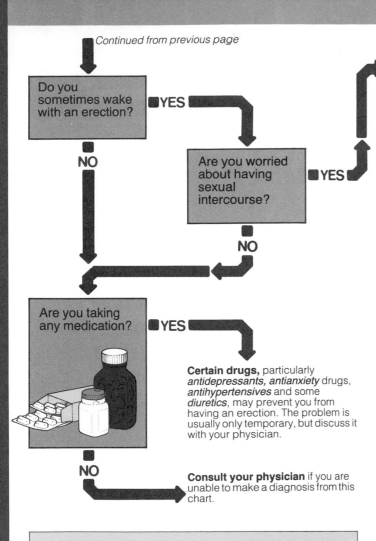

Do you sometimes wake with an erection?

— **YES** →

Are you worried about having sexual intercourse?

— **YES** →

NO ↓

NO ↓

Are you taking any medication?

— **YES** →

Certain drugs, particularly *antidepressants, antianxiety* drugs, *antihypertensives* and some *diuretics*, may prevent you from having an erection. The problem is usually only temporary, but discuss it with your physician.

NO ↓

Consult your physician if you are unable to make a diagnosis from this chart.

If you sometimes wake with an erection, a physical cause for your impotence is highly unlikely. Anxiety is a fairly common cause of erection difficulties. Worry about premature ejaculation, making your partner pregnant or catching a sexually transmitted disease, for example, are all common causes of sexual anxiety. In the majority of cases it is only a temporary difficulty.

Self-help: Discuss your feelings with your partner. You may find that your partner's reassurances are sufficient to help you overcome your difficulty. Meanwhile, try other forms of sexual contact such as mutual stimulation or oral sex. An erection may follow when you begin to feel less anxious. Try also the advice given in *Reducing sexual anxiety* (below). If, after you have tried these measures, the problem persists so that it interferes with you and your partner's sexual enjoyment, consult your physician, who may recommend that you receive counseling (see *Sex counseling,* opposite).

REDUCING SEXUAL ANXIETY

Many sexual difficulties arise out of anxiety in one or both partners, and most forms of *Sex counseling* (opposite) involve advice on reducing such anxiety as a basis for improving sexual enjoyment. Sensate focus is often successful in heightening sexual responsiveness without provoking anxiety about perfor-mance, and may help you overcome inhibitions and tensions that can mar sexual relationships. The first step is for both partners to agree to abstain from sexual intercourse for, say, 3 weeks.

Sensate focus
Set aside at least 3 evenings (or a period at another time of day) when you can be alone with your partner without fear of inter-ruption for at least 2 hours. Try to create an atmosphere in which you both feel relaxed – playing some favorite music may help. During the time when you are trying this therapy you and your partner must stick to your agreement to refrain from full sexual intercourse.

Stage 1
On the first evening, each partner should take turns gently mas-saging and caressing the other for a period of about 20 minutes. This is best carried out when you are both naked, and you can use a body lotion or oil if you like. The massage should involve a gentle exploration of all parts of the body except the genital and breast areas. The partner being caressed should concentrate on finding pleasure from being touched, and the partner giving the caresses should concentrate on his or her own pleasure from contact with the partner's body. Once you have gotten over any awkwardness and are finding enjoyment from the sensations you experience during this activity – this may take several sessions – go to stage 2.

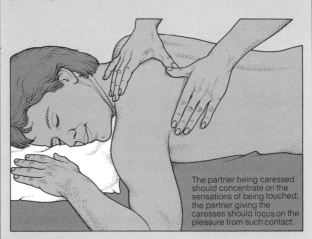

The partner being caressed should concentrate on the sensations of being touched; the partner giving the caresses should focus on the pleasure from such contact.

Stage 2
Stage 2 is similar to stage 1, but this time body massage may include genital and breast areas. Remember, however, to con-tinue to include other parts of the body in your caresses so that direct sexual stimulation can be felt in context with other body sensations.

Stage 3
Most couples find that soon after reaching stage 2 they are ready to resume sexual intercourse, and in most cases they find that they are more relaxed and are more able to enjoy a full range of physical and emotional sexual feelings.

SEX IN LATER LIFE

The majority of men reach their physical sexual peak in their late teens or early twenties. During sexual intercourse they reach orgasm quickly, ejaculate powerfully and are able to have another erection soon after. As a man gets older it may take him longer to get an erection, which may not be as hard as in the past, and more stimulation may be necessary. Ejaculation may be delayed slightly (this can be beneficial for men who have previously suffered from premature ejaculation). The time it takes to develop another erection may be longer. However, there is usually no physical reason why a man should not continue to have an active and happy sex life well into old age.

Possible problems
The changes described above occur only gradually and often go unnoticed. For many men sexual activity becomes more enjoyable with increased experience and confidence. A reduction in the frequency of orgasm is often more than compensated for by the enhanced quality of the sexual experience.

However, some men become anxious about their sexual per-formance as they approach middle age. This usually occurs when anxiety or depression, possibly connected with other aspects of life – for example, lack of job satisfaction or concern about the future – leads them to compare their current sex life unfavorably with how it was 20 or 30 years before. Some men who have experienced sexual difficulties in the past use their advancing years as an excuse for avoiding sex altogether in later life. This is no cause for concern if both partners are happy not to have sex. But if a reduction in sexual activity causes unhappiness in either partner, it is never too late to seek *Sex counseling* (opposite) for this or any other sex problem.

64 Premature ejaculation

There are occasions when men ejaculate before they wish to. This becomes a problem only if you consistently ejaculate so quickly that you and your partner become frustrated by the curtailment of sexual intercourse. The anxiety that often accompanies premature ejaculation tends to make the problem worse and may lead you to avoid sex. This may result in disharmony between you and your partner. However, the tendency to ejaculate prematurely can usually be overcome with time, patience and self-help.

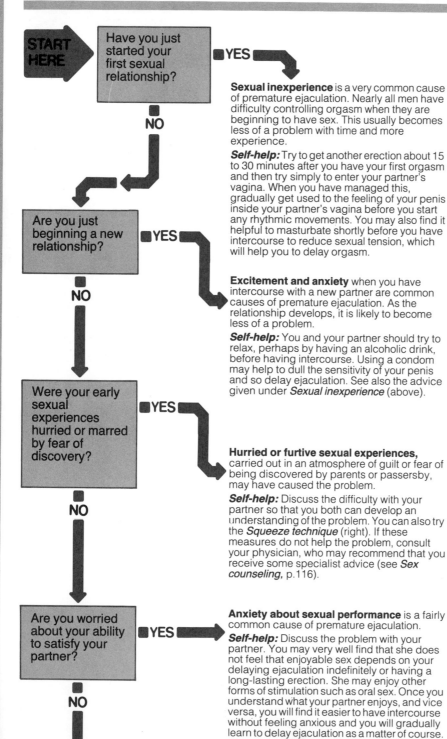

START HERE — Have you just started your first sexual relationship?

YES

NO

Are you just beginning a new relationship?

YES

NO

Were your early sexual experiences hurried or marred by fear of discovery?

YES

NO

Are you worried about your ability to satisfy your partner?

YES

NO

Consult your physician if you are unable to make a diagnosis from this chart or if the self-help measures do not help the problem.

Sexual inexperience is a very common cause of premature ejaculation. Nearly all men have difficulty controlling orgasm when they are beginning to have sex. This usually becomes less of a problem with time and more experience.

Self-help: Try to get another erection about 15 to 30 minutes after you have your first orgasm and then try simply to enter your partner's vagina. When you have managed this, gradually get used to the feeling of your penis inside your partner's vagina before you start any rhythmic movements. You may also find it helpful to masturbate shortly before you have intercourse to reduce sexual tension, which will help you to delay orgasm.

Excitement and anxiety when you have intercourse with a new partner are common causes of premature ejaculation. As the relationship develops, it is likely to become less of a problem.

Self-help: You and your partner should try to relax, perhaps by having an alcoholic drink, before having intercourse. Using a condom may help to dull the sensitivity of your penis and so delay ejaculation. See also the advice given under *Sexual inexperience* (above).

Hurried or furtive sexual experiences, carried out in an atmosphere of guilt or fear of being discovered by parents or passersby, may have caused the problem.

Self-help: Discuss the difficulty with your partner so that you both can develop an understanding of the problem. You can also try the *Squeeze technique* (right). If these measures do not help the problem, consult your physician, who may recommend that you receive some specialist advice (see *Sex counseling,* p.116).

Anxiety about sexual performance is a fairly common cause of premature ejaculation.

Self-help: Discuss the problem with your partner. You may very well find that she does not feel that enjoyable sex depends on your delaying ejaculation indefinitely or having a long-lasting erection. She may enjoy other forms of stimulation such as oral sex. Once you understand what your partner enjoys, and vice versa, you will find it easier to have intercourse without feeling anxious and you will gradually learn to delay ejaculation as a matter of course. Also, read *Reducing sexual anxiety* (p.117) and try the *Squeeze technique* described at right. If these measures fail and the problem persists so that it interferes with your sexual enjoyment, consult your physician, who may recommend that you seek specialist advice (see *Sex counseling,* p.116).

SQUEEZE TECHNIQUE

The squeeze technique is one of the most widely accepted methods for helping a man to delay and control orgasm. It teaches both partners to recognize the sensations that immediately precede ejaculation, so increasing control. Many couples find that it helps to try the technique of sensate focus (see *Reducing sexual anxiety,* p.117) before undertaking the squeeze technique.

Stage 1
Adopt a position that is comfortable for both you and your partner. Many couples find the best position is one in which the woman sits with her back to the head of the bed, her legs spread out in front. The man lies facing her, with his body between her legs, his legs over hers. Your partner should then caress your penis to full erection and continue until you are close to orgasm. When you feel ready to ejaculate, signal to your partner, who then stops stimulating you and grips the penis firmly with her thumb and index finger just below the glans until your erection subsides. After about half a minute, she can start to stimulate your penis again. Repeat this 2 or 3 times before allowing yourself to ejaculate. With practice, your partner will begin to sense without a signal when you are near to orgasm. After a few sessions, when you both have gained confidence about controlling ejaculation, it is possible to move on to the next stage.

Gripping below the glans delays orgasm

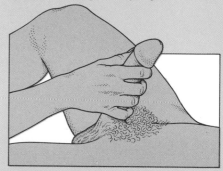

Stage 2
Lie on your back with your partner astride you and your erect penis inside her vagina. Practice holding this position without moving for as long as possible. If you feel you are about to ejaculate, signal to your partner. She then lifts herself away and applies the squeeze grip as before. Repeat this 2 or 3 times. If your erection begins to subside, stimulation of the penis will restore it so that it can be once again inserted into your partner's vagina.

After a few sessions, when you feel control has improved, normal full intercourse can be attempted so that both partners can reach orgasm. You may find that positions in which your partner is on top allow you to control orgasm most easily. If at any time you feel ready to ejaculate before your partner is ready, she can use the squeeze technique.

65 Delayed ejaculation

Consult this chart if you are able to have a normal erection but are unable to ejaculate as soon as you would like, or if you have lost the ability to ejaculate altogether. There may be physical or emotional reasons for this type of difficulty. Whatever you suspect may be the cause of the problem, frank discussion with your partner is essential so that she can help you to overcome the difficulty.

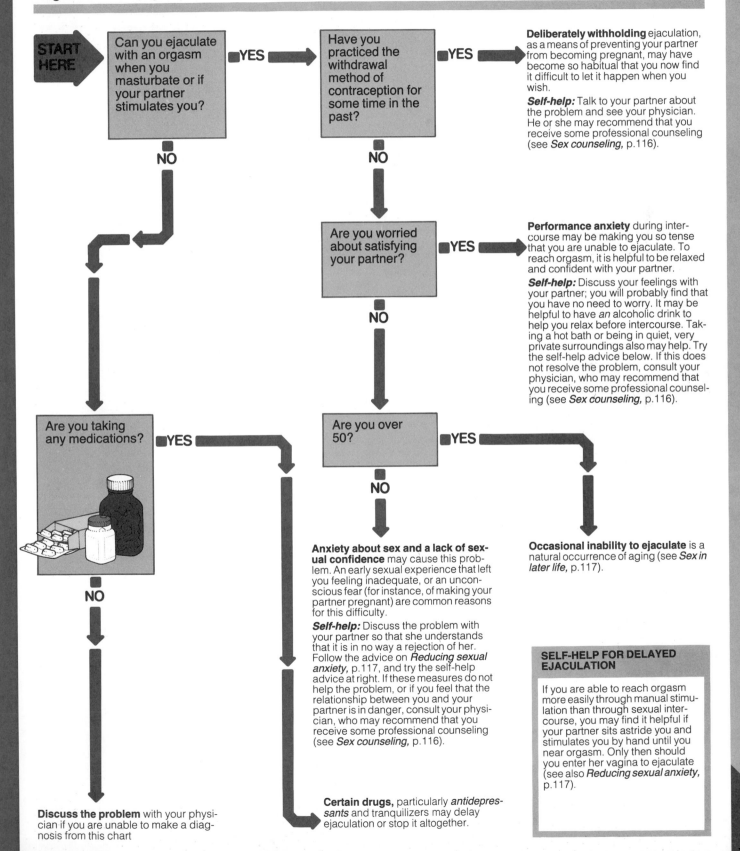

START HERE

Can you ejaculate with an orgasm when you masturbate or if your partner stimulates you?

YES → **Have you practiced the withdrawal method of contraception for some time in the past?**

YES → **Deliberately withholding** ejaculation, as a means of preventing your partner from becoming pregnant, may have become so habitual that you now find it difficult to let it happen when you wish.

Self-help: Talk to your partner about the problem and see your physician. He or she may recommend that you receive some professional counseling (see *Sex counseling,* p.116).

NO (from withdrawal question) → **Are you worried about satisfying your partner?**

YES → **Performance anxiety** during intercourse may be making you so tense that you are unable to ejaculate. To reach orgasm, it is helpful to be relaxed and confident with your partner.

Self-help: Discuss your feelings with your partner; you will probably find that you have no need to worry. It may be helpful to have *an* alcoholic drink to help you relax before intercourse. Taking a hot bath or being in quiet, very private surroundings also may help. Try the self-help advice below. If this does not resolve the problem, consult your physician, who may recommend that you receive some professional counseling (see *Sex counseling,* p.116).

Are you taking any medications?

YES → (continues to *Certain drugs*)

NO (from satisfying partner) → **Are you over 50?**

YES → **Occasional inability to ejaculate** is a natural occurrence of aging (see *Sex in later life,* p.117).

NO → **Anxiety about sex and a lack of sexual confidence** may cause this problem. An early sexual experience that left you feeling inadequate, or an unconscious fear (for instance, of making your partner pregnant) are common reasons for this difficulty.

Self-help: Discuss the problem with your partner so that she understands that it is in no way a rejection of her. Follow the advice on *Reducing sexual anxiety,* p.117, and try the self-help advice at right. If these measures do not help the problem, or if you feel that the relationship between you and your partner is in danger, consult your physician, who may recommend that you receive some professional counseling (see *Sex counseling,* p.116).

Certain drugs, particularly *antidepressants* and tranquilizers may delay ejaculation or stop it altogether.

Discuss the problem with your physician if you are unable to make a diagnosis from this chart

SELF-HELP FOR DELAYED EJACULATION

If you are able to reach orgasm more easily through manual stimulation than through sexual intercourse, you may find it helpful if your partner sits astride you and stimulates you by hand until you near orgasm. Only then should you enter her vagina to ejaculate (see also *Reducing sexual anxiety,* p.117).

66 Low sex drive

Male sexual arousal is governed by both psychological factors and by the male sex hormone testosterone. If a man has a very low level of testosterone he is unlikely to have a great interest in sex and may find it difficult to become sexually aroused. However, most cases of reduced sex drive are the result of nonhormonal factors including physical illness, depression, stress, sexual difficulties, boredom, and discontent with a relationship.

START HERE

Have you always had little interest in sex?
YES →

A naturally low level of interest in sex is a normal part of the personality of some men. This is unlikely to be a cause for concern if you and your partner are happy with your present level of sexual activity. However, if your low sex drive is causing difficulties within your relationship, consult your physician, who may recommend *Sex counseling* (p.116).

NO

Have you been overtired AND/OR under stress recently?
YES →

Fatigue and stress are very common reasons for a man's loss of interest in sex.
Self-help: Discuss the problem with your partner and explain why you are feeling the way you do. This will help your partner to understand that it is not because you find her unattractive in any way. You will probably find that she agrees that there is little satisfaction for either of you from sex attempted out of duty. When you are feeling better, the desire for sex will almost certainly return. Meanwhile, see chart 3, *Tiredness,* and/or chart 20, *Anxiety,* for advice on tackling the underlying reason for your loss of sex drive.

NO

Have you been feeling low or "blue" recently?
YES →

Depression is a possible cause of loss of interest in sex.

Go to chart

19 **Depression**

NO

Have you been drinking heavily in recent weeks?
YES →

Regular consumption of large amounts of alcohol is a common cause of loss of interest in sex and, in some cases, may lead to impotence. There is also the possibility of other health problems (see *The effects of alcohol,* p. 22).
Self-help: Cutting out alcohol altogether should help to restore your interest in sex. If you find it difficult to cut down on your alcohol intake or your enthusiasm for sex does not return, consult your physician.

NO

Do you or your partner have a specific sexual difficulty?
YES →

A sexual problem may unconsciously make you feel that you do not desire sex. When such an underlying problem is dealt with, sex drive usually returns to normal. Chart 64, *Premature ejaculation;* chart 65, *Delayed ejaculation;* and chart 63, *Erection difficulties* deal with the most common sex difficulties in men. If your problem is not covered in this book, ask your physician for advice. He or she may suggest that you and your partner receive professional advice (see *Sex counseling,* p.116).

NO

Do you only fail to get aroused by your regular partner?
YES →

NO

1 *Go to next page column 1*

2 *Go to next page column 2*

SEXUAL ORIENTATION

Sexual orientation — that is, whether you are heterosexual (attracted to people of the opposite sex), homosexual (attracted to people of the same sex) or bisexual (attracted to people of both sexes) is probably determined by a combination of inborn personality traits, upbringing, and family relationships. Some researchers have suggested that there may be hormonal factors that contribute to determining sexual orientation, but these findings have not been generally accepted. Few people are wholly heterosexual or homosexual. In particular, it is common for adolescents to go through a phase of experiencing homosexual feelings before becoming attracted to people of the opposite sex. Some people, however, remain homosexual in their sexual preferences.

Homosexuality
This variation from the mainly heterosexual orientation of the majority is no cause for medical concern among most physicians as long as the individual is happy with his homosexuality. Treatment to change sexual orientation is unlikely to be effective and is seldom recommended unless the individual is determined to make the attempt and has at least some interest in the opposite sex. However, society's attitude toward homosexuality frequently causes homosexuals to feel guilty and abnormal, and therefore leads them to repress their sexual feelings. This can be psychologically damaging. If you think that you are homosexual and are experiencing such problems, consult your physician, who may be able to offer helpful advice and/or refer you for counseling to one of the organizations that specializes in advising homosexuals.

1 *Continued from previous page, column 1*

Are you taking any medication?

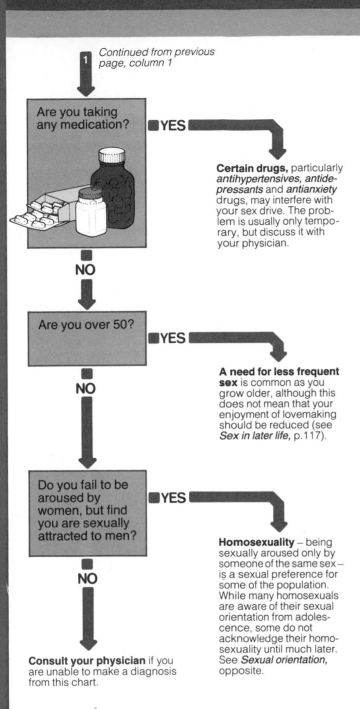

YES

Certain drugs, particularly *antihypertensives, antidepressants* and *antianxiety* drugs, may interfere with your sex drive. The problem is usually only temporary, but discuss it with your physician.

NO

Are you over 50?

YES

A need for less frequent sex is common as you grow older, although this does not mean that your enjoyment of lovemaking should be reduced (see *Sex in later life,* p.117).

NO

Do you fail to be aroused by women, but find you are sexually attracted to men?

YES

Homosexuality – being sexually aroused only by someone of the same sex – is a sexual preference for some of the population. While many homosexuals are aware of their sexual orientation from adolescence, some do not acknowledge their homosexuality until much later. See *Sexual orientation,* opposite.

NO

Consult your physician if you are unable to make a diagnosis from this chart.

---

2 *Continued from previous page, column 2*

Do you have any other cause for discontent in your relationship?

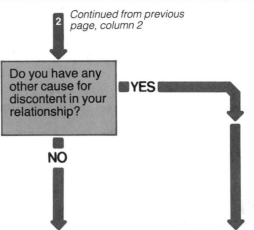

YES

NO

Loss of interest in a sexual relationship once the excitement and novelty have worn off is a common cause of loss of sexual desire.

Self-help: It may help to talk openly with your partner about how you feel so that there is no misunderstanding of the situation. If the relationship is a long-standing one, and sound in every other way, try to inject new life into it (for example, by going away for a weekend together or cooperating in some new venture). You may find trying new approaches to lovemaking helpful. If these measures do not help, consult your physician, who may suggest that you and your partner receive some professional advice (see *Sex counseling,* p.116).

Generalized antagonism or specific disagreements can lead to tension in a relationship that also affects your sexual feelings for each other. There may also be some lack of communication so that you do not fully understand each other's feelings and attitudes toward sex and other matters. This may produce conflict and damage your sexual relationship.

Self-help: Talk to your partner and explain how the problems with your relationship are affecting your feelings. If you find that things do not improve after full and frank discussion, consult your physician, who will examine you to find out if there is an underlying physical problem. If there is no physical disorder, he or she may suggest that you and your partner seek professional guidance about your general difficulties and possibly *Sex counseling* (p.116) for any specific problem you may have.

HORMONE DEFICIENCY AND LOW SEX DRIVE

In rare cases, low sex drive may be a symptom of a deficiency of the male sex hormone testosterone. This type of hormone deficiency often causes additional symptoms such as loss of body hair and unusually small testes. If your lack of interest in sex is accompanied by such additional symptoms, consult your physician.

Treatment

If tests confirm the diagnosis, hormone treatment will be prescribed and is usually successful in increasing sex drive and reversing such physical changes. Loss of sex drive that is not accompanied by the physical symptoms described here is not likely to be caused by lack of testosterone, and hormone supplements will have no beneficial effect.

MEDICAL PROBLEMS ASSOCIATED WITH HOMOSEXUALITY

While homosexual activity is not in itself a danger to physical or mental health, some diseases seem to be particularly prevalent among male homosexuals. These include hepatitis (liver infection) and all the sexually transmitted diseases, but especially syphilis and the much-publicized disorder of the immune system – AIDS (acquired immune deficiency syndrome). (See also *Sexually transmitted diseases,* p.99.)

The reason such diseases are more common among sexually active homosexuals is that homosexuals often have many different sexual contacts. Homosexual men who have many sexual partners are therefore advised to follow the advice given under *Multiple sex partners* (p.122) and to be especially vigilant for the following symptoms:

- unexplained tiredness
- yellowing of the skin
- unexplained rashes or sores
- abnormally frequent and persistent respiratory and/or digestive-tract infections (diarrhea)
- persistent swelling of the glands

If you notice any of the above symptoms, consult your physician without delay. It is advisable to avoid sexual contact until the cause of the symptoms has been diagnosed and treated.

67 Contraception

The complex process by which sperm is produced makes it very difficult for an effective male contraceptive to be developed. It is hard to interfere with the production and development of sperm without affecting male sex drive or reducing the volume of semen ejaculated. Various drugs are being investigated to find a method of reducing sperm count without altering sexual desire or performance, but it will be some time before they can be guaranteed to be safe and effective. Until such a contraceptive has been tried and tested, it is up to you, after reading this chart and discussing contraception with your partner, to decide which is the best method for you or your partner to use (see *Contraceptive methods,* opposite). The two methods currently available to you if you wish to take sole responsibility are the condom and the vasectomy.

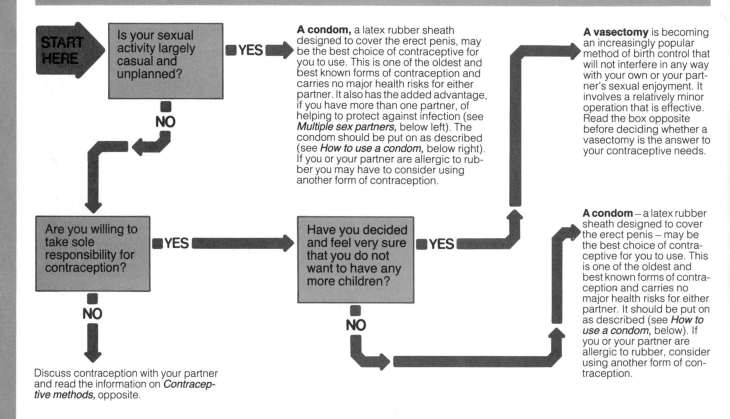

START HERE

Is your sexual activity largely casual and unplanned?

YES →

NO ↓

Are you willing to take sole responsibility for contraception?

YES →

NO ↓

Have you decided and feel very sure that you do not want to have any more children?

YES →

NO ↓

A condom, a latex rubber sheath designed to cover the erect penis, may be the best choice of contraceptive for you to use. This is one of the oldest and best known forms of contraception and carries no major health risks for either partner. It also has the added advantage, if you have more than one partner, of helping to protect against infection (see *Multiple sex partners,* below left). The condom should be put on as described (see *How to use a condom,* below right). If you or your partner are allergic to rubber you may have to consider using another form of contraception.

A vasectomy is becoming an increasingly popular method of birth control that will not interfere in any way with your own or your partner's sexual enjoyment. It involves a relatively minor operation that is effective. Read the box opposite before deciding whether a vasectomy is the answer to your contraceptive needs.

A condom – a latex rubber sheath designed to cover the erect penis – may be the best choice of contraceptive for you to use. This is one of the oldest and best known forms of contraception and carries no major health risks for either partner. It should be put on as described (see *How to use a condom,* below). If you or your partner are allergic to rubber, consider using another form of contraception.

Discuss contraception with your partner and read the information on *Contraceptive methods,* opposite.

MULTIPLE SEX PARTNERS

Many people enjoy an active and varied sex life with no ill effects. However, there are certain medical risks associated with having sex with a large number of different partners (female or male). The chief risk is contracting a sexually transmitted disease (p.99). There are, however, a number of precautions you can take to reduce the risk of becoming infected yourself or of passing on infections to your partners.

- Always wear a condom. This advice applies whether or not your partner is using other methods of contraception and to homosexuals. Wearing a condom may prevent bacteria from entering the urethra during intercourse and it will prevent the transmission of infection in semen.
- Pay particular attention to regular genital hygiene (p.113), washing carefully after sexual intercourse.
- Report any suspicious symptoms, such as discharge from the penis, pain when passing urine or sores in the genital or anal area, to your physician at once.

HOW TO USE A CONDOM

A condom is simple and easy to use and very reliable if you follow these instructions:

- Use a fresh condom each time you have intercourse.
- Check that it has no holes or tears.
- Make sure that you pinch a "teat" at the end, if there is not already one, so that semen can collect there rather

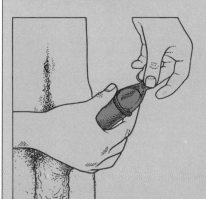

than burst through the condom at the time of ejaculation.
- Your partner is always well advised to use spermicidal foam, jelly or cream for added protection, just in case you do spill any sperm.
- After intercourse, withdraw your penis before your erection subsides, holding the rim of the condom as you do so, so that it does not slip off. This will help prevent the inadvertent deposit of semen in or near the vagina.
- If the condom is damaged or displaced during intercourse, your partner should ask her physician for a postcoital pill, which needs to be taken within 72 hours of intercourse. This will prevent an unwanted pregnancy.
- A condom is not only a reliable contraceptive, it also offers both partners protection from sexually transmitted diseases (STDs)

CONTRACEPTIVE METHODS

Method	For whom it is recommended	Possible side effects and risks
Barrier methods A barrier method is any device that prevents sperm from entering the uterus and so from fertilizing the egg. The condom (opposite) is a very popular method of temporary contraception for a man. Barrier methods used by women include the diaphragm, cervical cap and contraceptive sponge, which your partner places over the entrance to the cervix. Barrier methods are very effective, especially when used with a spermicidal foam, cream or jelly.	The condom is the only method of temporary contraception available for a man and is the best method if your partner is not taking any contraceptive precautions. It is also recommended for those who have many different partners (opposite). Condoms can readily be bought over-the-counter. Female barrier methods are useful for women who cannot or do not want to use the birth-control pill or IUD.	There are few side effects to barrier methods. You or your partner may be allergic to rubber in a condom or to certain chemicals in a spermicide, so you may need to switch brands (or, in the case of a condom, discontinue use and find another method of contraception).
Ovulation (rhythm) method This method of contraception is based on the principle that a woman can detect when ovulation (release of an egg) has occurred. Abstention from intercourse during the days surrounding ovulation prevents conception. Fertile days are detected by your partner monitoring changes in her body temperature and in the consistency and appearance of the mucus produced by the cervix.	This can be an effective form of contraception for those who do not wish to use "artificial" methods for any reason, if the relationship is stable, and if the woman has regular periods. But you may find the method unacceptable if you and your partner do not wish to abstain from sex for at least 7 days in each month.	There are none. However, this method is less effective than most others and you and your partner may feel frustrated if you cannot have intercourse during your partner's period.
Intrauterine contraceptive device (IUD) This is a device, usually made of plastic and sometimes covered with copper wire, which is inserted in the uterus. It prevents a fertilized egg from implanting in the uterine lining.	The IUD is usually recommended if you and your partner are in a stable relationship and your partner does not wish to take the birth-control pill. It may not be suitable if your partner has had an ectopic (outside the uterus) pregnancy or pelvic infections in the past.	Most women who use an IUD notice an increase in bleeding and sometimes pain during periods. There is also an increased risk of pelvic infections and of ectopic pregnancy. Occasionally, an IUD may be displaced or expelled from the uterus.
Birth-control pill There are two main types of oral birth-control pill taken by women: the combined estrogen and progesterone pill and the progesterone-only pill. The combined pill increases the level of the female sex hormones, estrogen and progesterone (progestogen is the synthetic form of the latter) and this prevents the release of an egg (ovulation). The most important contraceptive effect of the progesterone-only pill is that it causes thickening of the mucus at the entrance of the cervix, thus preventing penetration by sperm.	The combined pill is often recommended for young women. It may be particularly useful if your partner suffers from painful and heavy periods as it relieves both these symptoms. It may not be recommended if your partner is over 35, smokes, is overweight or has a history of circulatory disorders, migraine headaches, high blood pressure or heart or liver disease. The progesterone-only pill is usually recommended for women who want to use an oral contraceptive, but for whom one containing estrogen is unsuitable. This type of pill needs to be taken at precisely the same time each day to be effective, it may not be suitable for those who have an irregular life-style or who tend to be forgetful. It is particularly useful for breast-feeding mothers because it does not reduce milk production.	Possible side effects of the combined pill include "spotting" between periods, headaches, an increase in blood pressure, depression, loss of sex drive and slight weight gain. Regular combined pill-takers run a slightly increased risk of developing blood clots (thromboembolisms). The progesterone-only pill in general carries fewer risks and has fewer side effects than the combined pill. But there is an increased likelihood of spotting between periods.

VASECTOMY

Who should consider it

It is important to discuss the implications of a vasectomy with your partner. A vasectomy is usually a permanent form of contraception. Therefore, you and your partner need to be absolutely certain that you will not want to have any more children.

Remember that your present circumstances may change in the future. You may divorce and remarry and want to start a family. You may lose the children you already have. Or you may simply decide that you are no longer prepared to live without children. Couples under 30 years of age are usually discouraged from undertaking any form of sterilization. Your physician may suggest that you receive some professional counseling before you make a final decision.

The operation

A vasectomy is a straightforward operation that involves closing off the vas deferens so that sperm are no longer present in the semen. A vasectomy does not interfere with sperm production; sperm continue to be made and still travel along the vas deferens as far as they can but, because they cannot be ejaculated, they eventually dissolve and are absorbed into the system (see *Sperm production*, p.125). The operation does not affect sex drive or cause impotence. Ejaculation occurs normally because the blockage of the vas deferens does not affect the production of seminal fluid from the prostate gland. The only difference is that after the operation the seminal fluid contains no sperm (this can only be detected by the use of a microscope).

The operation is usually carried out with the help of a local anesthetic. Your pubic hair will be shaved and the surgeon will make two tiny cuts in the scrotum – one on each side, because you have two vas deferens, one for each testis. Each vas deferens is then tied or clipped in two places and the surgeon snips the length between each

knot or clip. You may feel slight discomfort in the groin, but this soon disappears. The whole operation lasts 15 to 25 minutes.

It is a safe procedure, but occasionally there is some bleeding within the scrotum, or a slight infection after the operation. If you notice any swelling in the scrotum in the days following a vasectomy, whether or not it is painful, consult your physician, who may refer you back to the hospital for treatment.

After the operation

A vasectomy does not make you sterile immediately. Sperm produced before the operation remain in the reproductive system beyond the break in the vas deferens until they are expelled by ejaculation over the course of the following months. In the meantime, you and your partner should use some alternative form of contraception until sperm counts (see *Sperm testing*, p.124) taken during the next three months or so confirm that your seminal fluid is free of sperm.

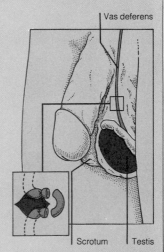

A tiny cut is made in the scrotum, and the vas deferens is tied in two places and snipped in between.

68 Fertility problems

Consult this chart if you and your partner have had sexual intercourse for more than 12 months without contraception and without your partner having become pregnant. Failure to conceive may be the result of a problem affecting the man or the woman (or both). Male infertility is nearly always the result of insufficient production of sperm or blockage of the passage of sperm during ejaculation. This may be caused by a temporary malfunction of the sperm-producing glands or by a long-term condition.

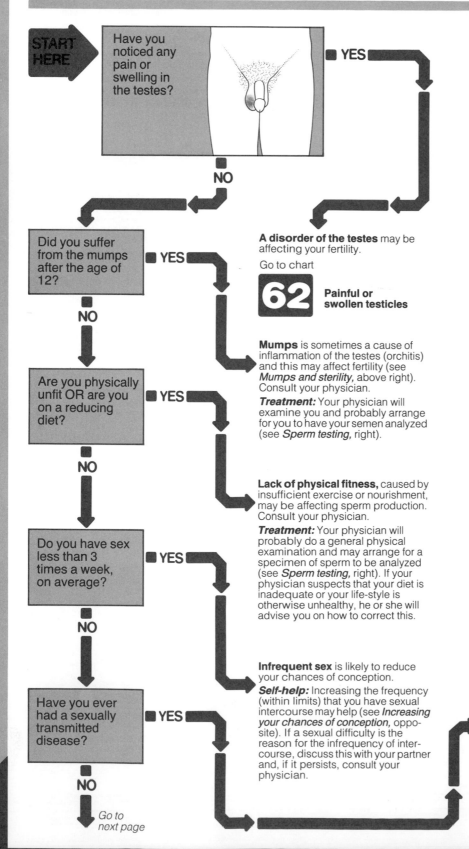

START HERE

Have you noticed any pain or swelling in the testes?

YES →

NO ↓

Did you suffer from the mumps after the age of 12?

YES →

NO ↓

Are you physically unfit OR are you on a reducing diet?

YES →

NO ↓

Do you have sex less than 3 times a week, on average?

YES →

NO ↓

Have you ever had a sexually transmitted disease?

YES →

NO ↓
Go to next page

A disorder of the testes may be affecting your fertility.

Go to chart

62 Painful or swollen testicles

Mumps is sometimes a cause of inflammation of the testes (orchitis) and this may affect fertility (see *Mumps and sterility,* above right). Consult your physician.

Treatment: Your physician will examine you and probably arrange for you to have your semen analyzed (see *Sperm testing,* right).

Lack of physical fitness, caused by insufficient exercise or nourishment, may be affecting sperm production. Consult your physician.

Treatment: Your physician will probably do a general physical examination and may arrange for a specimen of sperm to be analyzed (see *Sperm testing,* right). If your physician suspects that your diet is inadequate or your life-style is otherwise unhealthy, he or she will advise you on how to correct this.

Infrequent sex is likely to reduce your chances of conception.

Self-help: Increasing the frequency (within limits) that you have sexual intercourse may help (see *Increasing your chances of conception,* opposite). If a sexual difficulty is the reason for the infrequency of intercourse, discuss this with your partner and, if it persists, consult your physician.

Sexually transmitted diseases (see p.99) may sometimes cause infertility in both men and women. Consult your physician.

Treatment: If you currently have symptoms, your physician will examine you and take a sample from your blood or urethra. This will be analyzed and, if a sexually transmitted disease is diagnosed, you will probably be given *antibiotics.* If you have had such a disease in the past, tests on sperm (see *Sperm testing,* above) will determine whether or not it has affected your fertility.

MUMPS AND STERILITY

If you suffered from mumps after the age of 12 and you can remember that you had painful and/or swollen testes at the time, there is a possibility that the disease has interfered with your ability to produce normal sperm. Your physician will arrange for you to have a sperm count (see *Sperm testing,* below) and will offer you advice.

SPERM TESTING

A sperm count is the standard test for male fertility – that is, whether or not a man has a chance of successfully conceiving. For this test you will be asked to ejaculate into a container. For 2 days prior to the test you will need to refrain from ejaculating so that the number of sperm in the semen is at its highest level. From this sample the number of active, healthy sperm can be assessed.

A count of 100 million sperm per cubic centimeter of semen makes conception likely, providing that your partner is fertile. If a count of 200 million sperm per cubic centimeter is recorded, with 40 percent of them being active and the remainder being of normal shape, then conception is still possible. A "normal" sperm count (with good motility and shape) is considered to begin at about 50 million sperm per cubic centimeter. Because the sperm count varies greatly from day to day, a man found to have a low sperm count may need to have another test to confirm whether or not the result of the low count was a temporary fluctuation in sperm production.

Shape of a sperm

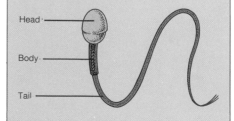

Head

Body

Tail

Continued from previous page

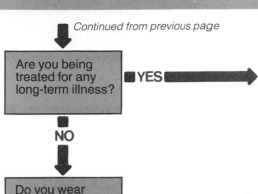

Are you being treated for any long-term illness? ■ YES ➡ **Certain illnesses** and the drugs used in their treatment may make it difficult for you to father a child. Liver and hormone disorders are particularly likely to have this effect. Discuss the problem with your physician.

■ NO

Do you wear underpants that are tight-fitting or made of an artificial fiber or do you use saunas or steam baths frequently? ■ YES ➡ **An increased temperature** within the scrotum may be making you less fertile. If the testes and the sperm they contain are not cooler than normal body temperature, fertility may be reduced (see *Sperm production,* below).

Self-help: Your chances of conception may be improved if you wear loose-fitting underpants made of a natural fiber such as cotton. This material allows air to circulate more freely so that the temperature around your testes does not get too high. Since there is some evidence that men who use saunas or steam baths often may have decreased sperm production due to high temperatures, it might be worthwhile to discontinue use of any saunas or steam baths for a while.

■ NO

Consult your physician if you are unable to make a diagnosis from this chart.

INCREASING YOUR CHANCES OF CONCEPTION

Although prolonged delay in achieving conception requires professional tests and treatment, you may be able to increase your chances of conception by following the self-help advice given below:

- Try to ensure that both you and your partner are in good health; eat plenty of fresh, vitamin-rich foods, get plenty of rest and keep alcohol consumption to a minimum.
- Have intercourse about 3 times a week; less frequent intercourse may mean that you miss your partner's fertile days, more frequent intercourse may reduce the number of sperm you ejaculate.
- Try to time intercourse to coincide with your partner's most fertile days (usually midway between menstrual periods).
- Following intercourse, encourage your partner to remain lying down for 10 to 15 minutes to allow the maximum number of sperm to enter the uterus.
- Avoid wearing tight-fitting underpants or those made of artificial fibers, which may damage the sperm by increasing the temperature in the scrotum.

SPERM PRODUCTION

Inside the scrotum (the baggy pouch resting beneath the penis) are the two testes. Sperm cells are formed in the tiny tubes inside each testis at the rate of 10 to 30 billion each month. Behind each testis is a coiled tube called the epididymis. Sperm mature here over a period of 2 to 4 weeks before they are transferred to the seminal vesicles for storage. When you have an orgasm, the sperm pass into the urethra and are then ejaculated in the seminal fluid. Sperm is only a small part of this seminal fluid. On the average, 60 percent of the fluid is produced in the seminal vesicle and 38 percent is produced in the prostate gland. The remaining 2 percent, although nearly all water, contain between 150 and 400 million sperm.

Sperm production is most effective at 6°F (3 to 4°C) below normal body temperature. This is why the testes are suspended outside the body in the scrotum. A high temperature prevents new sperm from forming and may kill those already in storage. The effect of this is usually only temporary infertility. Very low temperatures also prevent sperm from forming, but this does not damage those already in storage. Under normal conditions, sperm production is continuous, although there may be seasonal variations — sperm concentration seems to be lower in the warm summer months. Severe illness of any kind may temporarily suspend semen production for days or months (for example, in the case of severe infection).

Passage of sperm

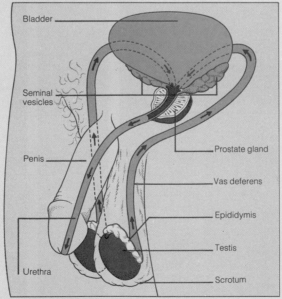

Bladder
Seminal vesicles
Penis
Urethra
Prostate gland
Vas deferens
Epididymis
Testis
Scrotum

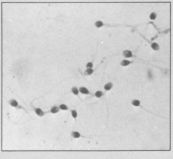

The prostate gland (left) surrounds the urethra at the point where it leaves the bladder. The exact function of the gland is unclear, but it is thought that the secretions it produces stimulate the movement of sperm (right) after ejaculation.

Bladder
Vas deferens
Seminal vesicles
Prostate gland
Urethra

Where sperm form and mature

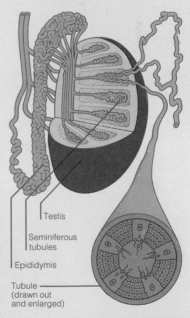

Testis
Seminiferous tubules
Epididymis
Tubule (drawn out and enlarged)

Index

Each of the symptom charts in this book is designed to help you discover the possible reason for your complaint. The book contains thousands of physiological references, and this index must of necessity be selective. For a full guide to the basic symptoms analyzed in the 68 charts and how to find the chart you need, see pp. 16-20. References within the following index are to page numbers of topics from the entire book, not just from the charts. Titles of information boxes within the charts and significant subtopics discussed in these boxes are italicized to emphasize their importance. Titles of the charts themselves and information contained within the introductory section preceding the charts are in **bold** typeface.

INDEX